Home Coffee Roasting

ALSO BY KENNETH DAVIDS

Coffee: A Guide to Brewing, Buying & Enjoying
Espresso: Ultimate Coffee

HOME COFFEE ROASTING:

Romance & Revival

REVISED, UPDATED EDITION

Kenneth Davids

ST. MARTIN'S GRIFFIN

New York

www.stmartins.com

Drawings and maps copyright © 1996 by Ginny Pruitt and Kenneth Davids except as follows: Courtesy of *Tea & Coffee Trade Journal*. Display ornament. Drawings on pages 3, 20, 27, 29, 30, 37, 41 (bottom), 44 (bottom), 45, 46, 49, 50 (top), 71, 72, 74, 82.

Courtesy of Idealibri, an imprint of Rusconi Libri, Milan. Drawing on page 6.

Courtesy of Kevin Sinnott. Engravings on pages 28 and 83.

The roast color tiles reproduced on the inside back cover appear courtesy of the Specialty Coffee Association of America and its executive director, Ted Lingle.

The long passage from Eduardo De Filippo in Chapter 1 appears courtesy of Idealibri, an imprint of Rusconi Libri, Milan. Reprinted by permission.

Design by Patrice Sheridan

LIBRARY OF CONGRESS CATALOGING-IN-PUBLICATION DATA

Davids, Kenneth, 1937–
        Home coffee roasting : romance and revival / Kenneth Davids.—Rev. updated ed.
        p. cm.
        ISBN 0-312-31219-9
        1. Coffee. 2. Coffee—Processing. 3. Coffee brewing. I. Title.

TX415.D43 2003
641.3'373—dc21

                                                                                    2003047159

First Edition: November 2003

10 9 8 7 6 5 4 3 2 1

CONTENTS

IMPATIENT?
To begin roasting immediately, turn to the "Quick Guide to
Home-Roasting Options and Procedures," p. 158.

Home Coffee Roasting

Chapter 1

WHY HOME ROASTING?

Authenticity, Economy, Alchemy

 When I produced the first edition of this book in 1996, roasting coffee at home was an obscure activity practiced by amiably caffeinated hobbyists who often lavished tremendous homespun ingenuity in figuring out how to get their beans properly brown.

Today, home—or, as some would have it, *alternative*—roasting is still obscure, but obscure on a much more substantial scale. No longer do home roasters need to assemble their own roasting apparatus or push beans around in an iron skillet. A dozen or more sleek new home-roasting devices have either nudged their way onto the market or are on the verge of nudging. Nor do alternative roasters need to satisfy themselves with lonely conversations with roasting beans, although some of us, doubtless, will want to continue that practice for therapeutic reasons. We now have the company of scores of Web sites and chat rooms devoted exclusively to our passion.

Nevertheless, home coffee roasting remains an oddball passion of the few, a practice that invariably provokes curiosity and long explanations.

Given its simplicity—once you know what you're doing, basic home coffee roasting ranks in difficulty somewhere between boiling an egg and making a good white sauce—why don't more people do it? Why isn't home coffee roasting already as popular as home baking, for example, or home pasta making or, for that matter, home corn popping?

First, most people simply don't know how vibrant truly fresh coffee tastes when compared to the partly stale version we usually drink. Almost everyone knows how exquisite fresh bread is or how much better home-popped popcorn is than the chewy, rubbery stuff that comes in bags. But the fragrance of coffee one day out of the roaster is a virtually forgotten pleasure.

Second, people don't know that roasting coffee at home is easy and fun, and something that everyone did before the victory of advertising and convenience foods.

Lettuce Comes from the Store

I once worked as a counselor in a day camp. One day while on a nature hike I invited the children to take bites of an edible weed Californians call *miner's lettuce*. Several refused, on the basis that the leaves came out of the dirt and bugs had crawled on them. When I pointed out that they all ate lettuce, and that lettuce also came out of the dirt and risked having bugs crawl on it, one child objected. "Lettuce doesn't come from the dirt," she declared. "Lettuce comes from the store!"

By the mid-twentieth century, Americans thought of "coffee" as granulated brown stuff that came from a can rather than the dried seeds of a tree requiring only a few relatively simple procedures to transform it into a beverage. As happened in the twentieth century with so many other foods and manufacturers, the actual facts about coffee's origin (it consists of vegetable matter that has been dried, roasted, and ground by human beings) were replaced by market-driven substitute facts (coffee is brown granules produced by the complex machinery of an all-knowing corporation).

Of course, at the very moment of victory for brand-name convenience foods (say about 1960), some of the individuals who had recently come to be called consumers began turning themselves back into cooks or wine makers or brewers or bakers, setting off a countermovement. In the world of coffee the return to more authentic foods took the form of the specialty-coffee movement, which advocated a revival of the nineteenth-century practice of selling freshly roasted coffee beans in bulk and encouraged coffee lovers to take their beans home and grind them themselves. It is unusual in America today to find anyone interested in eating and drinking well who doesn't buy coffee in bulk as whole beans and grind the beans themselves before brewing.

There is no doubt that whole-bean coffees handled well are a tremendous advance in flavor and variety over supermarket packaged blends, and certainly anyone not yet introduced to the adventure of fine coffee should start by simply buying whole-bean coffee at the local specialty-coffee store, learning to grind and brew it properly, and experiencing some of the variety and pleasures it affords.

However, for the committed coffee aficionado, home coffee roasting is a logical next step toward closer intimacy with the bean and a mastery of one's own pleasure.

Nostalgia, Balconies, and Roasting Smoke

Throughout most of coffee history people toasted their own beans. Even in the United States, the cradle of convenience, preroasted coffee did not catch on until the latter years of the nineteenth century. Home roasting persisted in Mediterranean countries like Italy until well after World War II, and many coffee drinkers in the Middle East and the horn of Africa still roast their own coffee as part of a leisurely ritual combining roasting, brewing, and drinking in one long sitting.

Museum collections are full of wonderful old home coffee-roasting devices. One of the options you could buy with your fashionable new wood stove in nineteenth-century America was a home coffee roaster, usually in the form of a hollow cast-iron globe that fit inside one of the burner openings.

For people in countries where home roasting was the norm through the first half of the twentieth century, the practice is rich with nostalgia. Listen to Eduardo De Filippo, for example, a well-known Italian writer and performer, recollecting coffee roasting in his childhood Naples in Mariarosa Schiaffino's *Le Ore del Caffè:*

In 1908 . . . in the streets and alleys of Naples, in the first hours of the morning, a very special ritual was celebrated, a ritual indispensable to less wealthy families as well as to better-off aficionados: the ceremony of coffee

An elaborate Italian home roaster from the seventeenth century. It probably doubled as a heat stove. A charcoal fire burned inside the double doors at the bottom of the device. When someone— doubtless a servant— wanted to roast coffee, the top lid with its elaborate tulip sculpture would be removed and replaced by the round roasting chamber with a crank pictured on the floor in front.

roasting. It saved money to buy raw coffee beans and then roast them at home, the only cost being personal skillfulness and patience. Every week (or every couple of weeks) a quantity of coffee was roasted, depending on the needs, finances, and appetites of each family.

And since these rituals were not simultaneous, every day somewhere in the neighborhood a woman or grandpa could be found sitting on the family balcony, turning the crank of the *abbrustulaturo*, or coffee roaster.

We now need to describe this object, today only a memory for most Neapolitans. It was a metal cylinder of thirty to sixty centimeters in length, with a diameter of about fifteen (twelve to twenty-four inches by six inches). Protruding from one end of the cylinder was a long pin; from the other a crank. Raw coffee beans were placed inside the cylinder through a small door in its side, which was firmly held closed by a little hook. The lower part of the device consisted of a rectangular steel box; inside the box a small charcoal fire was lit. At the top of either end of the box were grooves into which the pin and the crank fit, supporting the cylinder between them over the fire. Once the cylinder was placed atop the box the roasting could begin.

By the way: Why did I mention balconies? Because in the process of such roasting, the coffee beans, which are quite oily, release an intense smoke that could be quite unbearable in a closed space, yet no nuisance at all out-of-doors. Instead, dispersed in the air and transported by the wind, it was a source of great happiness for the entire neighborhood.

As the crank was turned the beans tossed up and down against the hot cylinder wall until they were roasted just right. Occasionally the cylinder had to be taken off the base and shaken a few times to check the sound the beans made, so as to judge their weight, since they became lighter as they roasted. But that was not enough . . . the color of the beans had to be checked through the small door in the side of the cylinder, and when they were the "color of a monk's tunic," as we said, the cylinder was quickly removed from the fire and the roasted beans poured onto a large tray or terra-cotta plate. There they were carefully stirred with a wooden ladle until they cooled. With every stroke the roasting smoke would permeate the air with a delicious, intense, irresistible aroma.

As for me—lingering about in bed during those early hours, trying to delay the moment when I would have to get up and go to school—as soon as this seductive smell reached my nose (it even penetrated the closed windows!) I would jump out of bed full of energy, happy to begin the day. And so it was that, even before I was allowed to drink it, coffee became my wake-up call and symbol for the new day. . . .

This freshly roasted coffee fragrance, one of the finest of aromas, would follow me as I washed myself, as I dressed, as I devoured my "'a zupp' e latte" or milk soup, and as I descended the stairs. . . . Down in the street the smell wouldn't be as strong . . . but I still would be made aware of it by the voices I heard. The comments crackled from window to window along my way from home to school. "Ah, what fragrance, what pleasure!" street vendors might shout.

One skinny old woman might ask another with a bun of black hair: "Have you roasted your coffee yet?" And the other would reply: "Of course! We roast it twice a week. Grandpa is so picky he has to do it himself." On the balcony of an elegant apartment a servant, who looked like a wasp with his black-yellow striped jacket and black greased whiskers, to an exquisite maid in the apartment next door: "I'll have to leave you shortly: the coffee must be removed." And she would reply: "Yes, of course . . . I roast it every Saturday; it is always a great responsibility, Ciro my dear. . . ."

Also, quite often, just before being swallowed up by the school gate, my ear would intercept an "Ahhhh . . . !" from a shoemaker nearby. Sipping his cup of coffee before starting work, his "Ahhhh . . . !" was so expressive— you could feel pleasure, satisfaction, happiness, appetite, even surprise and wonder. Later, as an adult, I would discover all of those things in coffee myself.*

Some Reasons to Roast

For those of us who weren't raised with the scent of roasting coffee filling the narrow streets and picturesque balconies of memory, and whose childhood recollections instead involve tract homes, Pepsi, and Maxwell House, what are the advantages of home roasting? It may be a simple but forgotten art, yet why bother at all? Here are a few reasons.

*Eduardo De Filippo, "Introduzione, *L'abbrustulaturo*," Mariarosa Schiaffino, *Le Ore del Caffe* (Milan: Idealibri, 1983), pp 6–8. This translation by Emanuela Aureli and Kenneth Davids.

Freshness and Flavor. Unlike stale bread, which rapidly becomes dramatically inedible, stale coffee still can be drunk and enjoyed. But what a difference a few days make! An absolutely fresh coffee, a day or two out of the roaster, explodes with perfume, an evanescent aroma that seems to resonate in the nervous system and vibrate around the head like a sort of coffee aura. The aftertaste of a truly fresh coffee can ring on the palate for an entire morning; the taste of a week-old coffee will vanish in a few minutes. Perhaps the persistent surprise and delight of De Filippo's shoemaker at the revelation of his morning coffee was partly owing to the fact that he had a grandpa who roasted it every week on the family balcony rather than buying it half stale at a supermarket.

Coffee is best about a day after it has been roasted. Once past that moment a rapid and relentless deterioration in flavor sets in as the protective envelope of carbon dioxide gas dissipates, allowing oxygen to penetrate the beans and stale the delicate flavor oils. For someone who genuinely loves coffee, the bouquet of optimally fresh beans is without doubt the most tangible of the many reasons to roast coffee at home.

Reasonably fresh coffee can be gotten at specialty stores if the roasting is done on the premises or close by, but with the growth of mammoth regional and national specialty-coffee chains, beans may be roasted hundreds or even thousands of miles from the store where you finally buy them. Coffee from these specialty chains will be infinitely better and fresher than the pre-ground stuff that comes in cans and bricks, but it won't—can't—be as fresh as the coffee you roast in your own kitchen.

Personal Satisfaction. Roasting coffee at home provides the gratification many of us derive from outflanking consumerism by gaining control of a heretofore mysterious process that was once imposed on us by others. Home roasting is also an art—a minor one perhaps, but an art nonetheless, and one that can provide considerable gratification.

Money. Obviously this issue is more important to some than to others. Depending on how and where you buy your green coffee, you can save anywhere from 25 to 50 percent of the cost per pound by roasting at home. See "Resources" for strategies on finding sources for green coffee.

Connoisseurship. The way to truly understand a coffee is to roast it. Furthermore, home roasting makes it possible to develop what amounts to a cellar of green coffees. Unroasted coffee doesn't quite last indefinitely, but for a year or two it registers only subtle changes in flavor and remains interesting and drinkable for years after that. Handled properly, some coffees even improve with age. Thus you can keep modest supplies of your favorite coffees around and select them for roasting according to your mood and your guests' inclinations. The coffee-cellar idea is discussed in more detail on pages 105–106.

Bragging Rights. So there you are, roasting a blend of Guatemalan Huehuetenango and Sumatran Lintong, your kitchen pungent with smelly yet glamorous smoke, when your friends arrive for dinner carrying that pathetic bag of week-old house blend from down the street. . . .

I won't add more because I don't want to encourage snobbery or one-upmanship, but you get the picture.

Romance. Finally, roasting your own coffee carries you deeper into the drama and romance of coffee, which I remain a sucker for despite twenty years of professional and semiprofessional involvement with the stuff. That romance is nowhere as vividly encapsulated as in that moment when a pile of hard, almost odorless gray-green seeds is suddenly and magically transformed into the fragrant vehicle of our dreams, reveries, and conversation. To be the magicians waving the wand of transformation makes that metamorphosis all the more stirring and resonant.

If You Can Read You Can Roast

And above all: *You can do it.* You couldn't get a job as a professional coffee roaster because professional roasters need to achieve precision and consistency as well as quality.

But anyone who can read this book can produce a decent to stunningly superb roast at home. Jabez Burns, probably the single greatest roasting innovator in American history, once said that some of the best coffee he had ever tasted was done in a home corn popper.

Liberating the Taste Genie

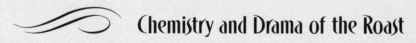 Chemistry and Drama of the Roast

What Happens to Coffee When It's Roasted?

In fact, no one knows—exactly. One of the many intriguing characteristics of coffee is the complexity of its aromatic agents: At this writing, 700 to 850 substances have been identified as possible contributors to the flavor of roasted coffee. The exact number of contributing substances varies from study to study and sample to sample, perhaps influenced by the geographical origin of the beans and how they are dried and prepared for market.

These figures do not include all of coffee's many additional non-flavor-influencing components. Over 2,000 substances have been identified in green *arabica* coffee beans.

These formidable numbers make coffee one of the most complex of commonly consumed foods and beverages. Wine, for example, has considerably fewer flavor-influencing constituents than coffee. Only about 150 components contribute to the taste of vanilla, considered by food chemists to be one of the more complicated of natural flavorings. To this day, the actual coffee part of "coffee-flavored" candies and other foods is derived from roasted coffee itself and not whipped up in a laboratory, a tribute to coffee's defiant complexity.

One thing is certain: The 700 to 850 flavor constituents of *arabica* coffee and their heady fragrance would not be available to us without roasting. Roasting is the act that liberates the taste genie of green coffee.

Very broadly, roasting: (1) forces water out of the bean; (2) dries out and expands its woody parts, making them more porous and reducing the total weight of the bean by 14 to 20 percent; (3) sets off a continuous transformation of some sugars into CO_2 gas, a process that continues after the coffee is roasted and only concludes when the coffee is definitely stale; (4) drives off some volatile substances, including a small part of the caffeine; and finally and most importantly, (5) caramelizes a portion of the bean's sugars and transforms some into what are popularly called the coffee's flavor oils: the tiny, fragile, yet potent mix of appetizing substances with unappetizing names like aldehydes, ketones, esters, and acetic, butyric, and valeric acids. It is the caramelized sugars, the flavor oils, and traces of other substances, like bitter trigonelline and quinic and nicotinic acids, that (along with the approximately 1 percent caffeine) give coffee drinkers the experience they pick up the cup for.

After roasting, the bean is in part reduced to a protective package for the caramelized sugars and flavor oils, which are secreted in tiny pockets throughout the bean's now woody, porous interior (or, in dark roasts, partly forced to the surface of the bean, giving these roasts their characteristic oily appearance). The carbon dioxide gas gradually works its way out of the bean in a process called degassing, which temporarily protects the flavor oils from the penetration of oxygen and staling. (Of course, when the CO_2 is finally gone, so is flavor. Vacuum cans, nitrogen-flushed bags, and so on are all artificial efforts to protect the coffee from the staling penetration of oxygen. And when the natural protective package formed by the bean is destroyed by grinding, the protective gas disappears even more quickly.)

The Drama of the Roast

If that's what happens inside the bean during roasting, what happens on the outside?

For the first few minutes after being introduced into the heat of the roasting chamber, nothing much. The beans remain grayish green and mute, then they begin to yellow and emit a grassy or burlaplike odor. Next comes a steam that smells vaguely like bread or grain.

Finally, anywhere from two to fifteen minutes into the roasting cycle (depending on the volume of beans being roasted and the intensity of the heat in the roasting chamber), the steam darkens slightly in color and begins to smell like coffee. Then the first popping or crackling sounds make themselves heard.

 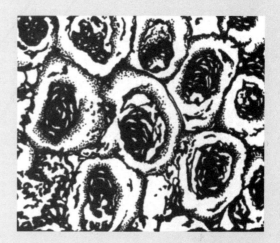

This *first crack,* as coffee people call it, signals the definite start of the roast transformation or *pyrolysis.* Inside the bean sugars begin to caramelize; water bound up in the structure of the bean begins to split off from carbon dioxide, causing the series of tiny internal cataclysms that provoke the crackling sound. The still moist, now increasingly oily roasting smoke continues to rise from the beans.

From this point forward the beans begin to produce their own inner heat, precise and measurable, rising from around 350°F/175°C at the beginning of pyrolysis to about 435°F/225°C for a medium roast, to as high as 475°F/245°C in a very dark roast.

The beans darken in color as the roast progresses, an effect mainly caused by the caramelization of sugars and secondarily by the transformation of certain acids. The roast may be terminated at any time after pyrolysis begins, from early on, when the beans are a very light brown in color, to late in the drama, when they reach a very dark brown, almost black color. The odor of the roasting smoke also subtly changes, reflecting (to experienced nostrils) the evolving roast style of the beans.

As the beans reach the middle ranges of brown the first wave of relatively subdued crackling gradually diminishes. Then, in roasts carried to a darker style, a second, more powerful wave of crackling sets in (the second crack), probably caused by the breakdown of the woody structures of the bean as still more substances volatilize. As this second round of crackling grows in intensity, so does the roasting smoke—now becoming dark, pungent, and even more abundant.

The drawing on the left depicts a magnification of a cross-section of a green coffee bean; the drawing on the right a similar section of a roasted bean. Note the irregular, rumpled forms and solid structure of the green bean, and the hollow, open cells (often harboring droplets of volatile flavor oils) of the roasted bean.

The progress of the roast can be measured in three ways: by the odor of the smoke (this was the favored approach to controlling the roast in the nineteenth century), by the inner temperature of the bean (the preferred approach of today's more technically inclined roasters), or by the surface color of the bean, color that can be read either by an experienced eye or by a sophisticated machine. The visual inspection of color is probably the most widely practiced method today, and the one most easily adopted by home roasters. Monitoring the roast by bean temperature dominates large-scale commercial roasting and is increasingly practiced by small-scale professional roasters as well, while controlling the roast through the changing fragrance of the roasting smoke is an almost lost art, carried on by only a handful of roasters trained in small shops during the earlier years of the twentieth century.

The same coffee bean brought to the same color or degree of roast by two different roasters will taste *roughly* similar; in other words, the *taste contributed by the roast* will be analogous if not identical. Differences in flavor among similar beans brought to the same degree of roast by different roasters are the result of variations in roasting equipment, method, and philosophy.

Some roasters prefer to develop a coffee slowly by subjecting it to relatively low temperatures in the roast chamber; others prefer a faster roast at higher temperatures. Still others vary the temperature as the roast progresses, raising the temperature in various increments at the moment the free moisture is eliminated from the bean and pyrolysis begins. These differences in method, a matter of pride and intense conviction on the part of individual coffee roasters, contribute to the richness and diversity of the world of fine coffee.

Chapter 2

FROM SPOON TO FLUID BEDS

Roasting History

The discovery that the seeds of the coffee fruit tasted good when roasted was undoubtedly the key moment in coffee history. It marked the beginning of the transformation of coffee from an obscure medicinal herb known only in the horn of Africa and southern Arabia to the most popular beverage in the world, a beverage so widely drunk that today its trade generates more money than any other commodity except oil.

A skeptic might counter that it is caffeine, not flavor (or the roasting necessary to develop that flavor), that made coffee into one of the world's most important commodities. This argument is difficult to sustain, however. Tea, yerba maté, cocoa, coca, and other less famous plants also contain substances that wake us up and make us feel good. Yet none has achieved quite the same universal success as coffee.

Furthermore coffee—coffee *without* the caffeine—figures as an important flavoring in countless candies, cakes, and confections. And people sensitive to caffeine happily choose to drink decaffeinated coffee in preference to other caffeine-free beverages.

So clearly the aromatics of roasted coffee have a great deal to do with its triumph. On the other hand, there is evidence that the taste of coffee takes some getting used to. Children do not spontaneously like coffee, for example. And from coffee's first appearances in human culture to the present, people have tended to add things to it. The first recorded coffee drinkers enhanced the beverage with cardamom and other spices, a tendency that continues today with flavored coffees and espresso drinks augmented with syrups, garnishes, and milk.

More than likely it is *both* the aromatic characteristics of roasted coffee and its stimulant properties that hooked humanity. At some point people began to associate the stimulating effect of coffee with the dark resonance of its taste, and combined those associations with the myriad social satisfactions that began to cluster around the beverage; coming to consciousness in the morning, hospitality, conversation, the reveries of cafés. Thus the entire package—stimulation, taste, and social ritual—came together to mean *coffee* in all of its complexity and richness.

Coffee-Leaf Tea and Coffee-Fruit Frappés

We can only speculate how coffee was consumed before the advent of roasting sometime in the sixteenth century. However, the practices of some African societies in the regions where the coffee tree grows wild give us clues.

Ethiopian tribal peoples make tea from the leaves of the coffee tree, for example. Other recorded customs include chewing the dried fruit, pressing it into cakes, infusing it, mashing the ripe coffee fruit into a drink, and eating the crushed seeds imbedded in animal fat.

It is difficult to believe that coffee would have become the beverage of choice of most of the world if the only way to experience it was by infusing its leaves; putting its rather meager, thin-pulped fruit in a blender; or chewing on its raw seeds. Furthermore, there is at least some evidence that coffee's accelerated success over the past two centuries may be in part the result of continuous improvements in the understanding and technology of roasting, which, inference suggests, have produced an increasingly attractive beverage.

Mysterious Origins

Who first thought of roasting the seeds of the coffee tree and why?

We will doubtless never know. The early history of coffee in human culture is as obscure as the origin of most of the world's great foods. All that is known is based on inferences drawn from a few scattered references in written documents of the fifteenth- and sixteenth-century Middle East.

When European travelers first encountered the beverage in the coffee-houses of Syria, Egypt, and Turkey in the sixteenth century, the beans from which it was brewed came from terraces in the mountains at the southern tip of the Arabian peninsula, in what is now Yemen. Consequently, when the European botanist Linnaeus began naming and categorizing the flora of the astounding new worlds his colleagues were encountering, he assigned the coffee tree the species name *Coffea arabica*.

Coffea arabica was the only coffee species known to world commerce for several centuries. It still provides the majority of the world's coffees. However, it did not originate in Arabia, as Linnaeus assumed, but in the high forests of central Ethiopia, a fact not confirmed by the Western scientific community until the mid-twentieth century. Well over a hundred species of coffee now have been identified growing wild in various parts of tropical Africa, Asia, and Madagascar. Probably about thirty are cultivated, most on a very small scale. One, *Coffea canephora* or *robusta*, has come to rival *Coffea arabica* in importance in commerce and culture.

No one knows how *Coffea arabica* first came to be cultivated, when, or even where. Some historians assume that it was first cultivated in Yemen, but a strong case has been made that it was first deliberately grown in its botanical home, Ethiopia, and was carried from there to South Arabia as an already domesticated species, perhaps as early as A.D. 575.

It is not clear what sort of drink the first recorded drinkers of hot coffee actually consumed. The coffee bean is the seed of a small, thin-fleshed, sweet fruit. The first hot coffee beverage may not have been brewed from the bean at all. More likely it was made by boiling the lightly toasted husks of the coffee fruit, producing a drink still widely consumed in Yemen under the name *qishr, kishr, kisher* (or several other spellings), and in Europe called *coffee sultan* or *sultana*. Or perhaps both dried fruit and beans were toasted, crushed, and boiled together. The dried husks are very sweet, so any drink involving the husks would be sweet as well as caffeinated.

Considerable speculation has been focused on what finally led someone in Syria, Persia, or possibly Turkey to subject the seeds of the coffee fruit alone to a sufficiently high temperature to induce pyrolysis, thus developing the delicate flavor oils that speak to the palate so eloquently and are undoubtedly responsible for the eventual cultural victory of coffee.

These explanations range from the poetic to the plausible. Muslim legends focus on Sheik Omar, who was exiled to an infertile region of Arabia in about 1260, and according to one version of his legend discovered the benefits of roasted coffee while trying to avoid starvation by making a soup of coffee seeds. Finding them bitter, he roasted them before boiling them.

Others have claimed that farmers in Yemen or Ethiopia, while burning branches cut from coffee trees to cook their meals, discovered the value in the seeds roasted by this serendipitous process. This theory, which began turning up in coffee literature of the early twentieth century, has a storyteller's rather than a historian's logic.

Ian Bersten, in his provocative history *Coffee Floats, Tea Sinks*, supposes that someone simply discovered that the light roasting given the husks of the coffee fruit to make qishr could be turned up a notch, as it were, to produce a truly roasted coffee bean. He further suggests that the Ottoman Turks, who assumed control of southern Arabia in the mid-sixteenth century, spread the habit of drinking the new kind of roasted coffee in order to make use of a heretofore useless by-product of qishr production, the previously discarded seeds.

Certainly the Ottoman Turks were the main instigators of the spread of coffee drinking and technology, since their expanding empire facilitated cultural and commercial exchange. Bersten also speculates that Syria is the likely location of the first truly roasted coffee, since the Syrians, particularly in the city of Damascus, had developed the technology necessary to produce metal cookware, which in turn facilitated a higher roasting temperature than the earthenware bowls used by the Yemenis.

Furthermore, Bersten suggests that the odor of roasting smoke, which is produced only by pyrolysis and which many people find more enticing than the beverage itself, may have been an incentive for someone to persist in the roasting process and push it beyond the temperature that produces the fruity-smelling qishr.

All such speculations remain impossible to prove or disprove. Seeds and nuts were roasted to improve their taste and digestibility early in history, long before the development of roasted coffee, and possibly someone simply tried the same trick with coffee seeds. Or perhaps some qishr drinker toasting coffee husks and seeds wandered away from the fire too long and came back to a pleasant surprise.

At any rate, by 1550 coffee seeds or beans were definitely being roasted in the true sense of the word in Syria and Turkey, and the spectacular rise of roasted coffee to worldwide prominence in culture and commerce had begun.

Ceremonial Roasting

Early coffee roasting in Arabia was doubtless simple in the extreme. We have no detailed accounts of these earliest roasting sessions, but they probably resemble the practices still found in Arabia today, and recorded by Europeans like William Palgrave in 1863 in his *Narrative of a Year's Journey Through Central and Eastern Arabia:*

> Without delay Soweylim begins his preparations for coffee. These open by about five minutes of blowing with the bellows and arranging the charcoal till a sufficient heat has been produced. . . . He then takes a dirty knotted rag out of a niche in the wall close by, and having untied it, empties out of it three or four handfuls of unroasted coffee, the which he places on a little trencher of platted grass, and picks carefully out any blackened grains, or other non-homologous substances, commonly to be found intermixed with the berries when purchased in gross; then, after much cleansing and shaking, he pours the grain so cleansed into a large open iron ladle, and places it over the mouth of the funnel, at the same time blowing the bellows and stirring the grains gently round and round till they crackle, redden, and smoke a little, but carefully withdrawing them from the heat long before they turn black or charred, after the erroneous fashion of Turkey and Europe; after which he puts them to cool a moment on the grass platter.

Among the inhabitants of the Arabian peninsula, roasting, pulverizing, brewing, and drinking the coffee all were (and often still are) performed in one long, leisurely sitting. Both roasting and brewing were carried out over the same small fire. The roasting beans were stirred with an iron rod flattened at one end. After cooling they were dumped into a mortar, where they were pulverized to a coarse powder. The coffee was boiled, usually with some cardamom or saffron added, then strained into cups. It was drunk unsweetened.

Variants of this coffee ritual continue throughout the horn of Africa and the Middle East. Ethiopian and Eritrean immigrants to the United States have carried a version of it to their urban kitchens and living rooms.

From Brown to Black: A New Coffee Cuisine

Attentive readers of the Palgrave passage will note that the Arabians roasted their coffee to a rather light brown color. At an early point in coffee history, probably before 1600, a somewhat different approach to coffee roasting and cuisine developed in Turkey, Syria, and Egypt. The beans were brought to a very dark, almost black color, ground to a very fine powder, using either a millstone or a grinder with metal burns, and boiled and served with sugar. No spices were added to the cup, and the coffee was not strained but delivered with some of the powdery grounds still floating in the coffee, suspended in the sweet liquid. It was served in small cups rather than the somewhat larger cups preferred by the Arabians.

The reasons for this change in style of roast, brewing, and serving are not known, but doubtless the very dark roast facilitated grinding the coffee to a fine powder. Lighter-roasted beans are tougher in texture and more difficult to pulverize than the more brittle darker roasts. And sugar, a native of India, which had been put into large-scale cultivation relatively recently in the Middle East, helped offset the bitterness of the dark roast and accentuate its sweet undertones. Thus a new technology (the hand grinder with metal burrs); a new, dark roasting style; and the availability of sugar all coincided to contribute to the development of the coffee cuisine we now call Turkish.

Why Turkish? Why not Egyptian, for example, or Syrian? Because this cuisine penetrated Europe via contacts with the Ottoman Turks, first through Venice into northern Italy and later through the Balkans and Vienna into Central Europe. Early European coffee drinkers all roasted their coffee very dark and drank it in the "Turkish" fashion, boiled with sugar.

Coffee Goes Global

During the seventeenth and early eighteenth centuries the habit of coffee drinking spread westward across Europe and eastward into India and what is now Indonesia. As a cultivated plant it burst out of Yemen: First a Muslim pilgrim carried it to India, then Europeans took it to Ceylon and Java. From Java they carried it to indoor botanical gardens in Amsterdam and Paris, then as a lucrative new crop to the Caribbean and South America. In a few short decades millions of trees were providing revenue for plantation owners and merchants, and mental fuel for a new generation of philosophers and thinkers gathering in the coffeehouses of London, Paris, and Vienna.

Throughout coffee's spread as one of the new commodity crops that fed the growing global trade network of the seventeenth and eighteenth centuries, it was associated with sugar. Coffee and sugar went hand in hand, both as sister tropical cash crops and as partners in the coffeehouses and coffee cups of the world. Coffee was undoubtedly a less destructive crop than sugar, both to the environment and to workers. It is a small tree typically grown under the shade of larger trees rather than in vast fields, and, unlike sugar, often provided a small cash crop for independent peasant farmers.

Nevertheless, in a global irony, coffee simultaneously became a symbol of both oppression and liberation. It developed as an instrument of social and economic exploitation in the tropics, as a plantation elite grew wealthy on the labor of darker-skinned workers, yet simultaneously fueled the intellectual revolution of the European Enlightenment and political revolutions in France and the United States. Coffee and coffeehouses were intimately associated with virtually all of the great cultural and political upheavals of the time.

It was also during the late seventeenth and early eighteenth centuries that Europeans introduced coffee to its second great companion: milk. The ancestor of America's latest favorite, the hot-milk-and-espresso *caffè latte*, was born in Vienna after the Turkish siege of 1683, when Franz Kolschitzky started Vienna's first coffeehouse with coffee left behind by the retreating Turks. Kolschitzky found that in order to woo the Viennese away from their breakfasts of warm beer he had to abandon the Turkish style of coffee brewing, strain the new drink, and serve it with milk.

From Vienna the practice of straining coffee, rather than serving it Turkish style as a suspension, spread westward through Europe, and with it the custom of serving coffee with hot milk. To this day the line between those European societies that strain their coffee and drink it with milk and those that drink their coffee Turkish style in a sweet suspension roughly corresponds to the seventeenth- and eighteenth-century border between the Ottoman Empire and Christian Europe. Austrians and Italians, for example, drink their coffee strained and with milk, whereas most coffee drinkers in the Balkans, which remained under the control of the Ottomans until well into the nineteenth century, take their coffee Turkish style.

Roasting in a Technological Rut

Despite these dramatic developments in coffee drinking and growing during the seventeenth and eighteenth centuries, roasting technology itself changed very little. The most common approach was a simple carryover from Middle Eastern practice: Beans were put in an iron pan over a fire and stirred until they were brown. Somewhat more sophisticated devices tumbled the beans inside metal cylinders or globes that were suspended over a fire and turned by hand. Some of these apparatuses could roast several pounds of coffee at a time and were used in coffeehouses and small retail shops; others roasted a pound or less over the embers of home fireplaces. See the illustration below and pages 40–50 for a sampling of these early roasting devices.

One of the earliest (c 1650) representations of a small cylindrical coffee roaster, ancestor of the devices that still roast much of the coffee we drink today. It was turned over the hot coals of a brazier or fireplace.

More Unanswerable Questions

Where did Europeans and Americans in the seventeenth and eighteenth centuries roast their coffee? Did they roast it at home or buy it in shops? How dark did they roast it? How might it have tasted when compared to our contemporary roasts?

Only the first two of these questions can be answered with any certainty. Coffee was roasted either in the home, often by servants, or in small shops or stalls and sold in bulk like any other produce. There is no evidence that roasting coffee was considered any more difficult or challenging than other kitchen chores. In fact, it appears that, in Europe at least, it was a job often given over to older children.

How well roasted was this coffee? What did it taste like? Iron pans, irregular heat, and children doing the roasting probably meant a technically poor roast: inconsistent and occasionally scorched. The storekeepers probably did better, though not by much.

But again, the coffee was definitely *fresh*. A case certainly could be made that kitchen-roasted coffee in these centuries tasted considerably better than today's instants and cheaper canned coffees.

Roast Style and Geography

Taste in darkness of roast doubtless differed from place to place according to cultural preference, much as it does today. In most of Europe during the sixteenth and seventeenth centuries coffee continued to be roasted in dark, Turkish style. A pamphlet from seventeenth-century England, for example, advises coffee lovers to "take what quantity [of coffee beans] you please and over a charcoal fire, in an old pudding pan or frying pan, keep them always stirring til they be quite black."

At some point, however, tastes in northern Europe—Germany, Scandinavia, and England—modulated to a roast lighter than that of the rest of Europe, which retained a preference for the somewhat darker roasts deriving from the Turkish tradition. This distinction carried over to the New World: North Americans largely adopted the lighter roasts of the dominant northern European colonists and Latin Americans the darker roasts of their southern European colonizers.

I have yet to come across a plausible explanation as to why northern Europe abandoned the darker roasts of the earlier Turkish-influenced tradition for the later lighter roasts. This shift in roast preference apparently occurred in the late seventeenth and early eighteenth centuries, and it probably was related in some way to the development of the taste for filtered coffee that took place during the same period. Some have connected it to the taste for lighter beverages like tea and beer in northern Europe, which (the theory goes) influenced tastes in coffee roasting and brewing.

Arabia and parts of the horn of Africa retained their original taste for a lighter-roast coffee, drunk with spices but without sugar.

Enter the Industrial Revolution

At the beginning of the nineteenth century most western Europeans and Americans lived in the countryside and made their living through agriculture; by the end of the century most resided in cities and earned their livelihood in industry and services. At the beginning of the century most spent their lives isolated inside an envelope of tradition; by 1900 many were literate and participated in a wider world in which newspapers and advertising profoundly influenced the details of their lives. At the beginning of the century machinery and tools were simple, and most power derived from renewable resources like water and wind; by the end complex machinery touched every facet of people's lives, and power overwhelmingly was provided by coal and oil.

Like everything else, coffee was swept along in these changes. As the nineteenth century began, coffee beans were toasted in small, simple machines, either at home or in shops and coffeehouses. By the end of the century the new urban middle class was increasingly buying coffee roasted in large, sophisticated machines and sold in packages by brand name.

Naturally this last development was uneven. Among industrialized nations the United States led in replacing home roasting with packaged preroasted and preground coffee. Germany and Great Britain were close behind, with France, Italy, and industrializing nations elsewhere hanging on to older, small-scale roasting traditions.

An example of one of the earliest advertisements intended to woo people away from home roasting to packaged, brand-name coffees is reproduced on page 29. This sort of advertising appeared at a time when increasing numbers of Americans and Europeans found themselves traveling farther and farther to their places of employment. In working-class families women as well as men worked away from home, and toward the end of the century somewhat better-off families, who once employed live-in servants to take care of tasks like coffee roasting, were forced to do it themselves. In this context it is easy to see why people might begin to prefer the costlier but more convenient option of preroasted coffee.

New preferences for store-bought bread and preroasted coffee also were driven by the myth of progress that infatuated the industrialized world throughout the nineteenth and early twentieth centuries. Packaged preroasted coffee was modern, clean, fashionable, and with-it. Roasting your own coffee was dirty, clumsy, grubby, and old-fashioned, something only your ignorant country cousins did.

The Pursuit of Consistency

With advertising and brand names came the need for a consistent, recognizable product. When a consumer bought your coffee in its fancy package, it was important to make the coffee inside the package taste the same way now as it did last week. The new commercial coffee roasters pursued consistency in both the green coffee they roasted and in the roast itself.

Consistency in green coffee was facilitated in several ways. The international coffee trade became better organized and more sophisticated in the language and categories it used to describe coffees and carry on its business. Countries where coffee was grown introduced complex standards for grading beans. The art of blending developed: Professionals learned how to juggle coffees from different crops and regions in order to maintain a consistent taste while controlling costs.

Meanwhile the American coffee industry developed a trade language for degree or style of roast: cinnamon, light, medium, high, city, full city, dark, heavy. Firms settled on a roast style and rigorously attempted to maintain it.

Tireless Tinkering: Nineteenth-Century Roasting Technology

It is never clear whether changes in technology drive changes in society or vice versa, but certainly the two went hand in hand in transforming nineteenth-century coffee roasting from a small-scale, personal act to a large-scale, industrial procedure fed by advertising and mass-marketing techniques. The consistency in roast style demanded by brand-name marketing could only be obtained through a more refined roasting technology.

The restless innovation of the Industrial Revolution, the tireless entrepreneurial tinkering aimed at coming up with yet another machine, still one more moneymaking technical wrinkle, claimed all aspects of coffee during the nineteenth century, from roasting through brewing. Proposals for new— or almost new—coffeemakers, coffee grinders, and coffee roasters streamed through the doors of patent offices in industrializing countries. Although only a few of the many patents had significant impact, enough did to totally transform roasting technology over the course of the century.

Coffee continued to be roasted in hollow cylinders or globes, but the cylinders and globes dramatically increased in size as coffee roasting moved from kitchens and small storefront shops to large roasting factories. See page 28 for a look at the interior of an American coffee-roasting plant from the mid-nineteenth century.

The roasting drums were now turned by machine, first by steam, then near the end of the century by electricity. Similarly, roasting heat was first provided by coal or wood, then by natural gas. By the end of the century a lively debate developed between adherents of "direct" gas roasting, which meant that the flame and the hot gases were literally present inside the roasting chamber, and "indirect" gas roasting, which meant that heat was applied only to the outside of the roasting chamber and sucked through the chamber by means of a fan or air pump.

Further technical innovations focused on two problems: (1) controlling the timing or duration of the roast with precision, and (2) achieving an even roast from bean to bean and around the circumference of each individual bean.

First the timing issue. As the drums and globes of commercial roasting machines grew larger it became more and more difficult to cool the large masses of roasting coffee with any precision because the beans continued to

Based on a turn-of-the-century photograph, this drawing depicts one of the many itinerant coffee roasters who with their simple equipment roamed the cities and towns of nineteenth- and early twentieth- century France, setting up in the street and roasting coffee for neighborhood house-holds. With his left hand he is turning the ball-shaped roasting chamber above a charcoal fire; in his right he holds a metal hook used to open the door in the roasting ball to check the color of the beans. The boxlike wooden object at his feet is his cooling tray. When he judged the coffee properly roasted, he flipped the ball on its hinged frame up and out of the top of the stove and over the cooling tray, into which it deposited its charge of hot beans.

roast from their own internal heat long after being dumped from the machine or removed from the heat source.

Solutions in the early part of the century tended to focus on ways of dumping the beans quickly and easily. With the Carter Pull-Out machines pictured in the engraving on page 28, for example, the selling point was exactly that: The roasting drum could be pulled out of the oven and easily emptied. However, as can be seen in the illustration, the beans still had to be stirred manually to hasten cooling.

Starting in 1867 fans or air pumps were introduced to automate the cooling. The beans were dumped into large pans or trays. While machine-driven paddles stirred the beans, fans pulled cool air through them, both reducing their surface temperature and carrying away the smoke produced by the freshly roasted beans.

The second technical problem addressed by late-nineteenth-century innovation was the question of even roasting. At the beginning of the century most roasting drums and globes were simple hollow chambers. The beans tended to collect in a relatively stable mass at the bottom of the turning drum or globe. Consequently some beans remained at the bottom of the pile in close contact with the hot metal of the drum and tended to scorch or roast darker than those at the top of the shifting mass. Furthermore the coating of oil produced by the roast often caused beans to stick to the hot metal walls of the roasting chamber.

Starting in the nineteenth century, vanes or blades that tossed the coffee as the drum or globe turned were added to the inside of the roasting chamber, facilitating a more even roast. And in 1864 Jabez Burns, an American roasting-technology innovator, further resolved the problem of dumping the beans by developing a double-screw arrangement of vanes inside the roasting drum that worked the beans up and down the length of the cylinder as it turned. The operator then had only to open the door of the roasting cylinder and the beans, rather than heading back away from the door for another trip up the cylinder, simply tumbled out into the cooling tray.

But the most effective answer to uneven roasting came toward the end of the century. To supplement the usual heat applied to the outside of the drum, hot air was drawn *through* the drum by a fan or air pump, often the same fan or pump used to suck air through the beans to cool them. The combination of moving air and vanes tossing the coffee meant the coffee was roasted more by contact with hot air than by contact with hot metal,

This nineteenth-century illustration suggests the outpouring of invention that was lavished on the simple act of coffee brewing during the early Industrial Revolution. Similar ingenuity was bestowed on coffee roasting. Scores of almost identical home-roasting devices were patented, as well as numerous variations on shop and factory machines.

improving both the consistency and the speed of the roast. Furthermore, efforts were made to deliver heat evenly around the entire circumference of the drum rather than only at the bottom, usually by enclosing the drum inside a second metal wall and circulating the heat between this wall and the outside of the drum.

The sum total of these innovations—gas heat directed evenly around the drum, a means of rapidly and precisely dumping the beans, vanes inside the drum, and air pumps to suck hot air through the roasting chamber and room-temperature air through the cooling beans—produced the basic configuration of the classic drum roaster. It is a configuration that endures today as the fundamental form of most smaller-scale roasting equipment. See pages 52–53 for an illustrated description of a representative drum roaster.

Of course there were (and are) many variations of this essential technology. Some turn-of-the-century machines put the gas flame inside the drum, for example. Most larger systems today spray the hot beans with a short burst of water to decisively kick off the cooling process, an approach called *water quenching,* as opposed to the pure *air quenching* described earlier.

In the nineteenth and early twentieth centuries, coating the hot

The interior of an American roasting plant in the mid-nineteenth century. Heat was provided by coal; brick ovens entirely surrounded the roasting drums, distributing heat more evenly around the drums than did earlier designs that heated the drums from the bottom only. The drums were perforated to vent the roasting smoke. These Carter Pull-Out roasters were turned by belts connecting to steam power, but were "pulled out" of the ovens by hand. The beans were dumped into wooden trays, where they were cooled by stirring with shovels.

beans with sugar to help preserve them was a popular practice. Today *sugar glazing* of coffee beans is practiced only in some regions of Latin America and Europe.

Throughout these decades of change some roasters stuck stubbornly to earlier technologies, as they still do today. Roasters in places as diverse as Japan, Brazil, and the United States continue to use wood or charcoal to roast their coffee, for example. They or their clients value the slow roast and the smoky nuance imparted to the beans by the process.

Nevertheless, the indirectly heated drum roaster using a convection system drawing hot air through the turning drum remains the norm today for all but the largest roasting apparatus.

An advertisement aimed at getting Americans of the 1870s to give up home roasting for packaged coffees. Arbuckles Brothers pioneered preroasted, brand-name coffee. Note the contrast between the up-to-date woman on the left, fashionably dressed and holding a package of preroasted coffee, and her distracted old-fashioned friend, tied to her stove and messing up the kitchen with coffee smoke.

The Jabez Burns Thermalo roaster of 1934. Previous machines supplemented the heat applied to the outside of the roasting drum with relatively gentle currents of hot air drawn through the drum. The Burns machine dispensed with the heat outside the drum, instead relying on a high-velocity blast of hot air roaring through the drum, thus roasting the coffee more by contact with hot air than by contact with hot metal. Burns machines like this one are still used in many American roasting establishments. The principle pioneered by the Thermalo reached its ultimate development in today's fluid-bed machines, which lift as well as roast the beans in the same rapidly moving, vertical column of hot air.

Twentieth-Century Innovations: Hot Air Only

Obviously the twentieth century could not leave coffee-roasting technology alone. The goal of roasting coffee beans as they fly through the air rather than rattling off hot metal or sizzling in a gas flame received two additional boosts in the middle years of the century.

In 1934 the Jabez Burns company developed a machine (the first model was called the Thermalo; see illustration above) that applied no heat whatsoever to the drum itself, instead relying entirely on a powerful stream of hot air howling through the drum. This arrangement permitted the use of a lower air temperature during roasting, since the rapidly moving air stripped the beans of their envelope of roasting gas and made the actual heat transfer from air to bean more efficient. Adherents of the new system argued that lower roasting temperatures and relatively rapid roasting burn off fewer flavor oils and produce a more aromatic coffee.

Also in the 1930s the first roasting device appeared that quite logically dispensed with the roasting drum altogether and instead used the same powerful column of hot air that roasted the beans to also agitate them. Such *fluid- (or fluidized-) bed* roasters work essentially like today's household hot-air corn poppers: The stream of hot air simultaneously tumbles and roasts the beans. The bed of beans seethes like fluid, hence the name. Fluid-bed roasters offer the same technical advantages as the Burns Thermalo machine: The rapidly moving air permits a lower roast temperature and a faster roast, theoretically driving off fewer flavor oils.

In the United States today the most widely used fluid-bed designs are the work of Michael Sivetz, an influential American coffee technician and writer. In the most popular Sivetz design the beans are forced upward along a vertical wall by the stream of hot air, then cascade back down again in a continuous rotation. See page 47 for an illustrated description of one style of Sivetz roaster.

Several other fluid-bed designs have been manufactured over the past fifty years, and more continue to enter the market. Some are simple variations on the original patents from fifty years ago, in which hot air rising from the bottom of a funnel-shaped roasting chamber creates a sort of fountain of beans that seethes upward in the middle before tumbling back down the sides of the chamber. Other designs, like Australian Ian Bersten's Roller Roaster and the Burns System 90 centrifugal, packed-bed roaster, are efforts to genuinely rethink the original fluid-bed principle. Still others are *display roasters*, which emphasize the drama of the procedure by enclosing the seething beans in glass. The idea is to draw customers into the store by flaunting roasting's technological and gourmet intrigue. All of the newer small fluid-bed shop roasters attempt to simplify and automate the roasting process as much as possible.

Electrified Roasting

Electricity came into use late in the nineteenth century to turn drums and pump air through conventional roasters. Electricity has not achieved great success as a heat source for large-scale roasting, however. As any cook knows, electric heat responds sluggishly to command compared to gas. Gas also is usually cheaper. For these reasons it has remained the preferred heat source in most larger shop and factory roasting installations.

Nevertheless, several shop roasting devices manufactured in the early part of the century provided roasting heat with electrical elements, and electricity continues in use in many small-scale roasting installations today.

Infrared and Microwaves

The use of electromagnetic waves or radiation to roast coffee has had mixed success.

Infrared is radiation with a wavelength greater than visible light but shorter than microwaves. It is used in outdoor-café heaters, portable home heaters, and similar applications.

The first infrared roasting machines appeared in the 1950s. Today one of the leading small American shop roasters, the Diedrich roaster, uses infrared heat. Like most drum roasters, the Diedrich machine combines heat applied to the outside of the roasting drum with currents of hot air drawn through it to roast the coffee. Unlike conventional drum roasters, however, the heat is supplied by radiating, gas-heated ceramic tiles. Metal heat exchangers apply some of the radiant heat to warm the air pulled through the drum. Proponents of the Diedrich machine admire its relative energy efficiency, low emissions, and clean-tasting roast.

Figuring out how to use microwaves to roast coffee has proven to be a tricky challenge, but sure enough, someone has figured out how to do it. The world's first genuine microwave coffee-roasting system, tentatively called Wave Roast, may appear about the time this book does. It is a small-scale roasting technology designed to make use of America's ubiquitous microwave ovens. See pages 168–170.

Roasting Without End: The Continuous Roaster

For large roasting companies time is money, and emptying beans from the roaster and reloading with more beans takes time. Such economic motives lay behind still another twentieth-century development, the *continuous roaster*, in which the roasting process never stops until the machine is turned off.

The most common continuous-roasting design elongates the typical roasting drum and puts a sort of screw arrangement inside it. As the drum turns, the screwlike vanes transport the coffee from one end of the drum to the other in a slow, one-way trip. Hot air is circulated across the drum at the front end and cool air at the far end. The movement of the beans through the drum is timed so that green coffee entering the drum is first roasted then cooled by the time it tumbles out at the end of its journey. Variations of this principle continue to be employed in machines used today in many large commercial roasting establishments. See page 50 for an illustrated description.

The fluid-bed principle has been pressed into service for continuous roasters as well. In these designs hot air simultaneously roasts and stirs large batches of coffee beans, which drop into a cooling chamber as soon as they are roasted, to be followed immediately by another batch of green coffee and still another, in continuous succession.

Conventional roasting machines that need to be stopped completely to be emptied and reloaded are now called *batch roasters* to distinguish them from continuous designs. Most specialty or fancy coffee-roasting establishments have stayed with batch roasters. If you are roasting a Kenyan coffee in the morning, a Sumatra at midday, and an espresso blend in the afternoon, the single-minded persistence of the continuous design makes no sense. On the other hand, large commercial roasting companies that roast a similar blend of coffee the same way every day find the consistent conveyor-belt approach embodied in such machines practical and desirable.

Chaff and Roasting Smoke

Some developments in nineteenth- and twentieth-century coffee-roasting technology have little to do with improving taste or the bottom line but instead respond to safety and environmental concerns.

The earliest of these issues to be faced involved roasting chaff. Green coffee arrives at the roaster with small, dry flakes of the innermost skin, or *silver skin*, still clinging to the bean. During roasting most of these flakes separate from the beans and float wherever air currents take them. They can be dangerous if they settle in one place and ignite, and are always annoying.

Recall that in the late nineteenth century fans were put into service to pull hot air through the roasting drum. This advance led to the development of the *cyclone*, a large, hollow, cone-shaped object that typically sits behind the roasting chamber. After the hot air is pulled from the roasting drum it is allowed to circulate inside the cyclone, where most of the chaff it has been carrying settles out. The chaff-free air and smoke then continue up and out of the chimney while the chaff collects at the base of the cyclone, where it can be removed and disposed of.

In the twentieth century the persistent odor of the roasting smoke and its potential pollutants became an issue. Technology came to the rescue with afterburners and catalytic devices that remove a good deal of the roasting by-products from the existing gases. Fuel was often conserved by recirculating at least a portion of the hot roasting air back through the roasting chamber.

A Revolution in Measurement and Control

At the arrival of the twenty-first century, there are signs that roasting technology may be undergoing still another revolution. Barring some breakthrough in the use of microwaves, it seems unlikely that the basic technologies for applying heat to the beans and keeping them moving will change. What is changing is the way the roast is monitored and controlled.

Traditionalists: Nose and Eye

Until recently small-scale roasting remained not too far removed from the hands-on approach of the Neapolitans cranking their *abbrustulaturo* on their balconies as recalled by Eduardo De Filippo in Chapter I.

Traditional roasters rely on a combination of eye (color of the beans), ear (sound of the crackling sounds emitted by the beans) and nose (the changing volume and scent of the roasting smoke). They take samples of the roasting beans by means of a little instrument called a *trier*, which they insert through a hole in the front of the roasting machine to collect a sample of the tumbling beans. The decision when to stop the roast is based on the color of the beans read in light of experience. Adjustments to the temperature inside the roast chamber also may be made on the basis of experience, both with roasting generally and with the idiosyncrasies of specific coffees.

For a traditionalist, roasting is an art in the old sense of the word: a hands-on experience unfolding again and again in the arena of memory and the senses.

Science Sneaks Up on Art

What was once a matter of art and the human senses, however, is increasingly becoming a matter of science and instrumentation in which individual memory is replaced by an externalized, collective memory of numbers and graphs.

Several instruments and controls are making this change possible. The first is a simple device that measures the approximate internal temperature of the roasting beans. Usually called a *thermocouple* or *heat probe,* it is an electronic thermometer whose sensing end is placed inside the roasting chamber so that it is entirely surrounded by the moving mass of beans. Although the air temperature inside the roasting chamber is different from the temperature of the beans, the beans tend to insulate the sensor from the air and transmit an approximate reading of their inner, collective heat to a display on the outside of the machine.

Once the chemical changes associated with roasting set in, the internal heat of the beans becomes a reasonably precise indicator of how far along the roast is. Think of the little thermometers that pop out of roasted turkeys when they're properly done. The inner temperature of roasting beans is a similar indicator of "doneness," or degree of roast. Thus the electronic thermometer can be used in place of the eye to gauge when to conclude the roast or make adjustments to the temperature inside the roast chamber. A chart matching approximate internal temperature with degree or style of roast appears on pages 68–69. With some contemporary roasting machinery it is possible to set the instrumentation to trigger the cooling cycle automatically when the beans have reached a predetermined internal temperature.

A second important control links the temperature inside the roasting chamber with the heat supply, automatically modifying the amount of heat to maintain a steady, predetermined temperature inside the chamber. This linkage is desirable because once the beans reach pyrolysis they emit their own heat, raising the temperature in the roasting chamber. If the amount of heat applied from outside the chamber remains uniform, as it does with the simpler conventional apparatus, then the heat inside the chamber begins to accelerate near the end of the roast, fed by the new heat supplied by the chemical changes in the beans. According to some roast philosophies, these spiraling, uncontrolled temperatures may roast the beans too quickly, burning off aromatics and weakening the structure of the bean.

A third instrument is the *near-infrared spectrophotometer.* This device, often called an *Agtron* after its manufacturers and developer, measures certain wavelengths of "color" or electromagnetic energy that are not visible to the human eye but that correlate particularly well with the degree of roast. Furthermore, the Agtron is not deceived by the changing quality of ambient light or by other sources of human fallibility like bad moods on talkative coworkers. The near-infrared spectrophotometer not only measures its narrow, telltale band of energy with consistency and precision, but translates it into a number as well. Thus two people thousands of miles apart can compare the development of their roasts by exchanging the readings on their instruments.

It has long been known that denser and/or moister coffees are slower to reach a given roast style than lighter or drier beans. Today's technically inclined roaster takes precise measurements of bean density and sets roast-chamber temperature and other variables to compensate for these differences according to a quantified system. The traditional roaster can only approximate such adjustments, basing them on past experience with the behavior of a given coffee in the roaster.

Finally, the velocity of the convection currents of air and gases moving through the roasting chamber can be controlled with great precision in some contemporary roasting equipment. Traditional roasters have always been able to control air currents in their drum roasters by adjusting a damper, much as we control convection currents in our home fireplaces and wood stoves. But again, this control was approximate rather than quantifiable and precise.

Thus today's systematic roaster has four to five quantifiable variables with which to work: original moisture content and density of the beans, temperature in the roasting chamber, internal temperature of the roasting beans, precisely measured color of the roasting beans, and (with some equipment) air velocity in the roasting chamber. Add in careful compensation for environmental factors like ambient temperature, altitude, and barometric pressure, and figures provided by these four or five variables can describe the progress and conclusion of a given roasting session for a given coffee, replacing

the ear, nose, eye, and memory with a set of hard data. With the use of computers, complex settings can be established to vary the temperature and other conditions inside the roast chamber on an almost second-by-second basis, permitting subtle modifications of the final taste of the roast, an approach called *profile roasting* by its proponents. Older, blander coffees can be made to taste somewhat more complex, for example, and rough or acidy coffees can be tamed and made smoother and sweeter.

This billboard from the 1930s dramatizes how preroasted, preground coffee was associated with modernity and progress in the early twentieth century.

But It Still Needs to Be Tasted

You may have patiently followed all of the preceding, or simply skimmed it to get to the punch line. Either way you can see how the use of instrumentation permits the translation of what was once an intuitive system held in the memory and nervous system of the roaster to a complex but precise series of numbers.

One human sense that hopefully will never become obsolete is taste. For even if the day arrives when roasting is performed entirely on the basis of system and number, the roaster (or *roastmaster* as he/she is increasingly called in these upscale days) still will need to taste the coffee when it comes out of the roasting apparatus and make some informed adjustments to those numbers based on personal preference and roasting philosophy. Thus the variety of taste achieved by different approaches to roasting may continue to surprise our palates and enrich the culture and connoisseurship of coffee. Roasting, perhaps, will remain art as well as science.

Social History: Quality Makes a Comeback

To conclude, let's return to the social history of roasting and bring it to its rather surprising conclusion in the twentieth century.

Although preroasted, preground coffee sold under brand names claimed more and more of the market in industrialized Europe and America during the first half of the twentieth century, older customs hung on. In southern Europe many people continued to roast their coffee at home well into the 1960s, and even in the United States small storefront roasting shops survived in urban neighborhoods.

As the century wore on, however, the trend toward convenience and standardization accelerated. By the 1960s packaged coffee identified by brand name dominated the urbanized world. Coffee was sold not only preroasted and preground, but in the case of soluble coffees, prebrewed. I recall visiting two of the world's most famous coffee-growing regions in the 1970s and finding only instant coffee served in restaurants and cafés. Most Americans and Europeans, who were now called *consumers*, had forgotten that coffee could be roasted at home, or even that it could be ground at home. Coffee doubtless appeared in their consciousness, perhaps even in their dreams, as round cans or bottles with familiar logos on the sides.

The simple process of home roasting became a lost art, pursued in industrialized societies only by a handful of cranky individualists and elsewhere by isolated rural people who roasted their own coffee as much from economic necessity as from habit or tradition.

Canned coffee became a favorite product to offer at great savings to lure people into large stores. The tendency to use coffee as an advertized loss leading sale item helped make it one of the most cost-sensitive food products of the 1950s and '60s, and understandably undercut the quality of the coffee inside those colorful cans. Commercial canned blends that were reasonably flavorful at the close of World War II became flat and lifeless by the end of the 1960s.

At that point, as mentioned in Chapter 1, a new phase of the coffee story began, a countermovement to the march toward uniformity and convenience at the cost of quality and variety. The few small shops that still roasted their own coffee and sold it in bulk provided a foundation for a revival of quality coffees that has gone far to transform coffee-consuming habits in the United States and many other parts of the industrialized world.

This revival is usually called the *specialty-coffee movement*. Thus the end of the twentieth century is witnessing a return to the coffee-roasting and -selling practices that dominated at its beginning, with people buying their coffee in bulk and grinding it themselves before brewing. Perhaps the United States, which has led the world down the superhighway of convenience, may be pointing it back along the slower road toward quality and authenticity.

From Gourmet Ghetto to Shopping Mall

However, a countertrend toward a new kind of standardization seems to be gaining momentum. The specialty-coffee movement began in the 1960s with small roasters selling their coffee as fresh as possible to neighborhood customers. However, specialty coffee has now moved out of gourmet ghettos and into suburban shopping malls. As it has, the stakes have risen. Neighborhood roasters have become regional chains, and regional chains have sold stock and gone national or international.

Today your neighborhood specialty-coffee store may well be one of a chain of fifty or, in the extraordinary case of Starbucks, one of thousands. Starbucks buys good-quality coffee, but roasts it in large plants and distributes it to a vast network of virtually identical retail outlets around the world.

Quirky and Individualistic

Starbucks is in many ways a happy marriage between the quality-conscious idealism of the specialty-coffee movement and rigorous corporate power and discipline. Nevertheless it does not entirely represent the world of coffee as I would like to see it enter the twenty-first century: quirky and individualistic, with local roasters selling their own styles of coffee in their own neighborhoods, a world full of choice and surprises.

For those who really love coffee, the moment may have come to leave both cans *and* enormous coffee-store chains behind, and enjoy coffee as people did before the advent of brand names, chain stores, and advertising: by roasting their own.

A Visual History of Roasting Machines

Home Roasters

For the first several hundred years of coffee history home roasters were the only kind of roaster. They remained a standard kitchen accessory until the early twentieth century.

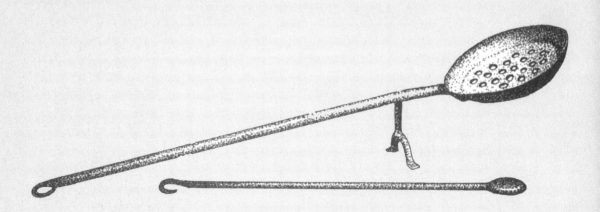

IRAQI ROASTING PAN, SIXTEENTH CENTURY

This simple implement projected over a small fire or the smoldering coals of a brazier, supported by the elongated handle and the two little legs. The bottom of the pan is perforated, and the beans were stirred with the long-handled spoon. According to coffee historian William Ukers, roasters like this one were in use in Iraq by the early sixteenth century.

AMERICAN FIREPLACE ROASTERS, EIGHTEENTH CENTURY

These three devices are typical of those used to roast coffee in fireplaces in the seventeenth and eighteenth centuries. The two round-bottomed pans on legs were called *spiders*. Much of the shop and commercial roasting apparatus in use today evolved from the simple cylinder pictured below the spiders, the point of which tested on an andiron or chink in the fireplace wall while someone (probably a servant or child) dutifully twirled it. Coffee was loaded through the little sliding door on the side of the cylinder.

AMERICAN STOVE ROASTERS, CA. 1860

These devices fit inside a burner opening in a wood or coal stove. In the middle years of the nineteenth century roasters like these were probably rather upscale appliances. Poorer or less fashion-able families roasted their coffee in the same iron skillet they used for the rest of their cooking.

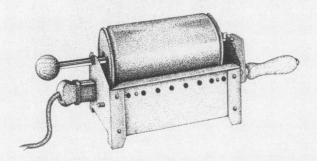

ITALIAN SPIRIT-LAMP ROASTER, EARLY NINETEENTH CENTURY

The glass cylinder of this decorative tabletop roaster usefully permits the operator to observe the developing color of the beans. A spirit lamp furnishes heat.

EUROPEAN ELECTRIC HOME ROASTER, EARLY TWENTIETH CENTURY

An electric element in the base provides heat in this countertop roaster. Despite the decline in home roasting in the early twentieth century, a number of devices like this one were marketed in Europe and Japan.

ELECTRIC FLUID-BED HOME ROASTER, 1980s

This little appliance reflects an effort to use the elegantly simple technology of the fluid bed to revive the practice of home roasting. A column of hot air rises from the base of the device, roasting and seething the beans inside the narrow cylinder that protrudes necklike from the base. The element that sits like a head atop the roasting chamber diverts and collects the chaff that otherwise would float out of the top of the unit. The AromaRoast was imported from Hong Kong by the Melitta Corporation during the 1980s.

ELECTRIC FLUID-BED HOME ROASTER, EARLY TWENTY-FIRST CENTURY

At the turn of the century several small home fluid-bed roasters appeared that improved on the Aroma-Roast design. The Fresh Roast incorporates features that have become standard for such handy little machines: a heating element and a fan (concealed inside the base) that forces the heated air up through the visually accessible roasting chamber, simultaneously agitating and roasting the beans; a chaff collector (the hatlike cylinder that sits atop the glass roasting chamber); and a timer that automatically turns off the heating element, allowing the fan to continue circulating room temperature air up through the beans, cooling them.

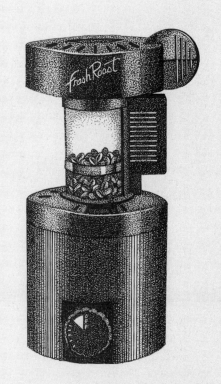

CONVECTION ROASTER, EARLY TWENTY-FIRST CENTURY

The Zach & Dani's Gourmet Coffee Roaster is an impressive effort to eliminate one of the main impediments to mainstream acceptance of home roasting: the troublesome roasting smoke. A screw in the middle of the glass roasting chamber agitates the beans. Because the hot roasting air that circulates from the bottom of the chamber is only required to roast the beans, not agitate them, as is the case with fluidized-bed devices, the air flow and roasting process can be slowed down, reducing smoke emission by stretching it out. Second, a catalytic converter, housed in the column opposite the roasting chamber, cleans the smoke from the air that flows out of the chamber.

Shop Roasters

Shop, retail, or micro roasters are small to medium-size machines used to roast coffee in stores and cafés. Most coffee not roasted in the home was prepared in shop roasters until the early twentieth century, when factory roasting and packaged preground coffees overwhelmed the market. In the late twentieth century shop roasting made a comeback as consumers in the United States and other industrialized countries rediscovered the pleasure of genuinely fresh coffee.

AMERICAN SHOP ROASTER, EIGHTEENTH CENTURY

Probably used in either a shop or coffeehouse, this little device is a simple elaboration on the cylinder roasters used in home fireplaces in the seventeenth and eighteenth centuries. It was placed inside a fireplace over the embers and turned by hand.

BRITISH SHOP ROASTERS, EIGHTEENTH CENTURY

The machines illustrated below were advances over the simpler fireplace designs in two respects: They were self-contained, with roasting heat provided by charcoal in the boxes beneath the drums, and they incorporated a hood that helped distribute heat around the entire circumference of the roasting drum.

AMERICAN SHOP ROASTER, 1862

This design, dating from 1862 and manufactured by E. J. Hyde of Philadelphia, is typical of more advanced mid-nineteenth-century shop roasters. It incorporated a swing-out roasting drum that facilitated dumping the coffee for cooling and vanes inside the drum that tossed the coffee as the drum turned. Heat continued to be provided by a coal fire under the drum, and the drum was turned by hand.

FRENCH GAS ROASTER, 1890s

According to William Ukers, the first patent for the use of gas heat for coffee roasting was filed in France in 1877. Today gas continues to roast most of the world's coffee. This gas-fired roaster, patented by M. Postulart in 1888, retains the globular roasting chamber to which the French remained loyal long after the Germans, British, and Americans had unanimously gone over to cylindrical designs. The hot roasted coffee was dumped by gravity from the globular roasting chamber down through a funnel to a cylindrical cooling chamber in the base, and from there into the drawer at the bottom of the machine.

GERMAN SHOP ROASTER, 1907

In this German Perfekt roaster from the first decade of the twentieth century, power is supplied by a belt connected to the pulley protruding at the left. This power turns the drum and, through a system of gears (visible at bottom right), rotates a set of paddles inside the circular cooling tray at the front of the roaster. These paddles agitate the beans and assist in their cooling.

Heat is provided by gas. An air pump, located in the base of the machine and powered by the descending belt at the left, pulls hot roasting air through and around the drum, ensuring a more even distribution of heat and faster roasting than could be obtained in earlier machines, in which only the metal of the drum itself was heated. These air currents also dispose of roasting smoke and chaff, the fine paperlike flakes of skin that adhere to green coffee beans. Finally, the pump, by moving fresh air through perforations at the bottom of the cooling tray, assists the turning paddles inside the tray to cool the roasted beans.

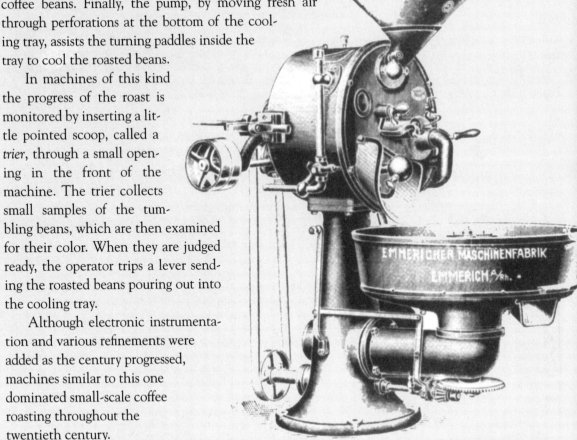

In machines of this kind the progress of the roast is monitored by inserting a little pointed scoop, called a *trier*, through a small opening in the front of the machine. The trier collects small samples of the tumbling beans, which are then examined for their color. When they are judged ready, the operator trips a lever sending the roasted beans pouring out into the cooling tray.

Although electronic instrumentation and various refinements were added as the century progressed, machines similar to this one dominated small-scale coffee roasting throughout the twentieth century.

SMALL GERMAN SHOP ROASTER, EARLY TWENTIETH CENTURY

Fashionably streamlined, compact little devices like the one on the right sat in the windows or near the front doors of many small shops in Germany and other European countries during the 1920s and '30s, enticing passersby with the odor of freshly roasting coffee. It worked almost exactly like the previously described machine.

FLUID-BED SHOP ROASTER, 1980S (CROSS SECTION)

Fluid-bed machines use the same powerful stream of hot air to simultaneously heat and agitate, or fluidize, the beans. In the design by American Michael Sivetz illustrated below, a column of hot air rises from the base of the machine through a sieve, driving the beans up the wall of the roasting chamber until they cascade back down again to the base in a continuous, fountainlike movement. A thermocouple, or heat

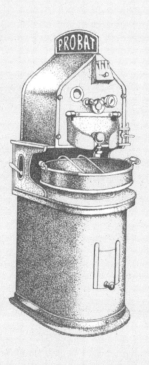

probe, roughly measures the internal temperature of the beans, enabling the operator to conclude the roast on the basis of bean temperature rather than color. The beans are then diverted into a separate chamber, where a column of room-temperature air cools them.

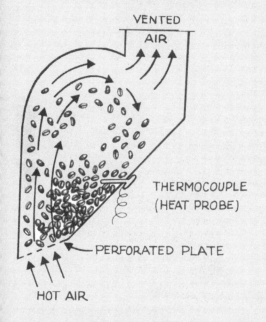

VENTED
AIR

THERMOCOUPLE
(HEAT PROBE)

PERFORATED PLATE

HOT AIR

There have been numerous other fluid-bed designs over the past fifty years, all similar in basic principle but varying how the air column and rotation of the beans is managed. Many incorporate a window or glass tube in the roast chamber to add interest to the rather bland-looking machine exteriors. Small fluid-bed roasters also introduced greater automation to the roast procedure, with sophisticated electronic controls making it possible to "instruct" the machine to terminate the roast when the thermocouple indicates that a predetermined bean temperature has been reached.

Factory Roasters

In the United States the first packaged coffees reached the expanding shelves of stores soon after the Civil War. By the end of World War II preroasted and preground coffees prepared in giant factories completely dominated the North American market. The technology of large roasting devices variously called plant, factory, or commercial roasters developed in tandem to this standardizing, centralizing trend. During the mid- to late-nineteenth century factory roasters were simply larger versions of shop machines, but near the end of the century the first continuous-roasting devices were developed, an approach that in one form or another continues to dominate large-scale coffee roasting.

BRITISH FACTORY ROASTER, 1848

The Dakin roaster pictured here was a more sophisticated version of the American Carter Pull-Out machines appearing in the engraving on page 28. As with the American machines, the drum was turned by steam power transmitted via pulleys, and was enclosed inside a brick oven. In the Dakin design, however, the drum was surrounded by a second inner metal shell to protect it from direct heat, and the pull-out mechanism was more elegant than the simple arrangement of the American machine.

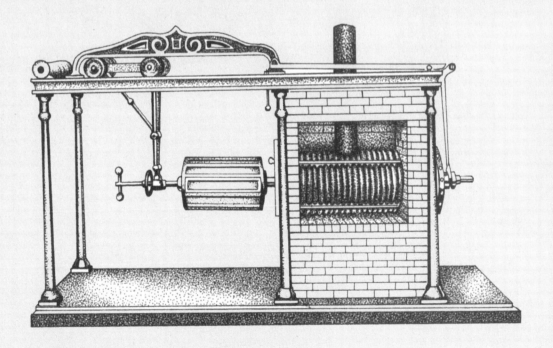

AMERICAN SMALL FACTORY ROASTER, 1864

The Jabez Burns roaster of 1864 introduced a double-screw arrangement that worked the coffee in a continuous forward-and-back movement inside the roasting cylinder. This innovation not only distributed the coffee in the cylinder more consistently than did earlier arrangements of vanes, but—more important—would work the coffee out the front of the cylinder when the door was opened. Most twentieth-century drum roasters propel the roasted coffee out of the drum using a similar arrangement. Note that the roasting cylinder is still surrounded by a brick oven and turned by steam.

FRENCH GAS FACTORY ROASTER, LATE NINETEENTH CENTURY

The new technology of gas began to appear in coffee-roasting apparatuses in the late decades of the nineteenth century. This French machine dumped the coffee by gravity from the bottom of the drum into the cooling tray.

GERMAN GAS CONTINUOUS ROASTER, LATE NINETEENTH CENTURY

The German Thurmer roaster of 1893 was probably the world's first continuous gas roaster. A screwlike arrangement of vanes inside the long roasting cylinder gradually moved green beans in one direction down the length of the gas-fired cylinder; by the time they reached the end of the cylinder they were roasted. Thus a continuous flow of beans could be roasted without stopping the process, as was necessary with batch roasting as represented in the previous machines and in retail or shop roasters. The Thurmer machine also introduced the concept of fast (three- to four-minute) roasting, an approach large roasting concerns immediately found appealing but which remains controversial in terms of its impact on quality.

CONTINUOUS ROASTER, LATE TWENTIETH CENTURY (CROSS SECTION)

Pictured here is a cross section of a contemporary continuous roaster, looking down the interior of the drum. The roasting is accomplished by a powerful stream of hot air moving from one side of the drum to the other. The beans are cooled near the end of their ride down the cylinder by a combination of cool air and a fine spray of water.

Large continuous roasters being installed today are increasingly likely to use the fluid-bed principle, however. They work much like oversized versions of the Sivetz shop roaster illustrated on page 47. After one batch of beans finishes rotating and roasting in the stream of hot air, it drops into a cooling chamber and a fresh batch of beans replaces it, thus implementing continuous roasting.

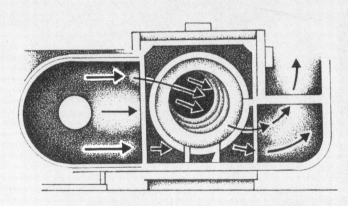

Chapter 3

FROM CINNAMON TO CHARCOAL

Roast Styles

 Nothing influences the taste of coffee more than roasting. The same green coffee can be roasted to taste grassy, baked, sour, bright and dry, full-bodied and mellow, rounded and bittersweet, or charred. In appearance roasted beans can range from light brown with a dry surface through dark brown with an increasingly oily surface to black with an almost greasy look.

These differences in appearance lead people to talk about differences in roast *color*, from *light* roast to *dark*. I prefer the term *style* to describe the varying taste characteristics that roast imparts to coffee, since a coffee carried to a medium roast slowly, for example, will taste subtly different from the same coffee brought to the same medium roast quickly at higher temperatures. Others call the gradual change in color and taste created by roast *degree of roast* or *degree of processing,* which are accurate terms but clumsy. In this book I'll generally stick with the term *style.*

Changing Roast Traditions

Until recently preferences in roast style, like so many other cultural choices, have been traditional. Style of coffee roast was a choice our par-

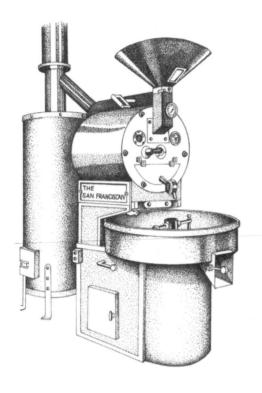

A shop-sized drum roaster of the classic design, in this case the San Franciscan, a product of a small American manufacturer, Coffee/PER. Most drum-style shop roasters, including those manufactured by Probat (Germany), Samiac (France) and others, are arranged much like this example. Larger, industrial-capacity drum roasters employ more sophisticated control of heat and airflow, and typically incorporate a water-quench system inside the drum, usually a pipe or nozzle that sprays the hot coffee with a quick burst of water to kick off the cooling process.

ticular time and place made for us. Thus Turks roast darker than Saudi Arabians; southern Italians roast darker than northern Italians; people in Normandy darker than people in central France. In the United States the Northwest has traditionally preferred a somewhat darker roast than New England, northern California darker than southern California, New Orleans darker than Atlanta.

These traditional preferences are the basis of many of the names used in the contemporary American coffee business to describe style of roast: New England (light), American (medium), Viennese (slightly darker), French (still darker), Italian (still darker again), and so on. Names for roasts are discussed in more detail later in this chapter, and are summarized along with other information on roast in a chart on pages 68–69. However, in our globally conscious, media-saturated times, regional uniformity in roast preference has begun to blur. Certainly in North American cities you can find virtually every possible style of roast sold by someone somewhere. The typical "American" roast style—medium brown in color, bright and dry in taste—is increasingly displaced by roast styles that are darker in color and more pungent, while the foamy nuances of cappuccinos and caffè lattes replace the bottomless cup.

What's Best?

Such cultural crossing and mixing makes it difficult to argue for any single "best" style of roast. According to the people who sell coffee, the "best" happens to be what they sell. Most roasters have clearly defined roasting and blending philosophies, arrived at after long experience. These dedicated professionals are certainly entitled to their positions, but to claim that a given approach to roasting is scientifically and objectively better than other approaches ultimately founders on the rocks of cultural difference. Who is to say to a French coffee drinker from Normandy who

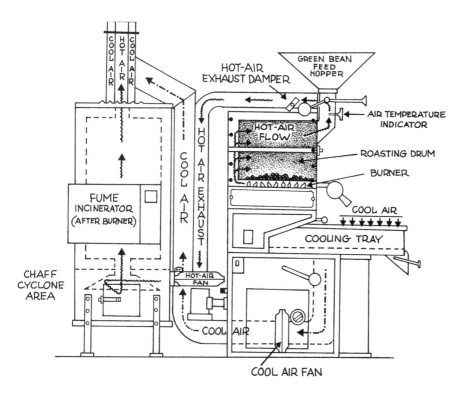

A cross-section view of the San Franciscan drum roaster pictured on page 52. The green beans are released from the cone-shaped hopper into the roasting drum. There they are roasted by a combination of heat applied to the outside of the drum and a flow of heated air drawn through the drum by the hot-air fan. A system of metal vanes (not shown) tumbles the beans inside the drum. When the beans achieve the desired roast a semicircular door is opened at the front of the drum enclosure, and the hot beans spill out into the cooling tray. The cool-air fan then pulls room-temperature air down through the hot beans while paddles inside the cooling tray gently stir them.

After leaving the roasting drum, the hot air, now carrying roasting chaff and smoke, circulates in the chaff-cyclone area, dropping its chaff as it does so. The chaff-free hot air then continues upward through the fume incinerator or afterburner to be cleansed of its smoke and odors.

prefers a thin-bodied black coffee that tastes mildly burned that a coffee carefully brought to a medium roast is objectively and universally better than his or hers because more of the flavor oils survive the roasting? Perhaps this French coffee drinker from Normandy prefers a charred taste to more flavor oils.

One of the many pleasures of home roasting is experimenting to determine what the "best" roasting style is *for you*. Of course one of the frustrations of home roasting is that once you get a batch of beans that taste exactly the way you want them to you may have trouble precisely duplicating the procedure that produced them. But if you are at all systematic you can come very close to consistency, and home roasting is for romantics and adventurers anyhow. Those concerned purely with uniformity probably should stick to buying coffee from the store.

Bad by Any Standard

There are some clear parameters to good roasting, however, boundaries which, if transgressed, produce roasts that are bad by almost anyone's standard.

Look at the table on pages 68-69. In roasts that are too light, in which the internal temperature of the beans never rises above 390°F/200°C and the color remains a pale brown, the flavor oils remain undeveloped, which gives the coffee a grassy, sour taste and no aroma. In roasts that are too dark, in which the internal temperature of the beans has soared above 480°F/250°C and the color is definitively black, most of the flavor oils will have been burned out of the bean and the woody parts of the bean itself may be charred. Such coffee tastes thin-bodied, burned, and industrial.

Another way coffee can be roasted badly is either by "baking" it by holding it too long at too low a temperature, or by scorching the outer surfaces of the beans. Fortunately, most store-bought home-roasting equipment makes it easy to avoid such mistakes, but home roasters using improvised equipment need to guard against them by following the relevant instructions in the "Quick Guide to Home Roasting Options, and Procedures."

But as long as a roast avoids such extremes, only cultural preference and personal taste can determine which style is ultimately "best."

Names and Roast Styles

Currently used names for roast styles come from two sources. One is the general roasting preferences of various nations of coffee drinkers—Italian, French, and so on. The other grew up within the American coffee profession during the late nineteenth and early twentieth centuries. Both nomenclatures are necessarily vague and are now being supplemented by a more objective numerical system based on instrument reading of color.

GEOGRAPHICAL ROAST NAMES

Let's take a quick run through the common roast names first, beginning with those that derive from coffee-drinking geography, since these are the names you are most likely to see on coffee bags and bins.

The lightest roast, *New England*, is hardly produced in North America anymore. The ordinary medium-brown roast that still dominates coffee taste in the United States is usually unnamed, but may be called *American*. A slightly darker roast, sometimes with tiny droplets of oil on the surface, may appear as *Viennese* or occasionally *light French*. *French* describes a moderately dark roast with more surface oil; *Italian* (sometimes *Spanish*, *Continental*, or *New Orleans*), darker and oilier still. A very dark brown, almost black roast, may be called *dark French* (since such a roast is favored in northwestern France), *Spanish*, *Turkish*, or *Neapolitan*. Lately a roast called *espresso* has been inserted between *French* and *Italian*, which roughly represents the current roast taste in northern Italy (moderately dark brown with some oil on the surface of the bean).

Thus we get something that looks like this (sticking to the more popular terms):

- *New England* (light brown; dry surface)
- *American* (medium brown; dry surface)
- *Viennese* (medium dark brown; possibly flecks of oil on surface)
- *French* (moderately dark brown; light oil on surface)
- *Espresso* (dark brown; surface can range from very oily to barely slick, depending on roast procedure)
- *Italian* (dark, blackish brown; definite oily surface—most roasting establishments stop here)
- *Dark French* or *Spanish* (very dark brown, almost black; very oily).

TRADITIONAL AMERICAN ROAST NAMES

There is another naming system haunting the aisles of coffee stores, however, one based on traditional American roasting terminology stretching back to the nineteenth century. It breaks out about like this:

- *Cinnamon* (very light brown)
- *Light* (light end of the American norm)
- *Medium*
- *Medium high* (American norm)
- *City high* (slightly darker than norm)
- *Full city* (definitely darker than norm; sometimes patches of oil on surface)
- *Dark* (dark brown; shiny surface—equivalent to *espresso* or *French*)
- *Heavy* (very dark brown; shiny surface—equivalent to *Italian*)

Of these terms *full city* is the only one used today with any frequency; roasters who bring most of their coffees to a style somewhat darker than the mid-twentieth-century American norm often describe their roast as *full city*.

Numbers to the Rescue: The Agtron/SCAA Roast Classification Color-Disk System

Confusing? True. To help save the roasting world from arbitrary naming and obfuscation, the Specialty Coffee Association of America (SCAA) has recently released a kit for classifying roast based on precise machine reading of color.

The eight reference points in this classification system have no names, only numbers, and are matched with eight carefully prepared color disks. A sample of a roasted coffee, when finely ground and pressed into a petri dish, can be matched with a color disk, thus assigning it an approximate number on a scale variously termed a *chemistry index* or *Agtron gourmet scale*. These *color-disk* (or *color-tile*) numbers run from #95 (lightest roast) to #85 (next lightest) and by intervals of ten down to #25 (darkest common roast).

Of course someone who owns an Agtron near-infrared spectrophotometer, an instrument that currently sells for between $7,000 and $20,000, can make very precise readings directly from the petri dishes of coffee.

At this writing, language deriving from the Agtron/SCAA system has not made much of an impression on the words used to communicate with consumers on signs and brochures. However, I have taken a stab at connecting the Agtron/SCAA classification-system numbers with common roast names in the comprehensive roast table on pages 68–69. Keep in mind, however, that the Agtron/SCAA system was designed without regard to the various traditions and preferences several generations of coffee roasters have attached to these names and is intended to create a separate and hopefully more objective basis for discussion of roast.

The four color samples printed on the inside back cover of the kit give a rough idea of the range of the eight roast colors represented in the Agtron/SCAA system. Remember, however, that there are eight colors in the system, not four, and that the vagaries of color printing, the glossiness of the ink, the variability of light sources, the distractions of adjacent colors, not to mention what you had for lunch, all combine to make this abridged version of the Agtron/SCAA color disks technically useless. In other words, don't expect to be able to hold up a handful of beans next to these four color samples and be able to assign the beans an Agtron number. The samples will give you some general visual reference for the system as a whole, however.

For information on obtaining the Agtron/SCAA Roast Classification Color Disk System, plus information on the SCAA and Agtron generally, see Resources. Carl Staub, an innovative practical scientist and president of Agtron, is the principal researcher behind the color-classification system.

Tasting Terms

At no time does language seem so puny as when it attempts to describe how things taste. Nevertheless, coffee professionals *can* talk sensibly about the taste of their beverage. They do so by sharing common definitions of certain key terms and categories. Around these terms and categories subtler observations about taste can be arranged.

Here are a few of the most important terms for talking about differences in taste among green coffees and roast styles. I've left out technical terms that relate to specific phases of professional coffee-cupping, or sensory evaluation. I have included only the most important and widely used of the many terms describing defects and related characteristics that green coffees acquire from idiosyncrasies in how they have been handled after picking (*fermented*, *musty*, *baggy*). Finally, I have disregarded terms that are self-evident or have no clear consensus meaning (*rich*, *floral*, *smooth*, *buttery*, and others).

The first three terms, *acidity*, *body*, and *aroma*, are relatively stable in meaning and almost universally used in coffee evaluation. Unless you understand them you can't properly talk coffee. The terms that follow those three are less likely to elicit consensus among tasters. They represent my selection from a large and growing list that includes traditional coffee terms dating back to the nineteenth century as well as new vocabulary being brought into coffee from wine and other tasting schemes.

Acidity, acidy. One of the most important tasting categories in coffee, and one of the most likely to be misunderstood. Neither acidic nor sour, an acidy coffee is brisk and bright. It is analogous to the dry sensation in wines. Coffees lacking acidity tend to taste bland and lifeless. Some coffees carry their identity wrapped in their acidy notes. For example, coffees from Yemen and from East Africa (Kenya, Zimbabwe) display a striking, fruity, red-wine–like acidity. The darker a coffee is roasted, the less acidy it becomes. However, strong acidity in a green coffee may show up in a dark roast as sharpness or pungency.

Body, mouthfeel. Body is the sensation of heaviness in the mouth; mouthfeel is the sensation of texture: *buttery*, *gritty*, *oily*, *smooth*, *thin*, *watery*, *lean*, *astringent*. Body is mainly a sensation rather than a measurable fact, although it roughly correlates with the quantity of dissolved solids the coffee releases into the cup.

As coffee approaches a medium- to dark brown roast, body *increases*, and mouthfeel becomes rounder and fatter. As it passes into a very dark roast (dark French or Spanish roast), body decreases again, and mouthfeel becomes lean and gritty.

Aroma. Although this term is self-evident in its general definition, it is important in discussions of roast. Aroma is less developed in very light roasts, peaks in intensity in medium to medium-dark roasts, and lessens and simplifies in very dark roasts. For professional coffee evaluators or cuppers, some qualities of coffees may be more immediately apparent in the aroma than in the taste of the coffee itself.

Complexity. Another obvious yet useful term. A complex coffee enables certain strong sensations such as acidity and sweetness to coexist. It presents a wide *range* of sensation and often doesn't reveal itself immediately and definitively. Complexity is undoubtedly at its peak in the middle ranges of roast style, from medium through the moderately dark to dark roasts used for espresso. Yet a good espresso roast is complex in a different way from a medium roast, since the elements that compose that complexity subtly change. Most blends (those that aren't designed simply to save the blender money) aim to increase complexity.

Depth, dimension. Depth describes the resonance or sensual power *behind* the sensations that drive the taste of the coffee. It is a tricky and subjective term, but one that profitably invites us to consider how certain coffees open up and support their sensations with a sort of ringing, echoing power, whereas others simply present themselves to the palate before standing pat or fading.

Origin distinction, varietal distinction, varietal character. These terms describe qualities that distinguish one unblended green coffee from another when the coffees are brought to the relatively light "cupping" roast used in professional coffee evaluation. Examples are the powerful, dry, berry-toned acidity of Kenyan coffees; the ringing acidy notes and clean balance of Costa Rica; the extravagant floral and citrus tones of Ethiopian Yirgacheffe; or the low-key, malty richness of traditional Sumatras. Some coffees do not display distinctive characteristics, which does not make them bad or boring. If they are particularly forceful yet balanced they might earn the epithet *classic*. Other coffees that are sweet and round may be praised as *good blenders* because they complement rather than compete with other, more distinctive coffees.

Strictly speaking, terms like "varietal distinction" are misleading, since most coffees are not marketed by botanical variety but by *origin*. Thus the proper term should be "origin distinction" or "growing-region distinction." But those phrases are not half as impressive as "varietal distinction," with its oak-toned, wine-world panache.

Whatever we choose to call it, this quality displays itself best in light to medium roasts, becomes progressively more obscured in darker roasts, and is virtually impossible to detect in very dark roasts.

Balance. Another self-evident term, this one describing coffees in which the acidity is strong but not overwhelming, the body substantial, and no taste idiosyncrasy dominates.

Processing-Related Terms

These are characteristics bestowed on the coffee by idiosyncrasies in how the fruit has been removed from the coffee beans (i.e., seeds) and how they have been dried and stored.

Clean. This frequently used term describes coffees whose cup characteristics come directly from the coffee fruit, without addition or interference from mistakes or idiosyncrasies in fruit removal or drying. The best Central American, Kenyan, Ethiopian wet-processed, and Hawaiian Kona coffees are examples of origins whose "varietal distinction" depends on a clean profile, with bright, clear articulation of flavor characteristics that come from no murky interference whatsoever from processing or drying. Sumatran Mandheling and Sulawesian coffees are just the opposite. Their "varietal distinction" depends in part on certain malty, musty, low-toned complexities that derive from the odd way they have been processed and dried.

Fruity, fermented, winey. Some coffees are naturally fruity, but often this flavor note derives from coffee fruit whose sugars have begun to ferment before the fruit was removed from the beans or from fruit residue that was allowed to remain on the beans while they dried. When this flavor is sweet and attractive without having attracted molds, it is often called *fruity,* but when the fermented taste begins to taste composty or rotten, the flavor is branded as *fermented,* a flavor defect. Somewhere between fruity and fermented are coffees whose fermented-fruit taste suggests the term *winey.* Some people enjoy fruity and winey coffees. I am among them.

Musty, malty. When coffees attract microorganisms while the beans are drying, the result is an aggressively flat taste that suggests the odor of mildewed leather left in a damp closet. When the underlying flavor profile of the coffee is sound and the musty taste is not too strong or dominant, this sensation can be quite agreeable and may merit the term *malty.* Some imaginative people may even romance the sensation with the term *chocolaty*. However, if the musty sensation is too dominant, the coffee is simply dismissed as definitively *musty*, an outright flavor defect.

Earthy. Often confused with mustiness, *earthiness* is the literal flavor of earth transmitted to the coffee when it is dried directly on the ground rather than on concrete, brick, or tarpaulins. Some coffee professionals judge this note exotically attractive; others condemn it as a defect.

Wild. An all-purpose term that describes coffees whose profiles have been influenced by any or all of the above factors: fermented fruit, mustiness, earthiness, or similar taints.

Storage-related taints: baggy, faded. When lower-grown, less dense–beaned coffees are stored in damp conditions, they tend to pick up a kind of flat mustiness, often with a rope- or burlaplike overlay, that coffee professionals call *baggy*. Baggy coffees also are typically *faded*, meaning their characteristics have become dull and subdued. These characteristics are almost always perceived as defects.

Picking-related characteristics: sweet, green, grassy. Coffees that have been picked when the fruit is ripe typically display a natural sweetness. Those that are dominated by beans that have been processed from unripe fruit will taste thin-bodied, *green*, and *grassy*, with an astringent mouthfeel.

Roast-Related Terms

These are words specifically related to the overlay of taste that style or degree of roast contributes to green coffees.

Sweet. In medium-dark through moderately dark roasts (Viennese through espresso) the development of sugars combined with the partial elimination of certain bitter flavor components, like trigonelline, give the cup a rounded, soft taste and rich body without flatness. As would be expected, naturally sweeter green coffees from fruit picked when it is ripe make sweeter dark roasts.

Pungent, pungency. These words are my choice to describe the distinctive, bitterish twist that dark roasting contributes to taste. Any lover of dark roasts knows and honors this sensation.

Roast taste, bittersweet. Terms describing the characteristic collective flavor complex of darker roasts. The acidy notes are gone, replaced by pungent notes combined with a subtle, caramel sweetness. "Bittersweet" is my term; some people call this often unnamed group of sensations "roast taste" or the "taste of the roast."

Bready. A bready taste manifests in coffees that have not been roasted long enough or at a high enough temperature to bring out the flavor oils.

Baked. Another term for maltreated coffee. The coffee has been held too long in the roaster at too low a temperature; the taste in the cup is flat and without aroma.

Roast Styles and Flavor

Now let's look at how some of these key categories—acidity, body, aroma, varietal distinction, and bittersweetness or roast taste—transform as coffee is brought in stages from a very light to a very dark roast style. Again, this information is summarized for easy reference in the chart on pages 68–69.

- The most lightly roasted coffee (usually called *cinnamon:* internal bean temperature at conclusion of roast below 400°F/205°C; SCAA color tile #95) is very light brown in color, will display a strong, sometimes sour *acidity,* little *aroma,* an often grainy taste, and thin *body.* The surface of the bean will be dry.

- As the coffee achieves a more complete but still relatively light roast (*New England, light:* concluding internal bean temperature around 400°F/205°C; SCAA color tile #85), the *acidy* notes will be powerful, and the *varietal characteristics,* which often are nuances of acidity, will be pronounced. The *body* will be developed but not as fully as it will become in a somewhat darker roast. The surface of the bean remains dry, as the flavor oils continue to develop in tiny pockets inside the bean.

- At a darker, moderately light to medium-brown roast (*light, medium,* unnamed, *American:* concluding internal bean temperature between 400°F/205°C and 415°F/215°C; SCAA color tiles #75 through #65), the *acidity* will be bright but less overpowering, the *varietal characteristics* still pronounced, and *body* fuller. For most traditional American East Coast coffee drinkers, this style represents a "good" coffee taste.

- At a slightly darker, medium-brown roast (*medium, medium high,* unnamed, *American, city:* concluding internal bean temperature 415°F/215°C to 435°F/225°C; SCAA color tile #55), *acidity* remains strong though perhaps richer, *varietal characteristics* muted but still clear, and *body* still fuller. This is the traditional roasting norm for most of the American West.

- At a slightly darker roast than the traditional North American norm, one coffee professionals often call *full city* (concluding internal bean temperature 435°F/225°C to 445°F/230°C; between SCAA color tiles #55 and #45), *acidity* is slightly more muted and *body* slightly heavier. At this roast, only the more pronounced *varietal characteristics,* like the winelike acidity of Kenyan coffees, will persist. Subtler notes, like the elusive smokiness of some Guatemalan coffees, will be lost.

  At this roast the first hints of an entirely new flavor appear: the taste taken on by darker roasts of coffee. This taste complex has no consensus name; in my list of tasting terms I call it *bittersweet.* Certain sugars are developed in the bean, giving it a subtle sweetness (*not* sugary but rather an understated caramellike quality), while the acidity begins to transform into a pleasant pungency. The combination is familiar to any drinker of darker-roasted coffees.

The surface of the bean may remain dry, or oils may appear in tiny droplets or patches as they begin to rise from pockets inside the bean to its surface. This is the preferred roast style of many coffee drinkers in the American Northwest and northern California, and is currently being carried nationwide by the successful Starbucks chain.

- At a moderately darker roast (*espresso, European, high:* concluding internal bean temperature 445°F/230°C to 455°F/235°C; between SCAA color tiles #45 and #35), the *acidity* is largely folded into a general impression of richness, the *varietal characteristics* muted virtually beyond recognition, the *body* full, and the *bittersweet* notes characteristic of dark-roasted coffees rich and resonant. At this roast the surface of the bean always displays some oil, ranging from a few droplets to a shiny coating.

- When coffee is brought to a definitely dark roast (*French, Italian, dark:* concluding internal bean temperature 455°F/235°C to 465°F/240°C; SCAA color tile #35), the *bittersweet* or dark-roast taste completely dominates, the *body* begins to thin again, and all remaining *varietal character* and *acidy* notes are transmuted inside the pungent richness of the dark-roast flavor, which may range from rounded and mellow (in less acidy coffees) to bordering on bitter (in coffees that begin very acidy). The surface of the bean will be bright with oil.

- With very dark brown roasts (*Italian, dark French, Spanish, heavy:* concluding internal bean temperature 465°F/240°C to 475°F/245°C; between SCAA color tiles #35 and #25), the *body* continues to thin as more and more of the oils are evaporated by the roast, the bitterish side of the *bittersweet* equation becomes more dominant, and a slight charred taste may appear. Needless to say, *acidy* notes and *varietal characteristics* have long since been transformed into nuances of the dark-roast flavor. The bean is shiny with flavor oils driven to the surface.

Despite the somewhat thinner body and dominance of the dark-roast flavor, such a coffee can be a bracing and pleasant experience for those who like it. It can be particularly pleasant drunk with hot milk as a caffè latte or similar espresso-and-milk drink.

- The ultimate dark roast, almost black (*dark French, Spanish;* concluding internal bean temperature 475°F/245°C to 480°F/250°C; SCAA color

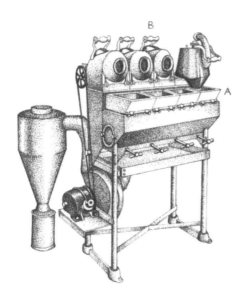

Sample roasters are used to prepare small quantities of green coffee for purposes of evaluation. Most are miniature drum roasters arranged in a battery, like this set dating from the early twentieth century. The roasted beans are dumped into the cooling trays (A) at the front of the drums by lifting the handles (B) at the back. The drum on the right is in the forward, dumping position. Heat is usually provided by gas, as it is here. An electric motor drives the drums, and a fan (here enclosed in a circular housing under the drums) sucks hot air through the drums, evacuating both roasting smoke and chaff. The chaff settles to the bottom of the cyclone at the rear of the machine. The fan also helps cool the beans by pulling fresh air down through perforations in the bottoms of the cooling trays.

tile #25) is definitely a special taste. The *body* is even thinner, the *bitter-sweetness* is still more bitter and less sweet, and burned or charred notes dominate. At this roast all coffees, regardless of origin, tend to taste about the same. The surface of the bean is glossy with oil. This unusual roast is not an espresso roast, by the way; espresso is best brewed with one of the dark-but-not-black, fuller-bodied, sweeter roasts described earlier. Home roasters typically have an opportunity to sample this ultimate dark roast, since sooner or later we all produce a batch whether we plan to or not.

- Beyond this point the coffee is definitively burned: It has no body, tastes like charred rubber, the oils are driven off the surface of the bean, and the roast is worthless.

Time/Temperature Ratio and Other Subtleties

All roast styles differ in taste depending on *how* the roast is achieved. Coffee brought to a given roast color quickly—by higher roast temperature or a combination of higher temperature and rapidly moving air currents—will usually preserve more acidy notes than will coffee brought to the same degree of roast at lower air temperatures over a longer period of time. On the other hand, a slower-roasted coffee tends to be fuller in body and more complex in taste.

These differences in approach are the source of often bitter controversy among proponents of various roasting systems. In particular, an intense behind-the-scenes struggle for the hearts and minds of newcomers to the coffee-roasting world is being carried on between what I like to call the slow-and-deliberate school of roasters versus the fast-but-gentle camp.

The slow-and-deliberate school likes to bring the coffee along in careful, methodical stages: first at relatively lower temperatures to force out free moisture from the bean, then at somewhat higher temperatures once the chemical transformation of pyrolysis has kicked in. The goal is to preserve as much as possible of the bean's original moisture and cellular structure during the roasting process by using temperatures just high enough to maintain the forward momentum of the roast, yet low enough to minimize damage to the cellular matrix of the bean and its bound moisture. The slow-and-deliberate camp tends to prefer drum roasters to fluid-bed equipment, because drum roasters typically permit a finer and more precise control over roast temperatures and air velocity than do fluid-bed roasters. Roast times for the slow-and-deliberate faction usually range in the twelve- to twenty-five-minute range.

On the other hand, the fast-but-gentle roasters argue that the longer the beans are in the roaster the more aromatic oils they lose. Consequently, they are usually proponents of fluid-bed systems, or those systems in which a column of hot air simultaneously agitates and roasts the beans. The fast schoolers contend that the high velocity of the roasting air in fluid-bed machines transfers heat to the beans so efficiently that you can bring a coffee along quickly without drying it out excessively or destroying its cellular structure, thereby preserving the maximum amount of its flavor components. Roast times among the fast-but-gentle contingent may be as short as five minutes, usually no more than fifteen.

Who's right? Perhaps both are. I have tasted superb coffees roasted quickly on fluid-bed machines, and slowly on drum roasters. The controversy simply may turn on what you consider a "good" coffee. If you favor an acidy but sweet cup (or a sweet, pungent cup in dark roasts) with a clean, straightforward flavor profile, you may weigh in as a backer of the fast-but-gentle school. On the other hand, if you prefer a fuller, less acidy cup, emphasizing complexity and depth rather than assertive brightness (with a bit more bitterness in dark roasts), you may back the slow-and-deliberate platform.

Both camps acknowledge that coffee held at too low a temperature for too long a time will taste baked and flat, while coffee brought to a given roast style too quickly at too high a temperature will lack complexity, resonance, and power. Thus both sides aim for quality; it simply may be that they nuance quality in different ways.

The nature of the roasting technology also influences the taste of a given roast. Proponents of fluid-bed roasting, for example, argue that their roasts taste better and cleaner because the roasting smoke and chaff are blown off the beans more decisively than is the case with most drum roasters. Other professionals may *like* the somewhat heavier, oilier taste imparted by smoke and burning chaff, and may deliberately stick with older roasting equipment that allows some of the smoke to work around the beans.

Time/Temperature Ratios and the Home Roaster

The foregoing nuances are best ignored by all but the most advanced of home roasters. Your first task is to learn how to control the timing of the roast so that you get the broadly defined roast style or color you prefer.

Your ability to experiment with subtler taste differences related to the *way* you achieve a given roast style depends above all on the equipment you use.

I survey several roasting technologies in this book. (See Chapter 5). Those who like a bright, acidy coffee probably are best served by a fluid-bed roasting technology as represented by either manufactured-from-scratch machines (see pages 129–130) or hot-air corn poppers (see pages 176–181). The temperature in the roasting chamber is usually fixed in these devices. They produce a relatively rapid roast (three to twelve minutes), and the roasting smoke is effectively blown off the beans, all promoting a clean, high-toned flavor profile.

Those who prefer a more idiosyncratic roast taste with heavier body and a fuller, more complexly layered profile would be best off with an old-fashioned stove-top roaster like the Aroma Pot (see pages 170–171), a stove-top popcorn popper (172–176), or an oven-roasting arrangement (181–189).

Dedicated drum or convection roasting machines like the Swissmar Alpenroast, the HotTop Bean Roaster, and the Zach & Dani's Gourmet Coffee Roaster produce a roast somewhere between these extremes: clean, without much smoky ambiguity, but lower-toned, less acidy, and also less sweet, often with more pronounced roasty pungency.

Quick Reference Guide to Roast Styles

Most of what you really need to know about roast styles can be determined from the following chart. Extended explanation of terminology and categories can be found in Chapter 3. (The roast colors associated with the tile numbers in column four are represented (roughly) on the inside back cover.)

Roast Color	Bean Surface	Approximate Bean Temperature at Termination of Roast	Agtron Gourmet Scale Numbers: SCAA Color Tile Number in boldface (see pages 55–57)	Common names
Very light brown	Dry	Around 380°F/195°C "First crack"	95–90 **Tile #95**	Cinnamon
Light brown	Dry	Below 400°F/205°C	90–80 **Tile #85**	Cinnamon New England
Moderately light brown	Dry	Around 400°F/205°C	80–70 **Tile #75**	**Light** New England
Light-medium brown	Dry	Between 400°F/205°C and 415°F/215°C	70–60 **Tile #65**	**Light-Medium** **American** Regular Brown
Medium brown	Dry	Between 415°F/215°C and 435°F/225°C "Second crack"	60–50 **Tile #55**	**Medium** **Medium-high** **American** Regular City
Medium-dark brown	Dry to tiny droplets or faint patches of oil	Between 435°F/225°C and 445°F/230°C	50–45 **Tile #45**	Viennese Full-City **Light French** **Espresso** Light espresso Continental After dinner
Moderately dark brown	Faint oily patches to entirely shiny surface	Between 445°F/230°C and 455°F/235°C	45–40	**Espresso** French European High Continental
Dark brown	Shiny surface	Between 455°F/235°C and 465°F/240°C	40–35 **Tile #35**	**French** **Espresso** Italian Dark Turkish
Very dark brown	Very shiny surface	Between 465°F/240°C and 475°F/245°C	35–30	**Italian** **Dark French** Neapolitan Spanish Heavy
Very dark (nearly black) brown	Shiny surface	Between 475°F/245°C and 480°F/250°C	30–25 **Tile #25**	**Dark French** Neapolitan Spanish

The most common of the common roast names listed in the fifth column (see page 68) are bold faced. The bullets under the tasting categories below indicate the following judgments:

- • characteristic is weak, thin, negligible.
- •• characteristic is moderately clear, discernible.
- ••• characteristic is clear, full, substantial.
- •••• characteristic is at its peak.

Acidity	Body	Aroma	Complexity	Depth	Varietal Distinction	Sweetness	Pungency	Comments
•••	•	••	••	•	••	•		Roasts at the extreme light end of the roast spectrum can taste sour and grainy.
•••	•	••	••	•	••	•		Used only for inexpensive commercial blends.
••••	••	•••	•••	••	••••	•		
•••	•••	•••	••••	•••	••••	••		The traditional norm for the eastern United States.
•••	•••	••••	••••	••••	•••	••	•	The traditional norm for most of the western United States.
••	••••	••••	•••	••••	••	•••	••	The traditional norm for northern California and the Northwestern United States.
•	••••	•••	•••	••••	•	••••	•••	The norm for northern Italian–style espresso cuisine and a normal roast for many newer American roasters.
	•••	••	••	•••		•••	••••	The norm for American espresso cuisine. Also a normal roast for many newer American roasters. Burned undertones.
	••	••	••	••		••	•••	Burned tones become more distinct.
	•	••	•	•		•	••	Burned tones dominate. Once rare, now an increasingly common roast in the U.S.

Chapter 4

WHAT TO ROAST

Choosing Green Beans

Every green coffee holds in its vegetable heart a slightly different collection of secrets. One of the pleasures of roasting at home is becoming acquainted with those intimacies in a far more direct and active way than by simply tasting someone else's roasted coffees.

Of course you may not care about the subtle differences among beans, only the general result: cheaper and fresher coffee. If so, you might simply buy a few pounds of green Colombia, Kenya, or Sumatra, skip to pages 158–194, and start roasting. Suggestions for obtaining green coffee beans and roasting paraphernalia can be found in "Resources."

Eventually, however, you may want to begin exploring the full range of taste distinctions among the world's fine coffees. You can explore a single great coffee in a variety of roast styles, for example. Or you can develop a sort of cellar of green coffees from which you can choose at your own and your guests' whims. Finally, you can experiment with composing personal blends in a far more thoroughgoing way than you can by relying on the already roasted coffees of others.

Green-Coffee Basics

The world's coffees are many and their differences complex. What follows is a general orientation to selecting green coffees. For more detail, consult my *Coffee: A Guide to Buying, Brewing & Enjoying* and Philippe Jobin's *The Coffees Produced Throughout the World*. See "Resources" for additional specialized books on coffee.

Keep in mind that the ultimate test of a coffee is not its name, or its grade, or any of the rest of the muttering that we attach to things, but rather its *taste*. If you try it and like it, then it's a good coffee. And if you don't like it, then you should be prepared to ignore all of the pontificating that tries to convince you otherwise.

An illustration from Jean La Roque's *Voyage de l'Arabie Heureuse* (*Voyage to Arabia Felix*), 1716. Coffee trees of the *arabica* varieties grown in Yemen, or historical Arabia Felix, do have a sparse, sturdy look like this one. Other *arabica* varieties may tend toward a fuller, droopier profile.

Narrowing the Field: Species and Market Category

Given the bewildering variety of the world's coffees, it is probably just as well that we can dismiss some categories at the outset.

First, our considerations can be narrowed on the basis of *species*. Botanists now recognize approximately one hundred species of coffee plant, but only one, *Coffea arabica*, is the source of all of the world's most celebrated coffees.

The coffee species second in importance in world coffee trade is *Coffea robusta*, or *Coffea canephora*, as it is known to botanists. *Robusta* grows at lower altitudes than *arabica* and is more disease resistant. *Robustas*, as coffees from the *robusta* tree are called commercially, generally lack the acidity and complexity of the best *arabica* coffees, although they often display a satisfyingly heavy body. They are used mainly as unnamed constituents of the cheaper coffee blends that line the aisles of supermarkets and fill the carafes of cost-conscious restaurants and corporate lunchrooms. Their only importance in the world of fine coffees occurs in relation to espresso. Small quantities of better-quality *robustas* are often used to give body and sweetness to espresso blends.

A second candidate for dismissal is coffee from *arabica* trees grown at relatively low altitudes in Brazil. Known in the trade as *Brazils*, these coffees are stripped from the trees rather than selectively picked, and handled carelessly. Together with *robustas* they contribute to the preponderance of

Another famous illustration from La Roque's *Voyage de l'Arabie Heureuse*, showing a coffee-tree branch of the *arabica* species with budding flowers at the top, modulating to fully opened flowers near the middle of the branch, to unripe and ripe fruit clustered together near the bottom. Although this illustration may stretch the point somewhat, flowers, unripe fruit, and ripe fruit typically do inhabit the same branch simultaneously.

the coffees used in packaged preground and soluble coffee blends. Similar low-quality *arabicas* grown in countries other than Brazil are sometimes called *hard* coffees. They compete with Brazils in price.

Other, better coffees are also grown in Brazil. These, together with all of the other better *arabica* coffees of the world, fall into the third great market classification, variously called *milds* or *high-grown milds*.

It is the many coffees making up this third category that we turn to now. These are the fancy coffees of the world, which appear in the bins and bags of specialty-coffee stores, and these are what you will be buying and roasting.

The Tortuous Question of Coffee Names

Before launching into a quick circumnavigation of the world of mild or fancy coffees, a word (actually quite a few words) about coffee names is in order.

Fancy or specialty coffees are sold in two forms: *blends*, mixtures of coffees from more than one crop or region, and *unblended* coffees from a single crop and region (often called *single-origin* or *varietal* coffees). Unblended coffees are of most interest to home roasters because they facilitate knowledge (you know what you're roasting), adventure (they often taste intriguingly different), and control (once you get a feel for various individual coffees you can begin to assemble your own blends).

Most unblended or single-origin coffees are labeled on the lists of exporters and importers by *country of origin*, by *market name*, and by *grade*. Grade often includes references to *processing methods* and occasionally to *growing conditions*, like altitude. An increasing number of coffees may be identified also (or alternatively) by the name of the *estate* or *cooperative* where they were grown and (occasionally) by their *botanical variety*. Let's look at each of these naming categories in order.

Country of Origin

This designator (Kenya, Colombia, and so on) is easy to understand. It is the one descriptive term that always appears on store labels and coffee bags. However, countries are large, coffees in any given country are many, and market forces complex. Hence the various names and categories that follow.

Mysterious Market Names

A market name is a traditional identifier that appears on burlap coffee bags and on exporters' and importers' lists. Most market names originated in the nineteenth century or even earlier. They derive from a variety of sources. Most refer to region (Guatemalan *Antigua* or Mexican *Oaxaca,*), a few to a port through which the coffee is traditionally shipped (Brazilian *Santos*) or even to a port through which the coffee once was shipped but isn't anymore (Yemeni *Mocha:* Mocha is a Red Sea port that hasn't shipped coffee for more than a century).

This illustration hints at the beauty of coffee trees in flower: The white blossoms with their delicate, jasminelike abandon contrast strikingly with the shiny, dark-green leaves.

However, market names ultimately describe a coffee, not a place. Market names carry specific associations that include not only growing regions, but certain taste characteristics. Some market names are more famous than the country of origin. Hawaiian Kona coffee is typically known by its market name, Kona, not by its country of origin, United States, or even by its state of origin, Hawaii.

Layers of Grade Names

Coffee is also sold by grade (Kenyan AA, Colombian Supremo, and so on). Grade names can be based on evaluative criteria ranging from how big the bean is to how high the coffee is grown, to how good it tastes (cup quality). Grading criteria are usually established by coffee bureaucracies in the growing nations in an effort to discipline growers and encourage quality. Grading also provides sellers and buyers with a framework for describing and negotiating their transactions. In general, the grading process tends to focus more on externals, like how many sticks or defective beans a coffee harbors, than on subjective criteria, like taste.

Bulking coffee in large generic lots according to grade traditionally has been a way for coffee bureaucracies of growing countries to maintain centralized control over the coffee enterprise. However, as more and more growing countries join the current global trend toward deregulation and allow individual growers and grower associations to cut their own deals with buyers, the importance of grading for the fancy-coffee business may be waning. In one growing country after another, the discipline of regulation as embodied in grading standards is being replaced or supplemented by the discipline of the market as embodied in competition among individual growers and grower associations for the attention of roasters and buyers in consuming countries.

Selective picking is crucial to quality coffee, since ripe and unripe fruit typically inhabit the same branches, and the unripe will spoil the ripe if both are allowed to commingle after picking. Machines that literally vibrate the ripe fruit off the tree are now in use in some parts of the world, but most coffee still is picked by skillful workers like this woman, whose hands deftly move down the branches, plucking the ripe fruit and allowing it to drop into the basket at her waist.

Nevertheless, grade names remain an important element of coffee nomenclature. The more informative coffee store may identify a coffee by country (Guatemala), by market name (Antigua), and finally by grade (Strictly Hard Bean). As a rule, however, stores qualify the country name of a bulk coffee with only one adjective, either grade or market name.

One particularly confusing grading term that often appears in importer and store literature is *peaberry*. The peaberry (*caracolillo* in Spanish) is a single oval bean that sometimes appears inside the coffee fruit in place of the usual two flat-sided beans. Peaberries may be mixed in with the normal beans, or separated and sold as a distinct grade of a given coffee. Peaberries generally embody the characteristics of a coffee with somewhat greater intensity than normal beans from the same crop.

For home roasters peaberries present a special advantage: They tend to roast more uniformly owing to their regular shape. In particular, roasters who use a stove-top roaster or corn popper will find that the rounded shape of peaberries makes them easier to agitate than normal beans with their motion-resistant flat side.

The Wet and the Dry: Processing Method and Grade Names

The coffee bean is actually a seed of a small fruit that coffee people call a *cherry*. How the fruit is removed from the bean and how the bean is dried are steps collectively known as *processing*. Since processing is one of the most important influences on coffee quality and taste it is no wonder that names for various processing methods figure so largely in grading and other descriptions of green coffees.

In the wet method the various layers of skin and fruit around the bean are stripped off gently and gradually, layer by layer, before the bean is dried. Such *wet-processed* or *washed* coffees tend to be more consistent, cleaner, and brighter, or more acidy in taste than *dry-processed*, *natural*, or *unwashed* coffees, which are dried with the coffee fruit still adhered to the bean. The dried fruit is subsequently removed from the dry beans, customarily by machine. Dry-processed coffees are generally more idiosyncratic in flavor, fruitier in taste, and heavier in body than wet-processed coffees.

Semidry or *pulped natural* coffees are a sort of compromise. The skin of the fruit is removed immediately after picking, but the flesh or pulp is allowed to dry on the bean. The dried pulp is later stripped off by machine. This method, developed in Brazil and now widely used there, has produced some exceptional and very distinctive coffees, with the clarity of wet processing but the fruity and floral notes we associate with dry processing.

See pages 79–80 for an illustrated review of these three main processing methods. Understanding the differences among the three methods is only a starting point. A staggering array of subtle variations can be played on the wet method in particular. Fruit pulp may be loosened by natural fermentation before being washed off the beans in channels of water (the traditional *ferment-and-wash* approach), or the fruit pulp may be stripped off the fruit by machine without the fermentation step (*mechanical demucilaging* or *aquapulping*).

Furthermore, additional clean water may be added to the beans during the fermentation step, a procedure called *wet fermentation*. Alternatively, the beans can be left to ferment in their own pulp with no added water, which is called *dry fermentation*. All Kenyan and Ethiopian washed coffees are wet fermented, whereas most Guatemalan coffees are dry fermented. Or coffees can be fermented and then washed, but not completely, so that some fruit residue still clings to the bean during drying, which typically contributes slight fermented or musty notes to the cup. This is the case with Sumatran Mandheling and other traditionally processed Indonesian coffees.

How coffees are dried also may affect flavor and quality. As a rule, *sun-dried* coffees are considered preferable to machine-dried coffees, although here again various compromises and combinations and nuances complicate the picture. Beans may be partly dried by the sun and partly by machine. Coffees dried by machine at somewhat lower temperatures are more desirable than those dried at higher temperatures. Handling during drying is also important. Sun-dried coffees that have been protected from nighttime moisture during drying may be favored over sun-dried coffees that have been left unprotected at night, for example.

Growing Conditions and Grade Names

Finally, the altitude at which coffee is grown figures in many grade names. *Arabica* coffee beans grown at higher altitudes typically mature more slowly than beans grown at lower altitudes, and the resulting denser bean may display more acidity and sometimes more complexity in the cup. As with most coffee generalizations, however, this one entertains many exceptions. Certainly growing altitude is only one aspect of many that influence coffee quality and flavor. In Mexico, the Caribbean, and Central America it figures in various grade names, ranging from the explicit *high grown* to the less explicit *altura* (height or altitude), a grading term in Mexico, and *Strictly Hard Bean*, a name for the highest grades of coffee in Guatemala and Costa Rica (the higher the altitude, the denser or "harder" the bean).

Estate and Cooperative Names

As the specialty-coffee trade matures, closer relationships are being established between individual growers and buyers. These direct relationships mean that a specific coffee often no longer needs to be combined or "bulked" with other coffees from the same region in large lots to reach roasters and their customers.

Owners of quality-conscious coffee farms enlist the aid of their colleagues in consumer countries to establish *estate identities* for their coffees. Estates also may be called *fincas* (in Spanish-speaking Latin America), *plantations*, or simply *farms*. These estates, fincas, or farms may be large establishments that remove the fruit from the bean and dry the coffee at their own facilities, or occasionally smaller enterprises that process their coffee through cooperatively run facilities but maintain control of their product. In either case, estates sell their coffees directly to dealers without mixing them with other coffees from the same region, in theory ensuring that these coffees reflect consistent growing conditions and processing practices.

A similar consistency is achieved by some cooperatives of smaller growers who market their coffees separately like estates through special arrangements with coffee dealers or roasting establishments. These designated cooperative coffees often support environmental and/or social agendas.

Occasional confusion and chicanery have developed around the estate concept, just as they have around other areas of coffee marketing. The sheer number of growers the currently scrambling to cash in on the estate idea has created confusion. Some estates may depend more on hype than on quality. Others may coast on a reputation that their coffees no longer merit.

Fortunately, however, well-established estate coffees are seldom counterfeited. Well-established estate coffees are handled by dealers and roasters

STAGES OF WET-PROCESSING COFFEE

The various steps in removing the skin and fruit from the coffee bean or seed are collectively called *processing*. Here, in cross section, are the main stages of traditional *wet processing*, the most common and also the most elaborate method of processing used for fancy coffee.

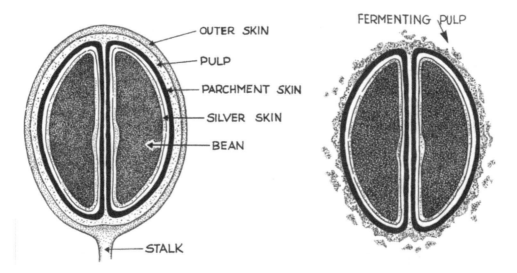

OUTER SKIN

PULP

PARCHMENT SKIN

SILVER SKIN

BEAN

STALK

FERMENTING PULP

1. Ripe coffee fruit
The coffee fruit is protected by pulp and several layers of skin. In wet processing, these layers are removed one by one.

2. Pulping and fermentation
The first stage of processing is called *pulping*. Immediately after the beans are picked, the outer skin of the fruit is slipped off by machine, exposing the sweet, sticky pulp. The pulp is then removed by fermentation: The fruit is held in open tanks, permitting enzymes and then bacteria naturally present in the fruit to literally consume much of the pulp from the beans. The remainder of the pulp is easily washed away.

STAGES OF WET-PROCESSING COFFEE (continued)

3. Drying in parchment

The beans, now separated and pulp-free but still in their parchment and silver skin, are dried, usually in the sun on open terraces but sometimes in machines. At this point the coffee is said to be *in parchment*.

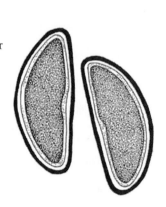

4. Hulling

Finally the parchment and silver skin, both now dry and brittle, are crumbled off the beans by machine, a stage called *hulling*. Fragments of the silver skin still adhere to the bean, however. These tiny, paperlike flakes float away from the beans during roasting, constituting the often troublesome *chaff*. In some cases the grower removes the chaff by subjecting the coffee to a last tumbling called *polishing*.

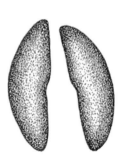
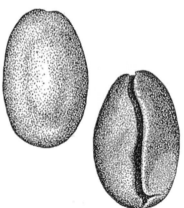

OTHER PROCESSING METHODS

Dry method. In this process the entire fruit is dried immediately after picking. The shriveled skins and pulp are then abraded from the beans in a single final step.

Semidry method. As in the wet method, the outer skin is first removed by machine. But the middle step in the wet method, fermentation, is skipped. Instead the beans are dried with pulp, parchment, and silver skin all still attached. These three layers later are removed by machine.

Processing influences both flavor and appearance. Wet-processed coffees are regular in appearance and typically display clean, consistent taste and aroma and bright acidity. Dry-processed and semi-dry coffees may have more broken beans, and may exhibit more idiosyncratic, often more complex flavor profiles because the beans were dried while in contact with the fruit.

who have too much pride and reputation at stake to play games with their customers. What have been counterfeited are high-priced regional origins like Hawaiian Kona and Jamaican Blue Mountain, where the path to market is more complex and harder to track than is the case with coffees from a single farm or mill.

Names for Certified and Other Coffees

Closer, person-to-person relationships between growers in producing countries and roasters and dealers in consuming countries have led to the development of various programs and niche-marketed coffees that attempt to blunt the destruction that a relentlessly price-driven agricultural commodity like coffee tends to inflict on the earth and people of regions where it is grown. In effect, these programs ask the consumer to pay a bit more for a coffee to support social and/or environmental agendas. Some of these "cause" coffees are *certified* by international agencies to have fulfilled certain specified health, environmental, or socioeconomic criteria. Others are not certified but represent long-term *partnerships* or *relationships* between roasters and growers.

Here are some certification programs:

Certified Organic Coffees. This certification assures the buyer that the coffee has been grown, transported, stored, and roasted without the use of manufactured or processed chemicals.

Certified Shade-Grown or "Bird Friendly" Coffees. Coffees that are both organically grown as well as grown in mixed-species shade may merit an additional *Bird Friendly* certification from The Smithsonian Institution's Migratory Bird Center.

The issue of shade growing in coffee is complex and contentious. Coffees roughly can be divided into four categories in regard to shade. True *shade-grown* coffees are interplanted among a variety of other trees and crops. Such mixed-species farms tend to look like miniature forests in which the coffee trees form a scraggly middle tier. However, the majority of the world's fine *arabica* coffees are grown in *managed shade*, a parklike arrangement wherein the coffee trees grow under a canopy of carefully tended single-species shade

An assortment of marks of the kind that appear on coffee bags, which ultimately are the origin of many of the terms used in importers' lists and coffee-store signs and brochures. The majority of the marks in this illustration, from the early twentieth century, are Colombian. Typically they display the name or initials of the exporter, the market name (Medellin, Armenia), and the grade name (Excelso). There are also marks from Sumatra (market name Mandheling), from Ethiopia (Djimah, Longberry Harrar), Venezuela (Mérida), and several from Brazil (Santos). In two cases the marks refer to botanical variety: the desirable "bourbons" or beans produced by trees of the bourbon variety.

trees. A third category is made up of coffees that are grown without shade but in traditional, relatively benign environmental conditions. These include coffees grown in regions with heavy cloud cover, for example (Jamaican Blue Mountain), or in semiarid regions (Yemen), or in cooler regions relatively far from the equator (most Brazilian and Hawaiian coffees)—all situations that make shade growing impractical. Finally, there is the true *bête noir* of environmentalists, *technified coffees*, which are grown like corn in full sun in often vast, otherwise barren fields. At this point there are very few fully technified coffee farms in the world, but if the price of coffee continues to decline we undoubtedly will see more of them.

Environmentalists support the first category of coffees, those grown in multispecies shade, because the often dense canopy of trees and other plants creates an environment that shelters migrating birds and other wildlife and reduces erosion and dependence on chemical fertilizers. The issue is most relevant in regard to Central American coffees, because many of these coffees have been traditionally grown in multispecies shade and historically have provided key shelter for migrating birds.

A nineteenth-century engraving of a Latin American coffee warehouse. It would appear to offer perfect conditions for storing green coffee: dark, as cool as the tropics permit, and presumably dry. In case you can't tell, the boss is the one counting the bags.

Certified Fair-Trade Coffees. Fair-trade coffees are produced by democratically run cooperatives whose members have been guaranteed a "fair" price for their coffees based on an internationally determined formula. Some of the extra money paid by coffee lovers for fair-trade coffees is used to promote the fair-trade principle in consuming countries, but most of the premium reaches the farmers directly. Almost all fair-trade coffees are also certified organically grown and many are shade grown. Therefore, buying a fair-trade coffee is probably the concerned coffee drinker's most impeccably progressive choice.

Certified Eco-OK Coffees. The Rainforest Alliance's Eco-OK seal certifies that inspectors have found that qualifying coffee farms and mills meet a wide variety of environmental criteria, including wildlife diversity, nonpolluting practices, and responsible and limited use of agrochemicals, as well as social and economic criteria that support the welfare of farmers and workers.

"Sustainable" Coffees. Various parties within the Specialty Coffee Association of America are attempting to come up with a big-tent, inclusive definition of *sustainability* that will combine criteria for environmental as well as social and economic sustainability. However, at this writing no certification program has been developed that reflects this goal, although conceivably there could be such a program in the future.

Partnership or Relationship Coffees. Roasting companies and coffee cooperatives frequently form partnerships, in which a fixed percentage of the retail price of a coffee is returned directly to the cooperative or village that produces the coffee. Other roasting companies may contribute to Coffee Kids, a development organization that sponsors projects in Latin American growing regions.

"Cause" Coffees and the Connoisseur

What are the trade-offs for a home roaster who wishes to support progressive environmental and socioeconomic programs by buying only certified and "cause" coffees?

Their main drawback is the limited number of options they currently offer to the aficionado. At this writing, most certified organic and fair-trade coffees come from Latin America, particularly Peru, Mexico, and Central America. Even from these regions, the choice is limited, and many of the world's most celebrated coffee-growing regions are not represented by any certification program whatsoever. To give only two examples: Kenyan coffees are almost entirely produced by cooperatives of small-holding peasant growers, yet no Kenyan coffees are certified fair-trade. Chemicals of any kind are virtually unheard of in the Harrar region of Ethiopia and in Yemen, yet virtually no coffees from those regions are certified organic.

Given that rather significant caveat, there are many fine fair-trade and certified organic coffees available at this writing. The best Nicaraguan and Peruvian coffees I cupped from the 2001–2002 crop year were certified organic and fair-trade, for example. But, for now, it is difficult for home roasters interested in fully exploring the world of coffee in its drama, range, and complexity to roast exclusively certified coffees.

Names for Botanical Varieties

All fine coffees derive from the *arabica* species, but not all coffees derive from the same botanical variety of that species. Think about the differences among apples: Golden Delicious versus McIntosh, for example: or wine grapes: Cabernet Sauvignon versus Pinot Noir, Sauvignon Blanc versus Chardonnay. There is little doubt that botanical variety is one of the main influences (along with climate, soil, altitude, and processing) on the taste characteristics of coffee. (Botanists often distinguish between cultivars or cultivated varieties of a species versus naturally occurring varieties, or between varieties and strains, groups of individuals within a variety that share common characteristics. Coffee professionals who are not botanists generally apply the term *variety* to all three: variety, cultivar, and strain. I use the term with the same inclusiveness here.)

The fine-coffee world is only beginning to market coffee by variety (or cultivar, or strain). At most we may learn that an estate's coffee trees are Bourbon and Typica, or Caturra and Catuai. Often we have no idea whatsoever which *arabica* varieties produced the fruit that produced the coffee we are drinking.

Variety is a source of conflict in the coffee world. The connoisseurs and traditionalists raise the banner of what they call "old" *arabica* varieties, while some scientists, coffee growers, and government officials defend the usefulness of new *arabicas*.

"Old" or Selected Varieties. In fact, the old varieties are often not that old, but they are spontaneous. Nature itself with its inscrutable processes caused these mutants to appear suddenly on someone's coffee farm at some point in the past, and human intervention was confined to merely taking advantage of that gift by preserving its seed through selection. Some of the most famous of traditional selected *arabica* varieties are the Moka (or Mocha) of Ethiopia and Yemen; Typica and Bourbon, which until recently dominated the coffee fields of Latin America; the Blue Mountain of the Caribbean; and Sumatra from Indonesia. The most striking of these spontaneous mutants is Maragogipe, a variety with very large beans (but low yields per tree) that appeared in about 1870 in Brazil.

Newer selected varieties include Mundo Novo (1920), Caturra (1935), and Catuai. Caturra has been planted widely in Latin America because of its compact growth and high yield. Although Caturra typically produces a rather simple, straightforward cup, Catuai often produces a more complex and complete cup than more traditional varieties like Typica.

"New" or Hybrid Varieties. The real source of the conflict between coffee snobs and coffee scientists is new (really new) *arabica* varieties that have been developed deliberately through cross-breeding programs. Some hybrids, like the famous SL28 cultivar widely planted in East Africa, are celebrated for their fine cup character. However, Colombia, Brazil, India, and Kenya have developed new disease-resistant or higher-bearing varieties that often introduce elements of other coffee species—usually *robusta*—into their genetic makeup.

The controversy is taste. Many coffee buyers claim that these concocted varieties may pay off for the farmer by producing more coffee at less risk of crop loss, but only at the cost of cup quality. Officials responsible for the cross-breeding programs tend to disagree, of course, arguing that the ecological and economic benefits of the new varieties outweigh any slight loss on the drinking end of things.

The most infamous of hybrids that include a bit of *robusta* in their parentage is Catimor, which most definitely produces a flatter, simpler cup than traditional varieties. However, the cup difference between traditional varieties and the newer, more sophisticated hybrids developed in places like India and Colombia is much less extreme and may be undetectable.

A final note: Even more disturbing for traditionalists than varieties produced by traditional cross-breeding is the prospect of coffee varieties that have been genetically engineered. Researchers at a private laboratory in Hawaii, for example are well along in developing a tree that will produce beans naturally free of caffeine, together with another variety whose fruit will ripen all at the same time, simplifying picking. It remains to be seen when and if either coffee will actually be approved for use. John Stiles, the main researcher responsible for the development of the Hawaiian caffeine-free coffee, argues that all he has done is to reverse one gene that is responsible for producing caffeine and that all of the remaining genetic material, including the genes that determine cup quality, will remain unaffected by this single alteration. If a coffee genetically engineered to be caffeine free does appear, I am sure we will hear about it and will have an opportunity to make our own judgment about the cup quality and character issue. Although, as usual, controversies about environmental impact doubtless will be decided for us.

The Ultimate Challenge: Adding Roast Names

Keep in mind that style of roast also can figure in the names that appear on store labels and signs. Most straight, unblended coffees are offered in whatever roast style the roasting company considers "regular" or normal. However, if an unblended coffee is offered in a style darker or lighter than the company's assumed norm, the name of the coffee and the roast style both may appear: Sumatran Mandheling Dark Roast, for example. Thus theoretically it might be possible to see a coffee designated Costa Rica (country), Tarrazú (market name), La Minita (estate), Washed (process), Strictly Hard Bean (grade), French Roast, although such lengthy and informative labeling is seldom seen for fear customers may nod off before buying the coffee, thus reducing sales.

Circumnavigating the Coffee Globe

To make the most of the quick tour around the coffee globe that follows make sure you understand the key tasting terms defined in Chapter 3 (pages

57–60), particularly acidity (the dry, bright sensation produced by a coffee brought to a medium roast), body (the sensation of weight and thickness imparted by a coffee), and regional or varietal distinction (the principal taste characteristics that distinguish one coffee from another at a medium to moderately dark roast).

CLASSIC COFFEES: LATIN AMERICA AND HAWAII

At their best, the classic coffees of Latin America and Hawaii manifest full body, bright acidity, and a clean, straightforward cup. They provide what for a North American is a normative good coffee experience.

The most admired of these coffees are balanced yet powerful: strong in all respects, from the rich vibrancy of the acidity through their full body and complex flavor. As a rule they are grown at high altitudes, although climatic conditions like latitude, cloud cover, and consistent moisture can mimic the effect of higher altitudes and produce a similar flavor profile.

Other classic coffees may be grown at lower altitudes or in conditions that encourage a softer, sweeter taste, with a lighter, brisker acidity rather than the powerful, vibrant acidity of the "bigger" classic coffees.

The classic Latin American/Hawaiian taste is based in part on the brightness and clarity of flavor achieved through wet processing. Almost all fine Latin American and Hawaiian coffees are washed or wet-processed, the exceptions being the better dry-processed and semidry-processed coffees of Brazil.

THE BIG CLASSICS

Generally, fine Costa Rican, Guatemalan, and Colombian coffees are "big" coffees: full-bodied, with a bracing, rich acidity.

The best Guatemalan coffees generally display a bit more intrigue and complexity than their Costa Rican counterparts, which are known for their powerful, bell-like clarity. This difference may be owing to botanical variety; most Costa Rican coffee derives from the newer Caturra variety of the *arabica* species while Guatemalan growers for the most part appear to have stuck with the traditional Typica and Bourbon cultivars.

Colombian coffees remain remarkably consistent, in part owing to the strong leadership of the Colombia Coffee Federation, a countrywide cooperative of tens of thousands of small coffee growers that supports one of the world's most sophisticated coffee research operations, the world's leading social and economic support system for growers, and (until recently) the world's most successful coffee marketing program, featuring Juan Valdez and his ubiquitous donkey. The massive and efficient apparatus of the federation assures buyers of a coffee that is typically clean tasting and free of defects, with an acidity ranging from austerely powerful to sweetly fruity, and a body ranging from medium to full. This generic Colombia typically is sold by grade only, either as Supremo (largest beans) or Excelso (somewhat smaller beans). Despite the impressive consistency of these coffees, specific lots may differ in character and quality, depending on the taste and skill of the green-coffee dealer who buys and sells them.

Other Colombia coffees are traded by private exporters and produced either by private mills or through the federation's specialty coffee program. These coffees, unlike the generic Supremo and Excelso grades, bear market names associated with the region, district, or mill that produces them. These Colombias work subtle variations on the cup character of the generic federation coffees, displaying cup character that may range from grandly acidy to softly fruity. Some estates or exporters may specify botanical variety in their promotional literature. Bourbon and Typica are the traditional and most prestigious Colombian varieties.

THE CARIBBEAN CLASSICS

The finest Caribbean coffees (best coffees of Puerto Rico, Jamaica, the Dominican Republic, and coastal Venezuela) are also powerful but generally lower-toned, with their acidity held inside a deep, sweet, long-finishing richness.

The best Jamaican Blue Mountain coffee is an intense but rounded, big, richly balanced example of the classic Caribbean taste. Unfortunately, this famous cup is difficult to turn up, as shortcut processing methods and dilution of higher-grown with lower-grown coffee has transformed most lots of standard Jamaican Blue Mountain to a rather ordinary Caribbean coffee, hardly worth prices that are triple to quadruple what one would pay for a fine coffee from another origin. However, individual lots of Jamaican Blue Mountain may display the expansive character that made this coffee famous. Some private-estate coffees, notably Old Tavern Estate and RSW Estates, typically offer a much better chance of finding a fine old-time–style Jamaican Blue Mountain than standard bulked or mill-designated versions. The most recent samples of Old Tavern Estate I cupped were extraordinary: rich, deep, sweet, and roundly full-bodied. However, at this writing the famous Wallensford Estate name is largely meaningless, since it now simply describes coffee from a mill that produces coffees similar to those produced by other government mills.

Do not pay high prices for coffees labeled "Jamaican Blue Mountain Style" or "Jamaican Blue Mountain Blend," by the way. The former will have no Blue Mountain in it whatsoever, and the latter will have very little.

A combination of relatively high labor costs and high local consumption has turned Puerto Rico from coffee exporter to importer during recent decades. Some fine Puerto Rican coffees can be found in mainland United States, however. The most notable in recent years is that marketed under the name Clou du Mont. The best estate Puerto Rican coffees embody the classic Caribbean cup at its finest: sweet, full-bodied, round, resonant.

Excellent to outstanding Caribbean-style coffees also are produced in the Dominican Republic (often marketed as Santo Domingo) and coastal Venezuela. Haitian coffee can be a fine version of the Caribbean mode, but it is often shadowed by musty and hard taints owing to processing or drying faults.

THE GENTLE CLASSICS

Good Panamanian, El Salvadoran, Honduran, Nicaraguan, Peruvian, and Mexican coffees generally are lively rather than overpowering in acidity and rounded in flavor. Their natural sweetness makes them excellent darker roasts for espresso drinks. Their gentler acidity also makes them attractive coffees for those who like to drink their coffee black and unsweetened. They may range in body from round and almost sugary sweet (the best Perus); to full-bodied and rich (the best Nicaraguas), to light, sweet, and buoyant (Salvadors). Some may display gentle fruit and floral tones, especially fine Panamas.

THE HAWAIIAN CLASSICS

In the big picture Hawaiian coffees may be somewhat overpriced and perhaps a bit overpublicized. However, the best estate Hawaiian Konas are often powerful, richly acidy representatives of the classic taste, while generic

Konas typically resemble the gentler Latin American classics, sweet, gently acidy, medium-bodied, with muted fruit and floral notes. The same warning regarding "style" and "blend" given earlier in regard to Jamaican coffees applies to Kona.

Premium coffees from the other Hawaiian islands are all lower-grown, gentler coffees in the classic styles and are often excellent. The most distinctive are the wet-processed Malulani Estate and the dry-processed Molokai Muleskinner from the Coffees of Hawaii estate on the island of Molokai, both of which display interesting variations on a flavor complex that can read as anything from spice through chocolate and pipe tobacco. Coffees sold by botanical variety from Kauai Coffee on the island of Kauai (particularly the Catuai varieties) often produce fine and intriguing, if understated, cups.

One of the great advantages of Hawaiian coffee for the aficionado is its accessibility. Growers are beginning to lavish the same attention on Hawaii coffee as vintners did a couple of decades ago on California wines. It has become relatively easy to visit the farms, and proprietors increasingly provide plentiful and detailed information on their coffees, including botanical variety and processing details. But remember, the ultimate proof is in the cup, not in the design of the four-color brochure.

THE BRAZILIAN CLASSICS

Brazil produces enormous quantities of coffee using a daunting variety of processing methods and botanical varieties. At this point, I think it is safe to divide Brazil coffees into three broad categories.

First, commercial coffees, which include cheap, mass-produced *arabica* coffees that are strip-picked and dried on vast patios, plus the smaller quantities of *robusta* species coffee grown in Brazil. Home roasters can feel safe in dismissing these coffees from their repertoires and cellars.

Second, the best Santos-style commercially traded coffees. These coffees, usually described in the trade as *Santos 2/3, good to fine cup*, have been picked and dry processed with more care than the lower grades of Brazilian coffees and are extraordinarily useful for the home roaster who is interested in blending, particularly for espresso. They are usually medium- to full-bodied, sweet, round, but heartier than similar wet-processed coffees from other coffee origins.

Finally, the true Brazilian specialty coffees, sold by estate name and by processing method, which can range from wet-processed or washed coffees that are light, bright, and gentle, to dry-processed or natural coffees that are rounder and fuller, to the often extraordinary *semi–dry-processed* or *pulped natural* coffees, which may glisten with subtle fruit and floral notes riding a delicate sweetness. As elsewhere in Latin America, trees of the traditional Bourbon variety produce the most sought-after and usually most complex lots of coffee, but other selected varieties like Mundo Novo and Catuai also can produce an outstanding cup.

ROMANCE COFFEES I: EAST AFRICA AND YEMEN

The coffees of Africa, Asia, and the Malay Archipelago (Indonesia, Timor, and Papua New Guinea) provide an array of romantic alternatives to the classic coffees of Latin America and Hawaii.

East Africa, together with Yemen, just across the Red Sea from Africa, produces some of the world's most distinctive coffees, characterized by vividly exciting floral, fruit, and wine tones and rich acidity. This fundamental East African profile can range from berry-toned and wild in dry-processed Ethiopian Harrar and Yemeni Mocha, to cleanly floral- and citrus-toned in wet-processed Ethiopian coffees like Sidamo and Yirgacheffe, to dry and winelike in Kenya. Similar wine and fruit notes enliven excellent *arabica* coffees from Zimbabwe and Uganda. The exceptions are washed or wet-processed coffees from Tanzania, Zambia, Rwanda and Malawi, which tend to be soft, full, rounded, and gently understated.

Probably the best place for home roasters to begin in their exploration of East African coffees is Kenya. The state-of-the-art Kenyan coffee industry produces a plentiful yet superb product that is relatively easy to obtain green. Kenya is a powerful example of the East African taste: intense in its dry, burgundylike acidity, medium-bodied but rich, with occasional berry tones.

Ethiopia, the original home of *Coffea arabica*, produces the most varied range of coffee taste experience of any country—or indeed any region—in the world.

After sampling a Kenya, I would try a sample of dry-processed Ethiopian Harrar. At this writing, the Harrar region is producing what may be the world's most distinguished and distinctive coffees, often dominated by intense blueberry notes exploding from a rich, complex cup alive with sweet, fruity acidity. Following that, perhaps an Ethiopian Yirgacheffe. In this impeccably wet-processed coffee the powerful dry fruit and wine notes of most East African coffees lift off and become buoyantly, often startlingly, floral and exhilaratingly lemony. Other southern Ethiopian washed or wet-processed coffees (Limu and washed Sidamo) offer somewhat less distinctive versions of the Yirgacheffe cup profile.

Among softer, fuller East African profiles I recommend starting with a Zambian estate coffee. As with Caribbean coffees, the pleasure here is in the sweetness and soft but resonant depth, with an occasional bonus of muted berry notes.

A last note of clarification: There are many variant spellings in English of Ethiopian and Yemeni names. Mocha may also appear as Moca, Mocca, or Moka; Harrar as Harer, Harar, or Harari; Jimma as Djimah or Jima; Gimbi as Ghimbi; Yirgacheffe as Yrgacheffe.

ROMANCE COFFEES II: INDIA, INDONESIA, NEW GUINEA

Coffees of the *arabica* species grown in a crescent stretching from southwestern India across the Indian Ocean and on through Sumatra, Sulawesi, and Java to New Guinea offer two kinds of romance.

The first is the intrigue of richness; heavy, resonant body; and idiosyncratic flavor notes. This character, owing in part to unorthodox processing and drying methods, reaches its peak in the traditional, peasant-processed coffees of Indonesia, Timor, and Papua New Guinea. The other version of Asian-Pacific coffee romance is the medium-bodied, sweet, occasionally brightly fruity, and floral wet-processed coffees of India, northern Sumatra, Java, and Papua New Guinea.

Processing and Asian-Pacific Coffees. There may be a wider variety of coffee-processing method in the India–Indonesia–New Guinea crescent than anywhere else in the world. Understanding the differences created by these processing methods is essential to getting what you want when you buy these coffees.

Almost every part of the Asian-Pacific region offers the option of coffees that have been simply processed by small growers and other coffees that have been classically wet-processed by large mills.

The small-holder–processed coffees, whether from Sumatra (Mandheling, Lintong), Sulawesi/Celebes (Toraja, Kalossi), East Timor, or Papua New Guinea (Y-Grade), share certain broad characteristics: heavy body, low-key acidity, and odd, unpredictable flavor notes that can range from repulsive (strong mildew or mustiness) to attractive (winey fruit, leather, sweet pipe tobacco, sweet earth). Although these small-holder coffees have been processed by a simple variant of the wet method, exporters typically describe them as "naturals" or "unwashed" to distinguish them from the standard, orthodox, wet-processed coffees from the same regions.

These standard wet-processed coffees have been prepared in large mills similar to mills in regions like Kenya and southern Ethiopia and tend to be medium-bodied, often with lovely floral and high-toned fruit tones and an acidity that can range from powerful and rich (Papua New Guinean estate coffees) to expansive and gentle (Indian washed coffees), with the washed or wet-processed coffees of northern Sumatra and Java falling somewhere between.

The confusion comes when a neophyte home roaster buys a Sumatra, for example, expecting the deep, rich tones of the traditional small-holder coffee he tasted at his local specialty store, and instead gets a wet-processed Sumatra from the big Gayo Mountain mill, with its lighter body and cleaner, brighter acidity.

Finally, to complicate the processing picture, some coffees from this region are subject to additional procedures after processing that further influence their cup character. Indian dry-processed coffees may be *monsooned*, a process whereby coffees are deliberately exposed to moisture-bearing winds, while some traditionally processed Indonesian coffees may be deliberately aged (see pages 96–97).

Buying Traditionally Processed Asian-Pacific Coffees. Where to start? Undoubtedly with a good, traditionally processed Sumatra or Sulawesi. These are the single-malt scotches of the coffee world—rich, complex, and full of deep, surprising, ambiguous flavor notes.

After having been the private pleasure of aficionados for years, the great coffees of Sumatra have been discovered by a larger clientele and have risen in price. New Sumatran coffees have entered the market that are wet-processed and fail to display the resonant idiosyncrasies of the traditionally processed Sumatras. Nevertheless, it is possible to find good Sumatran coffee (generally marked Lintong or Mandheling) at a reasonable price.

Even more surprising and challenging in flavor are traditionally processed Sulawesis marked as Toraja or Kalossi, which often display what some call the taste of the forest floor: earth, leaf mold, and mushroom notes.

Until the disruption of its coffee industry by its recent struggle for independence from Indonesia, East Timor produced some exceptional coffees in the traditional richly low-toned, Sumatra/Sulawesi mode, though usually a bit less idiosyncratic in flavor. Hopefully these coffees again will find their way to market.

Finally, the peasant coffees of Papua New Guinea offer still another, often intriguingly fruity, variant on the traditionally processed style of Pacific cup. These coffees are marketed either as Papua New Guinea Y-Grade or as organic cooperative coffees, and are quite different in cup character from the better-known estate washed coffees (usually AA Grade) of Papua New Guinea.

Buying Washed or Wet-Processed Asian-Pacific Coffees. The Java *arabica* coffee industry was wiped out by leaf-rust disease in the late nineteenth century and replaced by plantings of *robusta*, but the Indonesian government helped revive the tradition of fine *arabica* coffee in Java. These revival Javan coffees are marketed as Java Estate or Java Estate Arabica. They are medium-bodied, wet-processed coffees, ranging from rather ordinary and simple to sweetly round to high-toned, complex, and floral.

Most wet-processed Sumatran coffees available in the United States come from the Gayo Mountain mill in Aceh province. These Gayo Mountain washed coffees can be pleasantly round and mid-toned but probably will disappoint those expecting the full-throated richness of a traditionally processed Sumatra.

Papua New Guinea washed coffees are perhaps the most distinguished of wet-processed South Pacific coffees, and in some years rank with the world's finest. At best they display an echoingly resonant full body, bright acidity, and a complex high-toned intrigue that includes both floral and citrus (often grapefruit) tones.

Indian wet-processed coffees tend to be medium in body, with a sweet, low-key acidity and, at best, floral and fruit tones. The very best and rarest India estate coffees can be as fine as any in the world, with grace notes that range from Kenyalike wine to floral tones reminiscent of Ethiopian washed coffees to odd, striking spice notes that I have tasted nowhere else in the world.

ROMANCE COFFEES III:
AGED AND MONSOONED COFFEES

Aged and monsooned coffees constitute still another exotic possibility for the home roaster.

If green coffee is stored in relatively cool, dry conditions, it maintains its flavor rather well. As it ages, acidity slowly decreases and body increases. Thus a given coffee drunk as *new crop* (first year after harvest) generally will taste brighter, slightly more acidy, and slightly lighter in body than the same coffee consumed as *past* or *old crop* (a year or more past picking and processing). However, if coffees are held in hot, humid conditions, they often *fade* (lose their flavor and character) or become *baggy* (vaguely mildewed and ropy tasting) within a few months to a year after harvest. But, unlike such old-crop coffees, *aged* coffees are held for at least two years, often longer, before release and roasting.

There are two kinds of aged coffees: those aged inadvertently (allowed to sit in the corner of some warehouse because, for whatever reason, the owner failed to sell them) and those aged deliberately. Few inadvertently aged coffees come to market, but there is a lively business in the deliberate aging of Sumatran (and occasionally Sulawesian) coffees. The coffees, almost always traditionally processed, are purchased by exporters and held for periods ranging from two to as many as five years in special warehouses in Singapore, well ventilated and out of direct rain or sun, with the bags periodically rotated to even out exposure to moisture.

The very best aged coffees display heavy body and pronounced sweetness, yet preserve just enough acidity to add intrigue to the heaviness. Most aged coffees also develop mild musty notes, producing a sort of spicy mildew taste that can range from unpleasantly flat and sharp to pleasingly malty and hearty. Aged coffees relatively free of musty notes can be quite attractive as a single origin, and even those that display rough, musty notes can be invaluable in blending, where they add richness, power, and body to espresso and other dark-roast blends.

A taste profile somewhat similar to that of aged coffees is achieved in considerably less time by Indian exporters who *monsoon* their coffees. This exotic process involves holding dry-processed coffee in special warehouses open to moist monsoon winds. In a few weeks the beans yellow, swell up in size, and transform in taste. Although these big, yellow, smoothly fat monsooned beans are dramatically different in appearance from the shriveled brown beans produced by aging, the two cup profiles are rather similar. Both are heavy on the palate, sweet, with little acidity but with (usually) musty notes that can range from chocolate, malt, or carob to a flat, hard character.

Both aged and monsooned coffees are special tastes. The fondness for them among Europeans probably derives from the Java coffees brought to Europe in the eighteenth and nineteenth centuries in the holds of sailing ships. In the moist darkness of the long passage these coffees sweated and transformed in flavor much like monsooned coffees.

The tradition of such coffees in Europe doubtless accounts for the fact that most aged or specially handled coffees come out of India or Indonesia, regions that provided most of northwestern Europe's coffee during the eighteenth century. You may occasionally see aged African or Latin American coffees for sale, however.

At any rate, you may want to try an aged and a monsooned coffee, first straight, in order to understand their taste, then perhaps in a blend, where the weight and body of specially handled coffees can be used as a resonant counterpoint to brighter origins.

Buying Aged and Monsooned Coffees. Currently the most widely available specially handled coffee is Indian monsooned Malabar, which usually can be found on one of the Internet sites listed in "Resources." A bit more persistence is required to turn up aged coffees, but they, too, usually can be sourced via the Internet.

Home roasters who live in relatively warm, moist climates have the interesting option of pursuing their own experiments with aging coffees (see page 106).

Blending: An Overview

The goal of blending is simple: to achieve a more complete, complex, and pleasing coffee experience than can be gotten from brewing one coffee alone.

Blending can be a very subtle procedure. Some roasters blend new-crop and old-crop beans of the same coffee to obtain a fuller, more balanced version of that particular coffee's taste than could be obtained by roasting either new- or old-crop beans alone. In this case the goal is to make a certain coffee taste more like itself, to fulfill its inner potential, as it were.

Most often, however, the goal is to create an entirely new taste. For example, the world's oldest and most famous blend, Mocha-Java, combines one-third acidy, fruity Yemeni Mocha with two-thirds deeper-toned Java. The Yemeni Mocha enlivens the Java while the Java balances and enriches the Mocha. A new taste is created.

In still other circumstances the goal may be to produce a coffee appropriate to certain culturally defined tastes. Italians in Milan like a subtle, sweet, yet lively espresso. Italian-Americans in San Francisco's North Beach prefer a rougher, more bitter, pungent style. Thus, North Beach espressos are roasted darker than Milan espressos, and the blend of constituent beans is different as well. Most North Beach espresso blends combine rich, acidy coffees with a base of softer Mexican or Brazilian coffees. Most Milan blends are mainly *arabicas* with soft profiles, like Brazilian Santos, combined with high-quality *robustas* for sweetness and body, but with no sharp, acidy coffees whatsoever. In these cases the definition of "good coffee" in the respective cultures determines the goal of the blending project.

Yet, no matter what the goal of blending, the fundamental approach is the same: putting together coffees that fill in weaknesses without obscuring strengths.

BLENDING BY ROLE

The best way to begin blending is by understanding the basic roles that various categories of coffee can play in a blend. To facilitate that understanding, here is a list dividing some well-known coffees into categories according to the qualities they potentially contribute.

Category 1: Big Classic Coffees. These coffees contribute body, powerful acidity, and classic flavor and aroma to a blend. They may make too strong a statement for use as a base for blends but are excellent for strengthening and energizing coffees with softer profiles.

Guatemala: Antigua, Cobán, Huehuetenango, other high-grown
    Guatemalan coffees
Costa Rica: Tarrazú, Tres Rios, other high-grown Costa Rican coffees
Colombia

Category 2: Softer Classic Coffees. These are "good blenders"; they establish a solid, unobtrusive base for a blend and contribute body and acidity without competing with more individualistic coffees. When brought to a darker roast they often confer a satisfying sweetness and pleasing chocolate notes, making them favorites for espresso blends.

> Mexico: Oaxaca, Coatepec, Chiapas, Tapachula
> Dominican Republic (also called Santo Domingo)
> Peru: Chanchamayo
> Brazil: Santos
> Panama
> El Salvador
> Nicaragua
> India: wet-processed or washed *arabica* coffees

Category 3: Highlight and Exotic Coffees. Their often powerful fruit- and winelike acidity makes these coffees a distracting base for a blend but exciting contributors.

> Ethiopia: Harrar (This wild-tasting, complex, dry-processed coffee can contribute sweetness, fruit and berry notes, and rich acidity.)
> Yemen: Mocha (similar to Harrar but typically less intense)
> Ethiopia: wet-processed coffees (Yirgacheffe and Sidamo add extraordinary high-toned floral and citrus notes that survive even into a dark roast.)
> Kenya (adds powerful acidity and fruit, berry, and wine notes)
> Zimbabwe (same as Kenya but less intense)
> Uganda: Bugishu (same as Kenya but less intense)
> Papua New Guinea: AA, A, X (add powerful acidity and complex citrus notes)

Category 4: Base-Note Coffees. These add richness and body to a blend, and combine well with other coffees. Their deep-toned acidity will anchor and add resonance to the lighter, brisker coffees of category 2, and balance without blunting coffees in categories 1 and 3. Don't be put off by their occasional mildly mildewed, fermented, or earthy notes. These qualities may not please in a single-origin coffee but can contribute to a blend.

Sumatra: Mandheling, Lintong, and Aceh "natural" or traditionally
   processed
Sulawesi (also called Celebes)
Papua New Guinea: organic and Y grade
Timor
India: monsooned Malabar
Any aged coffee

Category 5: Robustas. *Robusta*, coffee from trees of the *robusta* or *Coffea canephora* species, is the notorious villain of the coffee world. It should be. The problem with *robusta* is twofold: the character of the coffee itself and the contemptuous way that coffee is treated once it is off the tree.

As for treatment, most *robusta* is strip picked and dried in piles, fruit and all, which means it often ends up both badly fermented (tastes like compost, owing to the rotting fruit) and badly musty (tastes like mildewed shoes, owing to molds that attack the half-rotting fruit).

There are, however, *robustas* that are both carefully picked and meticulously wet processed. These *washed robustas* (the best are from India) allow us to taste the essence of *robusta* coffee itself, free of foul tastes gotten from careless mass processing and drying.

So how does pure, clean *robusta* taste? Essentially, bland (no acidity and little nuance), neutral, vaguely sweet, slightly bitter, and very, very grain-like. In other words, washed *robustas* taste more like a coffee substitute made from nuts and grains than like coffee.

In that case, why are they included here? Because, in small percentages, say 10 to 15 percent, they add body, richness, and depth to espresso blends.

Definitely avoid dry-processed *robustas*, particularly Vietnamese robustas. At this writing they are almost universally foul-tasting. However, if you are blending for espresso, you may want to experiment with washed or wet-processed *robustas*. (Indian washed or Parchment *robustas* are best, Mexican washed *robustas* are a little sharper but still useful.)

COMPOSING YOUR PERSONAL BLENDS

There are two ways to approach blending: by system and by improvisation.

One systematic approach would be to start with a base coffee from category 2, roast and drink it long enough to really know it, then experiment with adding other coffees to it—a highlight coffee, a base coffee, etc.—keeping notes as you go along. Another approach might be to choose a coffee from each of the four categories, combine them in equal proportions, and then substitute one at a time from coffees of the same category until you achieve a combination that pleases you.

Or you can start the way professional cuppers do, by cup blending. Roast several coffees, say two from each of the four categories, then brew them all and let them sit on a table as they cool to room temperature and combine them in varying proportions, using a spoon. One spoonful of this, another of that, and so on, experimenting with various combinations until you have arrived at a formula that pleases you. Then roast the coffees that made up your preferred cup blend, combine them in the proportions that pleased you, brew up a pot, see how well you did, and adjust from there.

Although most blends are composed of coffees brought to roughly similar degrees of roast, you also can experiment blending coffees brought to dramatically different roast levels. A good way to start is by roasting the same coffee to two very different degrees—to a medium roast and to a dark, for example—then blend the two in varying proportions. If you enjoy the result, try varying the identity of the two coffees, then add a third, then perhaps a fourth. Go easy with extreme dark roasts in blends, however. Sometimes a very dark-roasted coffee simply sits on the rest of the coffees in a blend, turning them all simple and bitter.

As for blending by improvisation, no instruction is needed. Buy coffees from two or three of the categories noted above and combine them as moment and mood suggest. It probably still is a good idea to use one or two familiar coffees as a consistent base for your caprice, however.

BLENDING FOR ESPRESSO

When blending for espresso cuisine the first question to consider is how you and your guests take your espresso. If you tend to drink it without milk and with very little sugar, you should avoid the big, acidy coffees in categories 1 and 3, and rely mainly on coffees in categories 2 and 4. Italian blenders prefer a base of Brazilian Santos, whereas West Coast Americans typically rely on Mexican and Peruvian coffees. As I indicated earlier, some blenders like to use small quantities of high-quality, wet-processed *robustas* to smooth out and add body and richness to their straight-shot espresso blends.

On the other hand, if you drink your espresso with a good deal of hot milk and/or sugar, you may prefer a more pungent blend with some bitterness to balance the sweetness. On a base of Brazil, Peru, or Mexico, try adding a coffee or two from categories 1 and 3. Ethiopian Harrar or Yirgacheffe and New Guinean AA are particularly effective at adding complexity and energy to espresso blends. Then add a base coffee or two for milk-mastering power: Sumatra Mandheling or Lintong, for example, Papua New Guinea Y-Grade, monsooned Malabar, or an aged coffee. Finally, you may want to add a small quantity of wet-processed *robusta* to add even more body to your blend.

Of course how darkly you roast your espresso blend and what method you use to roast it also profoundly affects flavor. See Chapters 3 and 5.

Decaffeinated Coffees

Coffees are decaffeinated in their green state. Three principal processes are used today in specialty coffees to remove caffeine: the traditional or European process, the water-only or Swiss-water process, and the CO_2 process. All are consistently successful in removing all but a trace (2 to 3 percent) of the resident caffeine.

The European or Solvent Process. There are two variants of the solvent method. The direct solvent process opens the pores of the beans by steaming them and applies the solvent directly to the beans before removing both solvent and caffeine by further steaming. The indirect solvent process first removes virtually everything, including the caffeine, from the beans by soaking them in hot water, then separates the beans and water and strips the caffeine from the flavor-laden water by means of the caffeine-attracting solvent. The solvent-laden caffeine is then skimmed from the surface of the water, and the water, now free of both caffeine and solvent, is reunited with the beans, which soak up the flavor components again.

The Swiss Water or Water-Only Process. In this commercially successful process there are two phases. In the first, start-up phase, green beans are soaked in hot water, which removes both flavor components and caffeine from the beans. This first, start-up batch of beans is then discarded, while the caffeine is stripped from the water by means of activated charcoal filters, leaving the flavor components behind in the water and producing what the Swiss water-process people call "flavor-charged water"—water with the flavor but without the caffeine. This special water becomes the medium for the decaffeination of subsequent batches of green beans.

When soaked in the flavor-charged but caffeine-free water, new batches of beans give up their caffeine but not their flavor components, which remain more or less intact in the bean. Apparently the water is so charged with flavor components that it can absorb no more of them, whereas it can absorb the villainous caffeine.

Having thus been deprived of their caffeine but not their flavor components, the beans are then dried and sold, while the flavor-charged water is cleaned of its caffeine by another run through charcoal filters and sent back to decaffeinate another batch of beans.

The CO_2 Process. In the CO_2 method, the green beans are bathed in highly compressed carbon dioxide (CO_2), the same naturally occurring substance that plants consume and human beings produce. In its compressed form the carbon dioxide behaves partly like a gas and partly like a liquid, and has the ability to combine selectively with caffeine. The caffeine is stripped from the CO_2 by means of activated charcoal filters.

CHOOSING COFFEE BY DECAFFEINATION METHOD

If you are concerned only about health issues, I suggest that you buy the decaffeinated coffee that tastes good to you, regardless of process. Given the temperature at which all currently used solvents evaporate, it does not appear likely that enough of the chemical could possibly survive the roasting and brewing processes to be anything more than the tiniest pea under the health-conscious consumer's mattress.

If, however, you are concerned about the environment, there may be some reason to avoid coffees decaffeinated by methods using methylene chloride, which has been plausibly accused of attacking the ozone layer. Choose instead coffees decaffeinated by the Swiss water method, by solvent methods using ethyl acetate, or by CO_2 processes. Coffees decaffeinated by the Swiss water method are usually (though not always) so labeled. Signs and labels typically identify CO_2-decaffeinated coffees as well. When no decaffeination method is indicated, a good guess is that the coffee has been decaffeinated by a method involving use of a solvent.

DECAFFEINATION AND FLAVOR

However powerfully it may affect our nervous systems, caffeine has very little effect on flavor. Isolated, it is a bitter, almost tasteless white powder. Coffee without it should taste virtually the same as coffee with it.

Nevertheless, soaking green coffee beans in hot liquid and drying them out again is not a gentle process. It definitely affects the flavor of the abused beans. Affects how much? Depending on how careful the decaffeination process and how attentive the subsequent roasting, from a little to a lot.

If you buy decaffeinated beans to roast at home you may notice that they are no longer the common gray-green to blue-green color of unroasted coffee, but instead range from a rather sallow yellow to a light brown. This color change is due to the soaking and drying to which the beans have been subjected during decaffeination.

The result for roasting purposes is delicate beans that roast much less predictably than untreated beans. The combination of the loss of some flavor agents in the soaking process with the difficulty in roasting accounts for the fact that decaffeinated coffees purchased in the store may not taste as consistently good as coffee from untreated beans.

The main message for the home roaster is to buy green decaffeinated beans from a reliable source, and roast them carefully. See Chapter 5 (page 152) and the instructions following that chapter for suggestions on handling decaffeinated coffees.

You might also consider making blends of decaffeinated and untreated coffees. The untreated beans bolster the taste of the decaffeinated beans, yet still limit the amount of caffeine. Remember, however, that you may need to roast the decaffeinated beans in a separate session before blending, since they typically reach the same degree of roast 15 to 25 percent faster than untreated beans.

DECAFFEINATION METHOD AND FLAVOR

Which decaffeination method influences coffee flavor least?

My experience suggests that the Swiss water process tends to develop body while muting acidity and high notes, whereas the European, or solvent, process tends to preserve acidity, nuance, and high notes but may reduce body and dimension. As for coffees processed using the CO_2 method, I have tasted some excellent samples but not enough of them to generalize.

Your Own Coffee Cellar

For food romantics, *coffee cellar* has a fine ring to it. It resonates with the same combined pleasure of connoisseurship and security that motivates people to keep piles of dusty wine bottles piled deep in the hearts of their houses.

Correct storage for green coffees is cool but not cold, dark, dry, and, above all, well ventilated. Rather than cellar, think pantry. The storage cupboards in the kitchens of older houses, the kind that allow air to circulate among the shelves, represent an ideal environment in which to store green coffee.

Good, high-grown green coffees (Central American, Colombian, East African) kept in such conditions will change very little over two or three years. For the first year or so they will round and sweeten in flavor, then become fuller in body but gradually lose brightness and acidity.

Lower-grown, gentler coffees may change in flavor rather drastically. Brazilian Santos, for example, may begin to lose acidity as soon as six months after harvest and after a year or so often develops an additional flat, mildewy taste professional cuppers call *baggy*.

Coffees that arrive dark green or brown in color and high in moisture (particular Sumatras and Sulawesis) are also likely to develop mildewed or musty notes when stored for any length of time. For some, this heavy, malty flavor is attractive; others will not like it.

SETTING UP A COFFEE CELLAR

In what kind of container should you store your coffee? Plastic bags are fine for short-term storage, but if you plan to hold a coffee for more than a month or two you should transfer it to something porous. Cloth is doubtless best, but corrugated cardboard boxes probably work as well.

Burlap bags of the kind used to construct temporary levees during periods of flood are ideal for storing coffee at home. They are sold empty; they are a convenient size (not trivially small yet still luggable when full); and they include sewn-in drawstring closures. You can find them in obscure industrial parts of cities; look in the Yellow Pages under "Bags." Buy the cloth bags, not the plastic.

Green coffee is a living entity; it needs to breathe. Elevate the boxes or bags on a pallet or similar arrangement that allows air to circulate beneath them. Every few months shift the containers around. Turn them over, and if they are in a pile, shift the bottom containers toward the top of the pile and bring the top ones down, much as you would rotate tires on a car.

Fortunately for those of us who are weary of restaurants gotten up as tacky imitations of wine cellars, there is no symbolic architecture associated with storing coffee beyond a simple warehouse filled with burlap coffee bags piled on pallets. So when it comes to the interior design aspects of your coffee cellar (or coffee pantry), you are on your own.

Aging Coffee at Home

For the flavor impact of storing coffee, see the preceding pages. To achieve the more dramatic effect gotten by deliberate aging as it is practiced in Singapore, you need a warm, humid climate. Those in the tropics may want to store some coffee in cloth bags in the carport, rotate the bags occasionally, and taste the result after a year or two. The goal here is lots of humidity but no direct contact with rain or moist concrete, which should net you a coffee with little acidity, heavy body, and varying degrees of a leathery, roughly musty flavor.

Coffee Geography

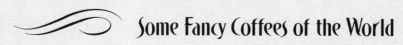

Some Fancy Coffees of the World

Maps are the beloved vehicles of armchair traveling. Here are a few, accompanied by descriptions of coffees to taste in the armchair while looking over the maps.

Cartographic precision is hard to come by in the world of coffees. I pieced together the information contained in these maps by pouring over text reference sources, general agricultural maps, information distributed by coffee growers and associations, and the rather general maps published by Bernhard Rothfos in his 1972 *Weltatlas der Kaffeeländer*. Most of these sources are vague, and few agree in detail. Consequently, I have fudged. If someone's farm is off in one of the white spaces, I apologize and invite correction.

Accompanying each map are brief descriptions of coffees that appear most frequently on the signs and lists of specialty-coffee roasters and importers. I have omitted lesser-known coffees, some of which may be excellent but have not yet made an impression on North American markets.

The information in these descriptions is a condensed summary. For more information see the preceding chapter. For still more see my book *Coffee: A Guide to Buying, Brewing & Enjoying* or Philippe Jobin's reference tome *The Coffees Produced Throughout the World* (available from the Specialty Coffee Association of America; see "Resources"). Also note that the increasing practice of marketing coffee by estate or cooperative means that we are likely to see more and more exceptions to the simple generalizations offered in this section.

And these generalizations are exactly that: cultural baggage that real experience drags along with it. All of the names, observations, and evaluations in this or any other book, not to mention various elegantly designed pamphlets on brown paper you may pick up in coffee stores, are meaningless unless they are confirmed by the senses—your senses. You need to experience these coffees, educate your taste, and ultimately trust it.

Finally, the following summary and its evaluations do not take into account the human and ecological dimensions of coffee growing. They focus on the quality, taste characteristics, and availability of the coffees themselves. There may be reasons other than cup character alone for choosing one coffee over another. You can make the environment a priority in your coffee buying, or migrating songbirds, or helping the often impoverished people who devote their lives to growing coffee. See pages 81–85 for a detailed discussion of social, economic, and ecological issues and coffee.

MEXICO

Most noted market names are Coatepec, Oaxaca, and Chiapas (also called Tapachula). Brisk, gently bright acidity, delicate flavor, medium body. Good blenders and dark roasters. Estates and numerous organic and progressive cooperatives. Some high-grown Mexican coffees share the fuller body and richer, more emphatic acidity of fine Guatemalan coffees.

GUATEMALA

The finest coffees (Strictly Hard Bean) of this very complex origin display rich acidity; often with floral, fruit, or spice nuance; medium to full body; and complex, understated authority. The most celebrated regional mark is Antigua, but other regions, including Cobán, Atitlán, Huehuetenango, and San Marcos, all can produce splendid coffees with a variety of profiles ranging from sweetly seductive to spicily complex to grandly and flintily acidy. Unlike many growing countries, Guatemala generally has stuck by the traditional botanical varieties of *arabica*. Many excellent estate and cooperative coffees.

HONDURAS

Not a celebrated origin, but the finest Honduran coffees are sweet, low-key, full-bodied, and superbly opulent.

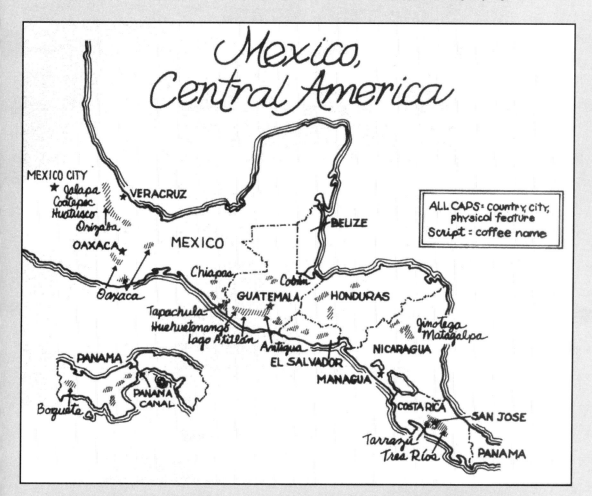

EL SALVADOR

Gentle acidity, delicate flavor, medium body. Their consistency, sweetness, and agreeable, understated balance make the El Salvadors outstanding blending coffees.

NICARAGUA

The best (usually marked Matagalpa, Jinotega, or Segovia) are splendid in their style: restrained acidity, richly low-key, with round, full, bouillonlike body and a variety of fruit-toned nuances. Excellent organic and cooperative coffees, including those from the huge Prodocoop group of small producers.

COSTA RICA

The best (Strictly Hard Bean) are big, clean, with bright to rich acidity and full body. They generally are authoritative, resonant, and emphatic rather than complex and nuanced. The most distinguished regions are Tariazú, Tres Rios, and West Valley, including the Volcan Poas district. Many outstanding estate coffees, including the celebrated La Minita.

PANAMA

Bouquete, the compact growing district on the slopes of Volcán Baru near the Costa Rican border, produces all of Panama's fine coffees. Most are subtle, sweet, and agreeable, with medium body, brisk to delicate acidity, occasional floral or fruit notes. Others may display more power in the cup, with big, winelike acidity, and can be as impressive as the very best Guatemalas or Costa Ricas. Several distinguished estates.

JAMAICA

True Jamaican Blue Mountain coffees (grown in the Blue Mountain district at over 3,000 feet) are full-bodied, moderately acidy, and richly complex yet balanced, though occasionally marred by a slight, shadow mustiness. The few genuine estate versions of Blue Mountain allowed to be exported, Old Tavern Estate, for example, are likely to be more impressive versions of the profile than generic Blue Mountain. Wallensford Estate is not a true estate coffee, by the way. The term simply describes coffee prepared by the Wallensford mill. Lesser, lower-grown coffees (Blue Mountain Valley, High Mountain) are medium in body, delicate to bland in flavor, brisk rather than rich in acidity.

HAITI

When available, wet-processed Haitian coffee is typically sweet, soft, and medium-bodied, though often marred by processing or drying faults that turn it mildly musty or fermented. An association made up of several thousand small growers (Cafeieres Natives S.A.) has been attempting to revive

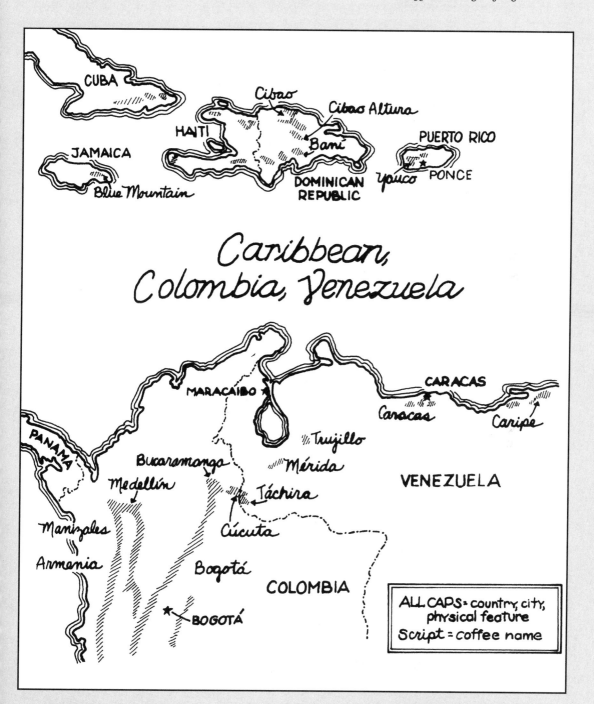

Caribbean, Colombia, Venezuela

ALL CAPS = country, city, physical feature
Script = coffee name

the Haitian coffee industry after its virtual destruction by the embargo of the early 1990s. The association's coffees are currently marketed under the name Haitian Bleu.

DOMINICAN REPUBLIC (MAY BE MARKETED AS SANTO DOMINGO)

Higher-grown Dominican coffees, like Cibao Altura, can be very fine examples of the Caribbean profile: soft, balanced, with a rich undercurrent of acidity. Lesser coffees may be mild and pleasant but lacking in authority.

PUERTO RICO

At this writing, a new limited-production Puerto Rican coffee branded Clou de Mont presents a fine example of the Caribbean taste: full bodied, balanced, and gentle yet alive, with a deep, vibrant complexity. Other Puerto Rican coffees are similarly vibrantly full and round but may be marred by shadow faults, particularly mild musty or mildew tones.

COLOMBIA

Colombian coffee sold without a qualifying market name usually originates with the National Federation of Colombian Coffee Growers, a mammoth, nationwide growers' cooperative association celebrated for its sophisticated control of quality, its progressive social programs, and, until recently, its successful marketing campaigns starring the photogenic Juan Valdez. Supremo designates the highest grade, Excelso is a smaller-beaned, more comprehensive grade. Such generic Colombian coffee tends to be balanced in flavor, richly acidy, authoritative, and relatively full-bodied. It may on occasion display winey tones or a lush, flirt-with-ferment fruitiness that many coffee drinkers (including me) enjoy but some coffee professionals deplore.

Colombian coffees from exporters and mills not associated with the Colombian Federation are often more distinctive (though not necessarily better) than the generic federation coffees and may include smaller lots from trees of the traditional "heirloom" Typica and Bourbon varieties marketed by specified estate, mill, or cooperative.

VENEZUELA

Most coffee produced is consumed locally. When available, Venezuela from the coastal regions (often marked Caracas) tends to reflect the Caribbean taste profile: mild, deep, low-toned, sweet. High-grown coffees from western Venezuela (Táchira, Mérida) resemble Colombian.

ECUADOR

Little Ecaudoran coffee reaches the North American specialty market. It typically is another smaller coffee in the Latin American style.

BOLIVIA

Although coffee generally has a long history in Bolivia, specialty Bolivian coffee is a new development, fueled in large part by idealistic efforts to assist indigenous communities in the Bolivian highlands. Bolivian specialty coffees tend to be impeccably clean, balanced, and sweet, often beautifully so.

PERU

In general Perus display a delicate to brisk acidity, medium body, and a sweet, round cup. The finest, often organically grown, are exquisite when fresh from origin: round, voluptuously sweet, quietly powerful, seductively gentle. Coffee is grown in the north (Northerns), center (Chanchamayo, Ayacucho), and south near Cuzco and Machu Picchu (Urubamba, Cuzco). The most admired name is Chanchamayo. There are a number of well-run cooperatives.

BRAZIL

In the past Brazil had a reputation for producing cheap *arabica* coffee that was carelessly picked and mass processed. However, the best Brazils always have been mild, sweet, and medium-bodied, with a relatively delicate acidity, making them favorites for espresso blends and other dark roasting. Of the better Brazilian coffees, the most familiar market name is Santos (dry-processed coffees traditionally shipped through the port of Santos, usually grown in the states of Minas Gerais or São Paulo).

However, a growing number of estates have managed to establish identities for their often excellent coffees in the North American specialty market. These estate Brazils are usually sold by one of three processing methods: wet-processed (*washed*), dry-processed (*naturals*), or semiwashed (*pulped naturals*). Typically, wet-processed Brazils display the brightest, cleanest taste, with the most distinct acidity; the better dry-processed coffees exhibit fuller body and greater complexity but lower acidity, with semiwashed agreeably positioned between the two: cleanly fruity, balanced, delicate but rich. Brazil estates also market their coffees by botanical variety: Coffees from trees of the traditional Bourbon variety are often more distinctive, though not necessarily better, than coffees from other, newer varieties. Like Perus, Brazils usually are best roasted and enjoyed while young; held longer than a year they often (though not always) fade and lose their sweetness.

YEMEN

Yemen Mocha. At best, a remarkable coffee in the traditional, dry-processed style: rich, intense, fruit- and wine-toned acidity; medium to full body; intriguing wild or natural notes. Most Yemeni coffee that reaches North America is marked as either Mattari (a region and coffee type) or Sanani (a blended type composed of coffees from various regions near the capital city of Sana'a). Sanani is generally more balanced; Mattari more acidy and distinctive. Ismaili describes both a coffee from a growing region and a botanical variety of *arabica* that produces a tiny, pealike bean and a rather delicate version of the Yemeni profile. Yemen fades very quickly and is best enjoyed as a fresh crop as it arrives in North America in the fall and winter months.

ETHIOPIA

Ethiopian dry-processed coffees. At this writing the dry-processed coffees of Harar (also Harer, Harriar, Harrer) are among the world's finest: balanced but explosively aromatic, shimmering with blueberry and wine notes. These splendid, distinctive coffees are often substituted for Yemen Mocha in good Mocha-Java blends. Gimbi (also Ghimbi), dry-processed or unwashed Jimma (also Djimah, Jima), and dry-processed Sidamo are usually lesser coffees, still wild and winey but lighter-bodied and considerably rougher in profile.

Ethiopian wet-processed coffees. Yirgacheffe (also Yrgacheffe) is one of the world's most distinctive coffees: overwhelmingly floral, lemony, with rich, soft-toned acidity, pungent mid-tones, and medium to light body. Coffee marked Limu and the washed or wet-processed versions of Sidamo and Jimma are similar to Yirgacheffe but usually less intensely floral and distinctive.

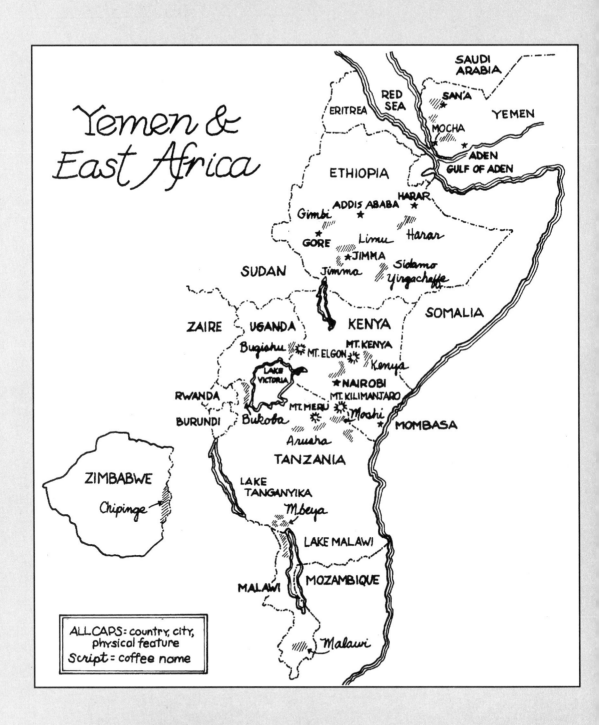

KENYA

Kenya's renowned small-grower coffee industry is in the midst of an awkward transition from a centrally managed model to a more open, market-driven model. Despite the confusion occasioned by this transition, Kenya continues to produce a splendid, consistent coffee displaying a rich, powerful, fruit- and berry-toned acidity energizing a cup of medium body and deep dimension. AA is the highest grade, but specific lots of AA sold at government auction differ, and one broker's or exporter's AA may be better than another's. Some fear that introduction of new, hardier hybrid varieties of *arabica* may begin to compromise Kenyan quality, but if so, it hasn't happened yet.

TANZANIA

The best Tanzanian coffees, grown mainly on the slopes of Mount Kilimanjaro and Mount Meru near the border with Kenya (usually marked Arusha, Moshi, or Kilimanjaro), resemble Kenyan coffees with their rich winelike acidity. Other wet-processed coffees, grown in the south near the town of Mbeya, tend to resemble the lesser Ethiopian wet-processed coffees: soft, ingratiatingly low-toned acidity, rounded taste, medium body. Dry-processed coffees grown near the western town of Bukoba are inexpensive "hard" *arabicas* that do not figure in the North American specialty trade.

MALAWI

Those few Malawian coffees to reach North America resemble the softer, full-bodied washed coffees of Tanzania.

UGANDA

Ugandan Bugishu in general profile resembles Kenya.

ZAMBIA

Some very fine coffees in the softer, fuller East African mode are emerging from Zambia. The most distinctive combine a rounded sweetness with berry tones reminiscent of Kenyas. Much of the best Zambian production comes from distinguished botanical varieties, including the hallowed Bourbon.

ZIMBABWE

Zimbabwe is another version of the powerfully acidy, wine-and-fruit–toned East African flavor profile. The Chipinge region on the eastern border with Mozambique produces the most and probably the best Zimbabwean coffee; 053 is the highest grade designation based on size of bean. there are several excellent estate coffees. At this writing, however, Zimbabwean coffee appears destined to dramatic change as traditional family coffee farmers are forced off their land and their farms expropriated by landless peasants.

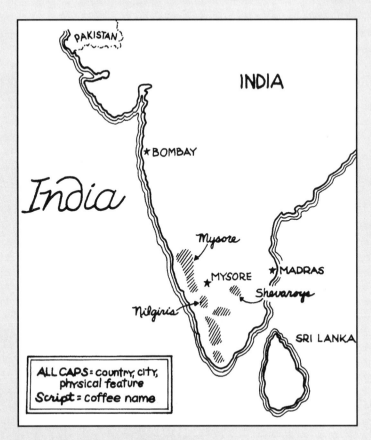

INDIA

Indian coffee is grown in the southern states of Karnataka, Tamil Nádu, and Kerala. Wet-processed Indian coffee (usually Plantation A grade, market name Mysore) is pleasant, low-keyed, and sweet, with medium body and occasional floral and chocolate-toned fruit notes. Coffees from the Shevaroys and Niligiris districts may display brighter acidity. The very finest estate Indias are unpredictably exceptional, with a character ranging from grandly winey to delicately spicy to vibrant, low-toned, and rich. Another origin best roasted and enjoyed young.

Indian monsooned Malabar. This is a dry-processed coffee exposed to monsoon winds in special warehouses on the southeastern coast of India before export. It displays a unique taste profile: heavy on the palate with a peculiar muted acidity and (usually) malty or musty notes. Splendid bottom-note coffee for espresso blends.

Indian washed robustas. These remarkably well-prepared coffees (Koapi Royale and parchment *robusta* A/B grade) are as good as it gets in the bitter to bland world of *robusta*: no acidity, grain and nut tones, a nice balance of sweetness and bitterness, and (the main reason for using them in quality blends) a deep, big body.

SUMATRA

Sumatran Traditionally Processed Coffees. The best (Mandheling, Lintong, Ankola, Aceh, and Gayo "unwashed" or "natural") are among the world's most distinctive coffees. They also are among the world's most frustrating coffees owing to their inconsistency from lot to lot and tendency to sharp mustiness. These traditionally processed Sumatran coffees are often labeled "natural" or dry-processed coffees but in fact are the product of a simple backyard wet-processing and sporadic, unorthodox drying, both of which undoubtedly contribute to the unique Sumatran cup character: resonant, deep, fruit-toned acidity, full body, and rich, idiosyncratic bottom notes.

Lintong, from a relatively small district near Lake Toba, is the most distinguished of traditional Sumatran coffee names. Mandheling, a designation encompassing the Lintong district plus other growing areas around Lake Toba, is the next most celebrated name. Aceh and Gayo, names describing coffees from the basin around Lake Biwa at the northernmost tip of Sumatra, are the least-well-known names. Nevertheless, coffees from any of these three regions can be outstanding. Furthermore, it is never entirely clear whether a given coffee actually comes from the region stenciled on the bag.

Sumatran Wet-processed Coffees. Sumatra also produces wet-processed coffees, which tend to be lighter in body, higher-toned, and less complex than traditionally processed Sumatras, though also more reliable in quality from lot to lot. The most widely available Sumatran wet-processed coffee is Gayo Mountain Washed, from the Lake Biwa region in Aceh province.

SULAWESI/CELEBES

Good, traditionally processed Sulawesian coffees display a deep, rich flavor profile similar to that of the best Sumatras but also exhibit an even greater tendency to display either idiosyncratic bottom notes (earth, humus, mushrooms, leather, pipe tobacco) or nasty taints (intense mustiness or compost-pile ferment). Of all the world's fine coffees, traditionally processed Sulawesis probably most reward the skill and discernment of a good green coffee buyer. Wet-processed Sulawesi is cleaner, lighter-bodied, and both less interesting and more predictable than traditionally processed Sulawesis. Virtually all specialty coffee from Sulawesi is grown in the Toraja (also called Kalossi) region.

JAVA ESTATE ARABICA

All Java *arabicas* are wet processed. The best are gently rich, medium-bodied, and rather delicately acidy, often with floral and high-toned fruit notes. They also are notoriously unreliable and often tainted by various drying and storage faults. There are five traditional government-sponsored estates, the best-known of which are Jampit and Blawan, plus additional private estates.

TIMOR

Before the disruptions of its recent independence struggle with Indonesia, Timor produced a typical and often fine Pacific-style traditionally processed coffee, a bit cleaner and less idiosyncratic perhaps than traditional Sumatras and Sulawesis but displaying the same deep dimension, low-toned richness, and nuance ranging from fruit to various malty/musty, leathery, and tobacco notes. It seems likely that the restored Timor coffee industry will return to producing these intriguing coffees. Most Timor coffees were and will continue to be certified organically grown.

PAPUA NEW GUINEA

There are two basic styles of coffee produced by this often undervalued but exciting origin: classically wet-processed coffees from larger farms or estates (Arona, Sigri) and small-grower coffees subjected to the same simple back-

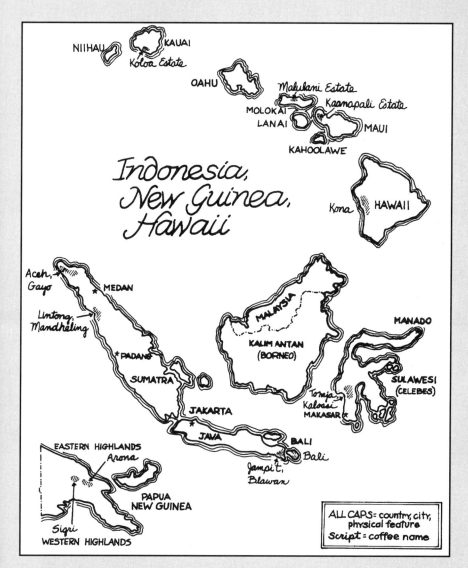

yard wet processing that gives the traditionally processed coffees of Sumatra and Sulawesi their unusual character.

The frequently magnificent and unique plantation wet-processed Papua New Guineas are acidy but balanced, with a variety of high-toned nuances, including flowers and citrus tones that often suggest grapefruit. The small-grower coffees (either marketed by organically certified cooperatives or bulked and sold as Papua New Guinean Y-Grade) are often a fine, fruity variation of the basic full-bodied, deep-toned, edging-on-musty-or-fermented Sumatran/Sulawesian cup.

AUSTRALIA

Australian estate coffees occasionally are seen on the American specialty market. The few samples I have cupped display good body and fundamental sweetness but lack authority and complexity.

HAWAII

The celebrated Kona coffees are grown on the west coast of the big island of Hawaii. They more resemble classic Latin American coffees like Costa Rica than they do other Pacific coffees like Indonesia or New Guinea. They are always clean and balanced but at best display a superb, rich, high-toned acidity; fruit notes; medium to full body; and complex aroma. The Kona coast is turning into the Napa Valley of coffee growing, as an increasing number of excellent small estates compete for the attention of visitors and aficionados.

Larger farms are now producing coffees on other islands in the Hawaiian chain. These are all relatively low-grown coffees with moderate acidity, but they are interesting and improving. Coffee from Molokai, both wet-processed (Malulani Estate) and dry-processed (Molokai Muleskinner), are particularly appealing with their spice-tobacco-malt nuance. Kauai coffee is less nuanced but sweet and rich.

Chapter 5

GETTING STARTED

Equipment, Methods, Issues

When I produced the first edition of this book there were virtually no home-roasting machines on the market. If you wanted to roast coffee at home, you had to improvise. Today, however, a growing number of home-roasting devices are available, all waiting for their big breakthrough to appliance-world stardom, meanwhile entertaining off-Broadway roasting aficionados like readers of this book.

True, the "perfect" home roasting device still eludes us. But perfection is boring anyhow, and the units currently on the market give the home roaster an engaging array of technologies that combine automated efficiency, good roasting practice, and an occasional whiff of coffee romance.

Plus there remain the many improvised home-roasting methods. For the coffee hobbyist who is patient and who doesn't require the security of walk-away-from-it automation, these improvised approaches offer certain advantages over dedicated roasting equipment as well as the creative satisfaction of doing it yourself. Improvised equipment also is cheaper. As of this writing, dedicated home-roasting machines vary in price from about $70 to $580, whereas most improvised home roasting setups cost less than $30.

The following pages outline a range of both dedicated and improvised home-roasting devices and approaches, describing the virtues and limitations of each, and give some hints for obtaining good results no matter which machine or method you use. Thereafter, you will find advice on controlling degree or color of roast, cooling roasted beans, dealing with roasting chaff and smoke, and, for serious aficionados, advice on approaching roasting systematically using a roasting log.

To save you having to make notes or turn down the corners of pages, the important practical information contained in this chapter is summarized in list format in the "Quick Guide to Home-Roasting Options and Procedures" on pages 158–194.

The Arabian coffee ceremony. The word *ceremony* may have originated with European commentators, who remarked on the similarities between this Arab (and the similar Ethiopian and Eritrean) practice to the better-known Japanese tea ceremony. The coffee ceremony is a bit less formal than its tea-drinking counterpart, but also technically more complex, since the coffee is not only brewed and drunk during the course of the event, but roasted and ground as well. Here the coffee beans, having already been roasted, are being pulverized in an ornate wooden mortar, while water for brewing is being heated in the open fire pit. The long-handled roasting ladle and spatula for stirring the roasting beans are neatly laid out on the far edge of the fire pit. From an early twentieth-century photograph.

Roasting Requirements

For orientation, let's review what needs to take place during coffee roasting.

- The beans must be subjected to temperatures between 460°F and 530°F (240°C and 275°C). These temperatures can be considerably lower if the air around the beans is moving faster, as in hot-air or fluid-bed roasting apparatuses, or higher if the air is moving sluggishly, as it does in home gas ovens.
- The beans (or the air around them) must be kept moving to avoid uneven roasting or scorching.
- The roasting must be stopped at the right moment and the beans cooled promptly. (Prompt and effective cooling is an often overlooked but crucial element in coffee roasting.)
- Some provision must be made to vent the roasting smoke.

Here are some of the machines and methods for achieving these simple goals at home.

Overview of Methods and Machines

Roasting machines transfer heat to the beans in three fundamental ways.

- By convection: Beans are roasted by contact with rapidly moving hot air.
- By conductivity: Beans touch a hot surface.
- By radiation: Beans are bathed in heat from a hot surface or heat source.

In addition, the world may soon have its first genuine microwave coffee-roasting system, which works by a combination of microwaves and radiation.

Although no roasting method or machine works absolutely exclusively by any one of these three (or four) principles, they form a good starting point for understanding the differences in home-roasting technology and how they affect final cup character.

HOT-AIR OR FLUID-BED ROASTERS

Such devices roast coffee almost entirely by convection. Fast-moving currents of hot air surge through the beans, both heating and agitating them. The smallest and least expensive home-roasting devices work on this principle, as do hot-air corn poppers pressed into service as improvised coffee-roasting machines. These devices, which blow off roasting smoke and roast beans rapidly owing to an efficient transfer of heat, tend to produce a relatively bright, clean, high-toned cup. Both sweetness and acidity are accentuated, while body may be somewhat lighter than with coffee roasted by other methods. At this writing, hot-air roasters on the market include the Fresh Roast (pages 43 and 159), the Brightway Caffé Rosto (pages 130 and 159) and the Hearthware Gourmet Coffee Roaster (pages 160 and 159).

The Sirocco home roaster, a small fluid-bed roaster manufactured in Germany and imported to the United States throughout the late 1970s and 1980s. Its cooling cycle is conveniently activated by a timer. A paper filter in the metal chaff collector atop the glass roasting chamber helps control roasting smoke. The Sirocco is no longer manufactured.

SLOWER CONVECTION ROASTERS

With Zach & Dani's Gourmet Coffee Roaster (pages 43 and 162–164), beans are roasted by convection but agitated mechanically by a screw in the middle of the roasting chamber. The gentler convection currents generated by the Zach & Dani's device induce a slower, more deliberate pace of roasting than that induced by pure fluid-bed devices.

Improvised roasting in a home oven also qualifies as slow convection roasting. The beans, held in a perforated pan, are subject to slow-moving (in ordinary ovens) to moderately strong (in convection-option ovens) currents of hot air.

With the Zach & Dani's device, with home ovens, and most likely with any other slow convection device that turns up on the market, the cup tends to be lower toned, with more muted acidity and sweetness, and body perhaps a bit heavier than with the fluid-bed method.

MICROWAVE ROASTERS

The latest wrinkle in home and small-batch roasting, Wave-Roast technology is an ingenious method for roasting coffee in microwave ovens. Beans are sealed inside a cardboard packet or cone that has an inner, heat-reflective lining. The beans are roasted by a combination of microwaves and heat radiated from the lining inside the cone, which converts microwaves to radiant heat. Most roasting smoke is trapped by the cardboard packet or cone, which acts as a filter. In the case of the more-sophisticated cone format, an attractive, rechargeable, battery-operated turntable rotates the cone inside the microwave, rolling it and thus tumbling the beans inside, assuring an even roast. In the case of the packets, the user (you) needs to agitate the beans by periodically opening the microwave and turning over the packet. The packets still produce a rather uneven roast.

At this writing the two roasting systems have not yet been released and are awaiting financial backers. I suspect that, short of further technological breakthroughs, the rather inconvenient packets will not enjoy much success on the market, although the clever cones may have a future.

Wave-Roast technology in general produces a low-toned, heavy-bodied cup, probably because the beans reabsorb moisture and roast smoke trapped inside the cone. Acidity, sweetness, and nuance are all muted; complexity is muddied. However, this technology comes into its own with dark-roast styles, which remain remarkably sweet and free of charred or burned flavor, deep and spicy rather than bitter or sharp.

DRUM ROASTERS

The most traditional of home-roasting technologies. Beans are mechanically agitated by tumbling inside a turning, perforated drum, while being roasted by a combination of direct radiation, conductivity, and gentle convection currents of hot air. At this writing two home drum roasters are available: the Swissmar Alpenrost (pages 132–133) and the Hottop Bean Roaster (pages 164–167).

The Alpenrost's especially gentle convection currents and relatively slow roasting produce a round, low-toned, full-bodied cup with muted acidity and a roasty complexity concentrated toward the bottom rather than the top of the profile. With the Hottop Bean Roaster, brisker air movement and decisive cooling produce a classic cup with impressive clarity and balance, medium body, good sweetness, and crisp but not overbearing acidity.

STOVE-TOP DEVICES

This method roasts the beans entirely by radiation and direct contact with hot metal. Beans are enclosed inside a potlike metal chamber that sits atop the stove. A crank protruding from the top of the device turns metal rods or paddles inside the chamber, agitating the beans. Slow roasting and smoke working around the beans during roasting together tend to produce a round, low-toned cup with muted acidity and complexity concentrated at the bottom rather than the top of the profile.

At this writing, the stove-top options include the Aroma Pot ½-Pound Coffee Roaster, a manufactured-from-scratch device of traditional design, and the Whirley Pop (formerly the Felknor Theatre II) popcorn popper, which must be modified to accept a candy thermometer (pages 173–174 and 180). At this writing, a version of the Whirley Pop already modified for coffee roasting is available for purchase on-line.

Which Is Best?

Choosing among these various roasting methods involves a trade-off among several factors: convenience (manufactured-from-scratch devices are easiest to use), volume of coffee roasted (drum roasters, stove-top devices, and oven methods all roast more coffee per batch than fluid-bed machines, microwave cones, or the Zach & Dani's device), attitude toward roasting smoke (Zach & Dani's produces the least smoke, the two drum roasters and stove-top devices by far the most), and preferences in cup (ranging from bright, clean, and crisp to low-toned and round). For some buyers, coffee romance and tradition may be an issue, with the old-fashioned looking Hottop drum roaster and the Aroma Pot stove-top roasters probably the leaders in this subjective arena. And then there is price: At this writing improvised equipment can cost as little as $30; drum roasters $280 to $580, with other options falling between these extremes.

A detailed summary of advantages and disadvantages of the various methods and devices is given in the "Quick Guide to Home-Roasting Options and Procedures" on pages 158–194.

Fluidized-Bed Approaches

To repeat, fluidized-bed or hot-air roasting means that the beans are both roasted and agitated by a powerful current of hot air, much like hot-air corn poppers heat and agitate corn kernels.

MANUFACTURED-FROM-SCRATCH FLUID-BED ROASTERS

All three home fluid-bed roasters available at this writing work in approximately the same way and offer similar features.

- All roast a relatively small volume of green beans (three to four ounces) in about four to ten minutes using a powerful current of hot air to both move and roast the beans.

- All incorporate a timer that automatically triggers a cooling cycle by turning off the heating element while allowing the fan to continue driving room-temperature air up through the beans.
- All permit you to watch the beans during roasting and cooling.
- All permit you to either stop the roast or add time to it on the fly, while the beans are roasting.
- All incorporate a filter near the top of the roasting chamber to trap chaff, the tiny flakes of silver skin liberated by roasting, preventing them from floating around the kitchen and gathering in corners or incorporating themselves into sauces.

See pages 158–164 for details about the three currently available machines (currently $65 to $150), their capabilities, and advice for using them. See "Resources" for purchase information.

IMPROVISED FLUID-BED ROASTING WITH A HOT-AIR CORN POPPER

Caffé Rosto fluid-bed home roasting machine. As in competing fluid-bed devices, a current of heated air generated from the base of the machine both agitates and roasts the beans. The dial at the front of the unit controls the time of the roast and triggers an automatic cooling cycle. The cover at the top is glass and allows the user to peer down at the roasting beans. The chaff is collected in the unit protruding above the dial.

A very effective home coffee roaster can be improvised from the appropriate design of a hot-air corn popper. The ease with which the right popper can be modified to incorporate a candy/deep-fry thermometer as bean-temperature probe makes this option particularly attractive. Adding the thermometer is a simple (five-minute) modification that enables you to monitor the progress of the roast by the inner temperature of the beans rather than their outer color or appearance. See pages 173–174. However, hot-air poppers require considerably more attention than their made-for-coffee fluid-bed counterparts. You need to unplug them to stop the roast, and you must cool the beans in a separate step.

Furthermore, hot-air corn poppers present particular issues in regard to chaff, the tiny paperlike flakes of coffee-fruit skin liberated by roasting. On the positive side, these devices, like store-bought fluid-bed roasting devices, blow the chaff up and out of the coffee beans while roasting them. On the negative side, the chaff blown out of the beans by hot-air poppers tends to float around the kitchen and complicate housekeeping rather than being trapped by a filter at the top of the machine as it is in dedicated home machines. The plastic hoods that fit over the top of hot-air poppers provide a fairly effective method for corralling the chaff, however. See page 177.

A more important chaff issue with hot-air poppers is the danger of combustion it poses with some designs. Use only poppers of the design recommended on page 176 for home coffee roasting, in other words, those machines that introduce the hot air from the sides of the popping/roasting chamber and circulate the beans in a circular pattern at the bottom of the roast/popping chamber. Do not use designs in which the hot air issues from grill-covered openings or slots on the bottom floor of the popping/roasting chamber. With such styles fragments of the roasting chaff can settle into the base of the popper, collect around the heating elements, and eventually cause the device to ignite.

Also keep in mind that if you use any unmodified hot-air popper for coffee roasting you void its warranty by employing it for a purpose other than the one for which it was originally intended. The recommended designs are sturdy as well as inexpensive, however, and stand up well when used to produce light through medium to Viennese roasts. If you enjoy darker roasts—espresso through very dark (dark French or Italian) styles—you should opt for a store-bought roasting machine.

Complete instructions for using a hot-air corn popper to roast coffee appear on pages 176–181, together with directions for adding a candy thermometer should you wish to. See "Resources" for information on buying hot-air poppers and thermometers.

Zach & Dani's Gourmet Coffee Roaster

Zach & Dani's new little roasting machine is unique among currently available home-roasting machines in two respects. First, it is a hybrid design that roasts the beans by means of a convection current of hot air but agitates them mechanically by means of a screw inside the roasting chamber that majestically stirs, lifts, and drops the beans. Second, it all but eliminates troublesome roasting smoke by means of a catalytic converter. No other home-roasting device employs such an effective way of reducing or diverting the roasting smoke.

The flow of hot air in the Zach & Dani's machine is less intense in both temperature and velocity than that generated by any of the fluid-bed devices, which means it roasts more slowly: twenty to thirty minutes, counting cooling time. On the other hand, it roasts a bit more coffee than any of the pure fluid-bed units. The slower roast time produces a cleanly articulated cup profile but one that is lower-toned and less acidy and sweet than the cup produced by faster-roasting fluid-bed devices like the Fresh Roast or the Hearthware Gourmet.

Controls for the Zach & Dani's machine are electronic rather than mechanical: You push buttons rather than twist a spring-loaded dial to control time of roast, and watch a digital readout as the roast counts down toward conclusion. The controls also allow you to prolong the roast as it is happening by adding time on the fly. Taken together, these features make the controls on the Zach & Dani's machine among the most flexible and sophisticated available on currently available home-roasting machines.

In price the Zach & Dani's (around $200 with grinder and green beans) falls between the simple little fluid-bed devices (around $70 to $150) and the larger-capacity, high-end drum roasters (currently around $280 to $580). See page 43 for an illustration of the Zach & Dani's device and pages 162–164 for details and some advice on using it. See "Resources" for purchase information.

Home Drum Roasters

So far the fledgling home-roasting industry has given us two small drum-style roasters for home use: the Swissmar Alpenrost and the Hottop Coffee Roaster. Both roast coffee much like traditional professional drum roasters do, making them attractive choices for coffee romantics.

They also roast eight or nine ounces of green beans per batch, considerably more than other dedicated home-roasting devices. On the other hand, they take a lot longer to roast each batch than the little fluid-bed machines do, and they produce *a lot* more roasting smoke, simply because they roast a lot more beans than competing devices. Furthermore, they also cost a good deal more than any of the smaller fluid-bed devices or the Zach & Dani's unit: around $280 for the Alpenrost and $580 for the Hottop. Finally, like the Zach & Dani's machine but unlike the compact little fluid-bed roasters, they are countertop space hogs.

Although both use similar technologies to roast about the same amount of coffee in about the same amount of time, and incorporate similar digital controls, they differ in several respects. The Hottop incorporates a window for observing the changing color of the beans, whereas the Alpenrost is entirely enclosed (you control the degree of roast by setting a timer and by trial and error or by listening to the crack and smelling the smoke). The Hottop dumps the beans into a pan outside the roasting chamber for cooling, a technical advantage; the Alpenrost cools the beans inside the roasting chamber with a current of room-temperature air. The Hottop is more traditional looking, the Alpenrost is rather sleekly high-tech. The exterior surfaces of the Alpenrost stay relatively cool to the touch during roasting, a unique safety feature among the current crop of home-roasting machines. By contrast, the exterior of the Hottop becomes very, very hot, although its manufacturers are promising an insulated version of their machine shortly.

See the illustration below of the Alpenrost, page 165 for a picture of the current Hottop model, and pages 164–167 for details on both of these devices. See "Resources" for ordering and availability.

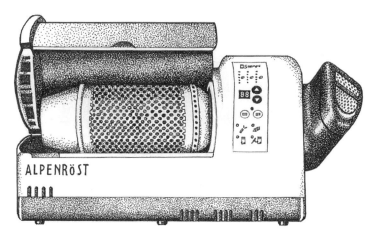

Swissmar Alpenrost home drum-roasting machine. Coffee is roasted inside the perforated drum revealed by the lifted hood, with heat provided by electric elements concealed beneath the drum. During roasting the hood is lowered over the drum, concentrating heat from the electric elements inside the machine and maintaining a safe surface temperature on the outside. The protruding component on the right can be turned to direct roasting smoke toward an exhaust fan or open window.

Microwave-Oven Roasting

Roasting coffee by simply microwaving the beans does not work. However, some persistent and ingenious technicians have developed a microwave coffee-roasting method that does work—remarkably well.

It should be mentioned that at this writing another organization calling itself Smiles Coffee is distributing *preroasted* coffee in microwave packages. Essentially you heat the already roasted coffee in the microwave to give the impression of fresh roasting. Hopefully this bizarre parody of home roasting will be off the market by the time these words appear in print, but if not, don't be taken in.

On the other hand, technicians behind a system called Wave Roast have mastered the challenge of actually roasting coffee in a microwave oven. The trick is a lining inside the microwave packet that converts some of the microwave energy into radiant heat. The radiant heat roasts the outside of the beans while the remaining microwave energy roasts the inside.

At this writing it is not clear which of the several trial versions of Wave-Roast products finally will make it to market. The simplest form of the Wave Roast system involves packets of green coffee ready to be popped into the oven and roasted. The sealed but porous cardboard packet absorbs some roasting smoke and contains the rest, releasing only a little puff when the packet is opened to liberate the roasted beans. In order to prevent the beans from roasting unevenly, however, you need to wait for the first popping sounds that signal the beginning of the roast, then begin opening the oven and flipping the (rather hot) packet. The beans still roast unevenly, and the result is a cup much like the one achieved by oven roasting: either complex and layered or muddy and confusing, depending on your point of view.

More complex versions of the Wave Roast system eliminate the problem of uneven roast by sealing the beans inside a cone that is rapidly rotated inside a microwave oven by a roller device. One prototype (illustrated on page 168) rotates the cone inside the microwave oven by means of a cute little rechargeable batter-operated roller device. Another tentative design involves a small, dedicated microwave with the roller device built into the microwave.

Assuming that the final released product works as well as the demonstration versions I reviewed for this book, the cone system could constitute the world's easiest coffee-roasting method. And, although the coffee it produces is a bit flat and muddy at medium through medium-dark roast levels, at darker roast levels Wave Roast cone coffee is impressive: sweeter, deeper, and more complex than dark roasts produced by most other methods.

However, it remains to be seen whether investors will be willing to commit the money necessary to bring this system to market. And, if they are, whether consumers are willing to pick up the cost added to the green beans by the packets and cones: Two ounces of green beans inside a packet may sell for an average of one dollar, for example, and inside a cone for two or three dollars, versus about fifty cents if the same beans were bought through normal channels. I hope that some buyers will pop for the cones, at least, enough of them to keep this interesting product on the market and reward the ingenuity of its creators.

Stove-top Roasting

Stirring the beans in a pan over heat undoubtedly was the earliest method of coffee roasting, a method that is still practiced in many parts of the world. In Ethiopia and Eritrea the roasting device of choice is a shallow metal pan that looks much like a wok and sits atop a charcoal fire. In rural Latin America and Indonesia roasting is typically performed using a large, round-bottomed earthenware bowl that accumulates a shiny patina of coffee oils.

Although it is possible to do a passable roast in similar fashion at home by stirring beans in a wok or cast-iron skillet on a range top, I recommend instead stove-top methods that help raise the heat around the beans by keeping them covered during roasting. This is the principle behind the little devices that, until World War II, were the roasting method of choice in much of continental Europe. These picturesque little appliances look like heavy covered saucepans with cranks protruding from the top. You put the beans into the interior of the device through a little door and stir the beans during roasting by turning the crank.

STOVE-TOP ROASTING WITH THE AROMA POT
½-POUND COFFEE ROASTER

The sturdy Aroma Pot revives this time-honored design. Aside from being fabricated in stainless steel rather than cast iron, the Aroma Pot pretty much duplicates a typical stove-top roaster of the nineteenth or early twentieth centuries.

Which is unfortunate, perhaps, because this traditional design has some problems. The optimum roasting temperature inside the pot must be determined by very rough trial and error, for example. You put the beans into the interior of the pot through a tiny door. It is possible to open the door during roasting to check the developing color of the beans, but awkward. The closed design of the roaster makes it difficult to impossible to repair the vanes that push the beans around should they lose alignment owing to jamming on wayward beans. Most important, the vanes essentially push the beans around in a pile rather than mixing or agitating them, which means you need to lift the roaster occasionally and shake it to make sure the same beans do not remain rolling around at the bottom of the pile, overroasting.

Nevertheless, those who don't mind standing over the stove and turning a crank for several minutes, plus administering a bonus shake now and then, may enjoy the Aroma Pot's large capacity and simple, nostalgic design.

The Aroma Pot with a large kit of accessories sells for $140 via the Internet. See "Resources" for purchase information and 170–171 for more advice and details on using the Aroma Pot.

ROASTING WITH THE WHIRLEY POP CORN POPPER

A second option for stove-top coffee roasting is an old-fashioned corn popper, the kind that looks like a covered saucepan with a crank protruding from the top or side. The crank turns a pair of wire vanes that rotate just above the bottom of the pan, agitating the corn kernels (in our case the coffee beans) to keep them from scorching.

There are several stove-top poppers on the market at this writing, but the one that I find works best for coffee roasting is the Whirley Pop (around $25). The suggestions and instructions here and on pages 172–175 are all based on my experience with the Whirley Pop.

Do not buy the somewhat similar West Bend electric countertop Stir

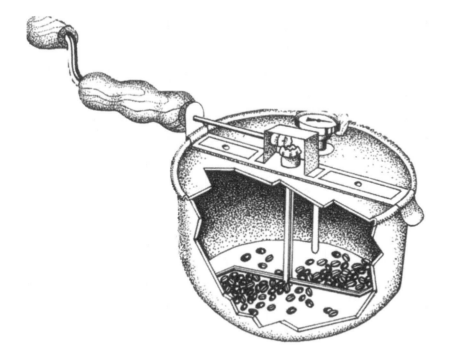

Whirley pop stove-top corn popper with candy thermometer installed to permit monitoring of roast-chamber temperature.

Crazy corn popper to roast coffee, by the way. It does not generate quite enough heat and ends up baking the coffee rather than roasting it.

Although the manufacturer obviously designed the Whirley Pop to pop corn rather than roast coffee, it actually turns out to be superior to traditional stove-top coffee roasters like the Aroma Pot in two respects. First, it enables you to easily watch the beans while they roast. With the Whirley Pop, half of the lid opens and folds back, making dumping the beans and keeping an eye on them while they're roasting relatively simple. A second advantage to the Whirley Pop is the ease with which it can be modified to accept an inexpensive candy thermometer (around $5). The candy thermometer provides rough readings of the temperature inside the popper, allowing you to safely and decisively manipulate burner settings to maintain optimum temperatures during the roast. Adding a candy thermometer to the Whirley Pop is a very easy procedure, requiring only a drill, a single drill bit, some odd nuts and washers as spacers, and about two minutes of elementary fiddling. Even better, at this writing one Internet supplier currently offers the Whirley Pop already modified with the thermometer (see "Resources").

A caution: The body of the Whirley Pop popper is constructed of aluminum, and like all light-bodied aluminum cookware it will melt if abandoned over high heat for an extended period of time. Not that the Whirley Pop is shabbily made. It is very well made and, used following the instructions in this book, will last through years of coffee roasting. But for those who read quickly or are inattentive I offer the following warning: *Never use a stove-top corn popper on burner settings above medium (with an electric range) or low (with a gas range), and never leave the popper unattended with the heat on.*

Given that warning, I find the Whirley Pop popper does an excellent job, particularly with darker roasts. I've cupped coffees I've roasted in it against equally fresh, professionally roasted coffees from the same crop, and found the Whirley Pop–roasted beans often better than their professionally roasted counterparts, and at worst only slightly inferior in acidity and aroma. The edge in home-roasted freshness will completely outweigh any such slight deficiencies. And the Whirley Pop roasts a half-pound of coffee per session, so you needn't hover over the stove cranking all that often.

Detailed instructions for using the Whirley Pop to roast coffee appear on pages 172–175 with illustrations on pages 137 and 173. If you have trouble finding the Whirley Pop see "Resources" for ordering information, including a source for a version with the thermometer already installed.

Roasting in Gas and Convection Ovens

Three kinds of ovens can be used to roast coffee using improvised methods: most ordinary kitchen gas range ovens, electric range ovens offering a combination of *both* convection and conventional thermal operation, and some electric convection ovens. Microwave ovens *only* can be used to roast coffee with Wave-Roast packets or cones (see page 168 and pages 168–170). Toaster ovens and conventional electric ovens without convection should not be used to roast coffee; you will be disappointed by the results.

ROASTING IN A GAS OVEN

A single layer of coffee beans spread densely over a perforated surface, say a perforated baking pan, will permit the gentle air currents moving inside gas ovens to flow through the beans and roast them fairly evenly.

Some beans may roast more darkly than others, but (this will sound like heresy to many professionals) I'm not sure that matters. In fact, the added complexity achieved by mixing beans brought to slightly varying degrees of roast in the same cup often dramatically enhances flavor. During my experiments with gas ovens I've turned out some rather funky-looking roasts that have tasted superb, with a wide, deep flavor palette that no professional roast I've tasted has ever matched.

It is true, however, that achieving an acceptable roast in a given gas oven usually requires patient experimentation with that particular appliance. And precise control of roast style can be difficult under any circumstances. This means that gas-oven roasting may not be a good idea for those who prefer roast styles at the very light or the very dark ends of the spectrum, since with a very light roast some beans may hardly be roasted at all, while at the dark end some beans may end up literally burned. But for those who prefer medium through moderately dark styles, gas-oven roasting can produce a remarkably rich, complex cup, a gustatory surprise that can only be experienced through home roasting.

Monitoring the progress of the roast also can be tricky with a kitchen oven, since the smoke and crackling that signal the onset of pyrolysis are muted by the barrier of the oven door, and you may need to use a flashlight to check the color of the beans as you peek inside.

Nevertheless, the flexible, precise control of temperature provided by gas ovens is an advantage, as are the venting arrangements, which usually carry the roasting smoke outside. Most gas ovens will roast up to a pound or more of coffee at a time, and again, the flavor of oven-roasted coffee can be startlingly good.

Detailed, illustrated instructions for gas-oven roasting appear on pages 180–186.

ROASTING IN AN ELECTRIC CONVECTION OVEN

Ordinary electric ovens do not generate sufficient air movement to properly roast coffee evenly, but many convection ovens, which bake by means of rapidly moving currents of heated air, can be pressed into service as ad hoc coffee roasters.

The majority of convection ovens manufactured today have a maximum heat setting of 450°F/232°C. This temperature is barely enough to bring coffee beans to a proper roast. Smaller convection ovens, those that resemble toaster ovens, typically have maximum settings lower than 450°F/230°C and cannot be used to roast coffee successfully. Those few ovens built with a maximum setting of 500°F/260°C or higher usually will produce a good, if mild-tasting, roast.

If you own a convection oven, test its heat output with an oven thermometer before attempting to use it to roast coffee. Instructions for this simple evaluation are given on pages 186–189, along with detailed instructions for convection-oven roasting. If you decide to purchase a convection oven especially for use in roasting coffee, look for a model that provides a maximum heat setting of 500°F/260°C or higher and permits easy visual inspection of the roasting beans through nontinted glass.

Even those convection ovens that generate reasonable roast temperatures tend to produce long, slow roasts of eighteen to twenty-five minutes. This deliberate pace yields a rather mild-tasting coffee with low acidity and muted aroma in medium roasts and a rather sweet, gentle profile in dark roasts. Some coffee drinkers, particularly those who take their coffee black and unsweetened, may prefer the taste of coffee roasted in a convection oven to the more complex, acidy taste of coffees roasted by other methods. And those few Americans who sip their espresso straight, without frothed milk, also may find the smooth flavor profile of convection-oven dark roasts attractive. However, I suspect that the majority of American coffee fanciers will find convection-oven coffee bland.

OVENS WITH COMBINED THERMAL AND CONVECTION FUNCTIONS

Some sophisticated electric ovens now convert from conventional operation to convection mode at the touch of a button. Such ovens also permit simultaneous use of both conventional and convection functions. For coffee roasting the combination setting works best. Complete instructions for roasting with these versatile devices is included with the instructions for general oven roasting on pages 181–189.

Higher-Priced Professional Equipment

For the serious aficionado, professional sample and small shop roasters may offer an interesting alternative despite their high price. Small professional roasting machines are usually divided into two categories: sample roasters, which typically roast anywhere from four ounces to one pound of coffee per batch, and tabletop roasters, which roast from one pound up to anywhere from five to seven pounds at a time.

In fact, many of the home-roasting devices described here do an excellent job of sample roasting, especially sample roasting for green coffee evaluation. In particular, the fast-roasting Fresh Roast and Hearthware Gourmet fluid-bed machines produce a style of cup ideal for evaluating green coffees: clearly articulated without distracting smoky or roasty notes. A hot-air corn popper with thermometer installed as bean temperature probe (pages 173–174) also works very well as a sample roaster for evaluation of green coffee, particularly because the thermometer makes it possible to achieve considerably more consistency in degree of roast than is possible with roasting equipment not equipped with thermometers or heat probes.

Nevertheless, the classic professional drum sample roaster, constructed of cast iron and brass and virtually indestructible, has many advantages over cheaper home equipment, including style, flexible control of heat and air flow, and, above all, durability. These handsome apparatuses start at around $4,200 for a "one-barrel" or single-cylinder model. See page 30 for an illustration of the simplest and still most widely used style, most closely associated with the name Jabez Burns. Sample roasters from Probat, CoffeePER, and Quantik go beyond the Burns design by reproducing most of the features of the traditional full-scale drum-roasting machine (see diagram on page 52). Unlike the Jabez Burns-style machines, the Probat, CoffeePER, and Quantik roasters enable you to control the velocity of airflow through the roasting chamber as well as the degree of heat applied to the coffee. The Quantik, manufactured in Colombia, adds to the basic drum-roaster design a heat probe inside the roasting drum (though not inside the bed of roasting beans) with digital readout. A heat probe that registers the temperature of the roasting beans themselves can be added as an option to the CoffeePER sample roaster. Both the Probat one-barrel and the Quantik run on ordinary household current. Models from other manufacturers typically require natural gas or a 220-volt connection.

Tabletop roasters, which roast a pound or more per batch, offer a considerable range of choice, too great a range to outline here. There are automated fluid-bed designs, like the simple, rugged, and relatively inexpensive one-pound-batch Sonofresco ($4,000); standard-configuration drum-style roasters for anywhere from $4,000 to $8,000, depending on features and batch size; and technically outstanding but awkwardly designed fluid-bed machines from Sivitz Coffee ($2,000 to $10,000). All run on natural gas, propane, or 220-volt current. See "Resources" for details.

Style of Roast

Different roasts for different folks. Some prefer an extremely light, brisk, almost tealike roast. Others prefer a dark, oily, nearly burned style. Between these two extremes the classicists range themselves, from those who prefer sweetly acidy medium roasts to those who enjoy a rich but balanced espresso. To review how these roast styles work out in terms of taste and terminology see the chart on pages 68–69.

The main trick in home coffee roasting is figuring out where to stop to achieve the roast style you prefer. One way to translate your personal taste in roast into home practice is to find a store that sells a whole-bean coffee roasted in a style you like, buy some, and attempt to duplicate it at home. However, those who want to fully explore the nuances of home roasting may prefer to experiment and taste, even carry out systematic tests to determine their preferences in roast, and along the way learn in detail about green coffees and roast styles. See pages 208–214 near the end of this chapter for suggestions on how to carry out such experiments.

Controlling the Roast

The following section offers an orientation to the issues involved in controlling degree or darkness of roast. Detailed and sequential instructions for various specific home-roasting procedures are given in the section following this chapter.

Whichever roasting method you use or roast style you prefer, you will eventually develop a feel for timing through experience with your particular method and equipment. Again, only our general unfamiliarity with roasting technique makes these instructions any more intimidating than directions for broiling a steak or preparing an egg over easy.

CONTROLLING THE ROAST BY TIME, TRIAL, AND ERROR

One way to control degree of roast, particularly with store-bought roasting machines, is simply to set the timer or other control to the setting the manufacturer recommends for a "medium" roast, taste what you get, and begin adding or subtracting time accordingly. If the roast tastes too bright, acidy, or grainy, add time to make your next roast longer. If the cup is too pungent, bitter, or burned tasting, or if it seems too dull or low-toned, shorten the next roast to brighten and lighten the cup.

The problem with the trial-and-error approach is that every green coffee roasts somewhat differently, so you may need to go through the same procedure for each new green coffee you add to your repertory.

Also, keep in mind that whatever time range you come up with is relevant to your roasting machine and method *only* and not to other technologies and methods. Don't be fooled by the illusion that there is some absolute "right" time for a good roast. Some small fluid-bed machines do a splendid roast in three or four minutes. If you tried to roast coffee in three or four minutes in a large drum roaster you would utterly destroy the coffee. Depending on the nature of the roasting equipment, a "good roast" can be achieved in as few as three minutes to as long as thirty minutes.

CONTROLLING THE ROAST BY SIGHT, SOUND, AND SMELL

The best and most versatile approach to controlling degree of roast is using your senses to follow the drama of the roast and ending it when the drama reaches the moment that produces the cup you prefer.

Recall that roasting coffee beans communicate to us by sight (gradually changing color from light brown to almost black), by sound (the "first crack" and "second crack"), and by smell (volume and scent of the roasting smoke).

Although both color and smoke are helpful indicators of roast development, the sound of the two cracks are the most telling and dramatic of indicators.

Here are the acts in the roasting drama and what they mean for roast flavor. For more detail see the chart on pages 68–69.

Overture. As the roast begins, beans silently turn brownish yellow and smell like bread or burlap. *Never stop the roast at this point because the coffee has not yet started to roast.*

First Act. Beans turn light brown, begin to smoke slightly, and start smelling more like coffee than bread. Most important, the beans begin to produce a rather loud popping or crackling sound. This is the onset of the "first crack," the moment the roast transformation begins.

Second Act. Beans turn light to medium brown and the popping of the first crack reaches a crescendo. *Stop the roast here, in the middle of the first crack, for a cup that is acidy and sweet but also grainlike and tealike in flavor.*

Third Act. Popping gradually trails away in frequency. Beans turn medium brown. As the popping stops completely the roast smoke may begin to darken slightly and smell sweeter and fuller. *Stop the roast here, in the lull at the end of the first crack, if you want a bright, acidy, high-toned, classic "breakfast"-style medium-roast cup.*

Fourth Act. A new, more subdued crackling begins. If the first crack sounds like corn popping, the second crack sounds more like paper being crinkled. Immediately before the second crack begins, the roast smoke increases in volume and becomes sweeter and more pungent. *Stop the roast here, just at the beginning of the second crack, if you prefer a round, sweet, but still bright cup of the kind roasters often call "full city" or "Viennese."*

Fifth Act. From here on, we enter the realm of "dark" roasts. The crackling or crinkling of the second crack becomes almost continuous. The smoke thickens and becomes dark and intensely pungent-smelling. The beans turn dark brown in color. *Stop the roast here, just as the second crack rises toward a crescendo, if you enjoy a balanced dark-roast cup without acidity, pungent yet sweet, full-bodied, with a roasty but not burned flavor.*

Denouement. As the second crack reaches a frenzied climax and a dark, heavy, sweet-smelling smoke fills the air, we reach the end of the roast story. Go no further. *Stop the roast here if you enjoy the ultimate dark roast, the kind often called "dark French": burned-tasting, thin-bodied, with only a vague overlay of sweetness and little nuance.*

The Story Is Over. After this final point in the roast has been reached, the coffee's aromatics have gone up in smoke entirely, the beans are completely black, the roasting chamber is oily, the neighbors have called the fire department, and the coffee, if you cared to sample it, would taste literally like burned rubber.

An Obvious Warning. Never abandon roasting beans if your roasting device lacks an automatic cool-down cycle or timer. *This is a particularly important caution with the stove-top and improvised hot-air popper methods.* With these approaches you should not even leave the room until the heat is off and the session is over. If coffee beans are abandoned inside a hot roasting chamber long enough they turn into semiflammable charcoal, not nearly as dangerous as many foods become when left over heat but flammable nevertheless.

CONTROLLING THE ROAST BY INSTRUMENT

In this case the "instrument" simply means a heat probe or thermometer arranged so that it is completely surrounded by the beans as they roast. The thermometer measures the approximate internal temperature of the mass of roasting beans, or "pseudo bean temperature" in professional roasting jargon. Since internal bean temperature is a measurement of roast style (see the chart on pages 68–69), the reading on the heat probe will tell the operator when to conclude a roast so as to achieve a given style.

Unfortunately, the instrument approach is difficult to realize with most home-roasting methods. Inexpensive metal thermometers intended for candy making and deep frying can be used to measure bean temperature in hot-air poppers by means of a very simple, two-minute modification (see pages 173–174). But with most other home-roasting setups the physical arrangements of the machine or method make it difficult to get the thermometer and beans into sustained and meaningful contact.

Concluding and Cooling the Roast

Cooling the hot beans rapidly and efficiently is one of the most important steps in home roasting, since coffee continues to roast from its own internal heat long after it has been removed from external heat. Coffee that is allowed to coast down to room temperature of its own accord will taste dramatically inferior to coffee that is promptly and decisively cooled.

COOLING THE ROAST WITH BUILT-FROM-SCRATCH EQUIPMENT

All dedicated, store-bought home-roasting devices cool the roast by circulating currents of room-temperature air through the hot beans. In all cases except the Hottop Coffee Roaster the cooling is performed inside the same chamber where the roasting occurred, which means the air is cooling both beans and chamber—a lousy idea technically; but given the small volume of beans being roasted it does not seem to compromise flavor.

IMPROVISED COOLING

Most hobbyist roasters who use improvised equipment prepare small batches of a few ounces of beans per session, so simply dumping the beans into a colander and stirring or tossing them is sufficient cooling procedure. This procedure is best performed over a sink or out-of-doors, so that the toasting chaff that floats free of the beans will not litter the kitchen.

If you have a kitchen range with an exhaust fan built into the stove-top, the kind that evacuates kitchen odors downward, you are in great luck. Simply place the colander full of hot beans over the exhaust fan and swirl or toss them. They will be warm to the touch within a minute or two.

Many exhaust fans located in hoods *above* kitchen ranges also can be used to air-quench beans. Simply dump the hot beans into a colander and hold the colander flush up against the filter or grill that covers the fan. (In the unlikely event the fan has no grill or covering, be careful not to touch the whirling fan blades!) The fan pulls air through the holes in the colander and up through the hot beans, typically cooling them within a couple of minutes.

You also can initiate the cooling process by water quenching, just as professional roasters often do. A pump- or trigger-spray dispenser, the kind with a nozzle that adjusts to a fine mist (illustrated on page 191), works very well. Simply fill the dispenser with distilled or filtered water, and while stirring or tossing the hot beans, subject them to a few seconds of light, intermittent mist. You must perform this procedure immediately after roasting and be careful not to overdo the application of water by spraying too long or by using too coarse a spray. Complete instructions for water quenching are given on pages 191–192.

Why water quench? There are two reasons. If you roast a half-pound or more of coffee at a time using improvised methods you probably should water quench to hasten the cooling process, since the more coffee you roast the slower it cools. Second, I find that coffee water quenched with care and restraint tastes better than coffee that has been cooled simply by stirring or tossing.

But if you do water quench, don't overdo it. Follow my instructions on pages 191–192 with care and sensitivity. And, obviously, *don't spritz the beans while they are still inside an electric appliance.* Liberate them and then apply the mist of water.

THE FREEZER STRATEGY

Another favorite cooling strategy among home roasters is sticking the hot beans into a freezer immediately after roasting. Make sure you take them out again well before they freeze, however. Like water quenching, freezer quenching shortens cooling and helps preserve aromatics.

Getting Out the Chaff

Chaff is paperlike stuff that appears as though by magic during roasting, apparently materializing straight out of the roasting beans. In fact these little brown flakes are fragments of the innermost skin (the silver skin) of the coffee fruit that still cling to the beans after processing has been completed. Roasting causes these bits of skin to lift off the bean.

With dedicated, manufactured-from-scratch home equipment, chaff is no problem. All you need to do is remember to follow the instructions that come with your roaster and empty the chaff receptacle after every roast batch.

CHAFF REMOVAL WITH IMPROVISED EQUIPMENT

With improvised equipment, chaff presents contrasting issues depending on which roasting method you employ.

With hot-air corn poppers the chaff will be blown free of the seething beans during roasting, creating one kind of problem: how to keep it from wafting around the kitchen and landing on the counter or in the soup. Solutions for this problem appear with the roasting instructions following this chapter.

If, on the other hand, you are using any other home-roasting method the chaff will remain mixed with the beans, presenting the problem of getting it out. Fortunately, the same tossing or stirring process that facilitates cooling will rid the beans of most of their chaff. Any amount that is left in the beans will have little to no effect on flavor. Only in very large amounts can chaff be detected at all, then only as a slight muting or dulling of the cup.

In fact, probably the single most important piece of advice to improvising home roasters in regard to chaff is to not become obsessive about it. However, advice for dealing with the occasional stubbornly chaff-retentive coffee is given on page 193.

The Troublesome Roasting Smoke

Finally, there is the roasting smoke. The good news is, it smells wonderful while you're roasting. To some people it still smells wonderful two hours later, but to most of us it turns stale and cloying.

Of the current crop of manufactured-from-scratch home-roasting devices, only one offers a solution to roaster smoke: Zach & Dani's Gourmet Coffee Roaster, with its smoke-thinning catalytic converter. All of the others require positioning either under a kitchen exhaust fan or next to an open window. They also can be used on a porch or balcony in clement weather, much like the Neapolitans and their *abbrustulaturi* celebrated by Eduardo De Filippo in Chapter 1. Don't try to use them outside in temperatures below 50°F/10°C, however. The cold may prevent them from achieving effective roast temperatures.

Improvising home roasters who use gas ovens and built-in convection ovens are in luck; typically ovens in kitchen ranges are well vented and carry the smoke outside. However, improvising roasters using hot-air poppers, stove-top apparatuses, or countertop convection ovens also need either a good kitchen exhaust fan or a partly open window.

Those who like light-to-medium roast styles will have less to be concerned about than those who prefer darker roasts, since beans produce their most voluminous and intense smoke as they are carried to darker styles. Also, keep in mind that the more coffee you roast the more roasting smoke you produce. Thus, those who roast a few ounces of coffee to a medium roast will have little to be concerned about. Those who roast a half-pound of coffee to a very dark "French" roast will need to make careful ventilating arrangements to avoid setting off the smoke alarm.

After-Roast Resting

Resting doesn't refer to what you yourself do after several minutes of vigilant home roasting but to what you do to the coffee. Freshly roasted beans are at their best anywhere from four hours to a day after roasting. Coffee fresh out of the roaster is superb, however, so don't deprive yourself of enjoying it owing to gourmet obsessiveness.

Systematic Roasting: Controlling Variables

Most home roasters rely on trial and error and accumulated experience to achieve the roast style they enjoy, with excellent results. Others relish the challenge of precision based on system and record keeping. A methodical approach also may be the best way to achieve intimate knowledge of roast and coffee taste.

Informative experiment depends on control of four roasting variables:

- the amount of coffee roasted
- the temperature inside the roasting chamber
- the identity of the green coffee (in particular its approximate moisture content)
- the time or duration of the roast.

With most home-roasting devices the first two variables are controlled for you and cannot be adjusted. The second two variables are controllable in all circumstances, however, and constitute a good starting point for home-roasting experiment.

Of course this list of variables assumes that you are using the same roasting method or technology (i.e., gas oven, hot-air corn popper, etc.) for all of your experiments. The taste of a given roast style gotten by different technologies will vary, sometimes greatly.

Like any good investigator, you need to control three of the four variables while systematically varying the fourth, meanwhile keeping careful record of the results. A sample form for recording notes on your roasting experiments appears on pages 156–157.

Again, the two variables with which you are most likely to experiment are the identity of the green coffee and the length of time the roast is sustained. In other words, if you want to find out how two green coffees or blends of green coffees compare when brought to roughly the same style of roast you should alter the identity of the coffees themselves while keeping the other three variables, including the approximate elapsed time of roast, constant. If, on the other hand, you are interested in how a single given coffee tastes at different styles or degrees of roast, obviously you should use the same green coffee or blend of coffees but increase the length of time you sustain the roast in regular, recorded increments.

THE FOUR VARIABLES IN DETAIL

Here is a closer look at the four variables, again assuming that the method or equipment you are using for your experiments remains constant.

Amount of Coffee You Roast. The more coffee you roast the slower the beans respond to heat, so if you vary the amount of coffee you roast from session to session you will not be able to make any meaningful connection between how long you have roasted a coffee and how it ends up looking and tasting. Fluid-bed roasters and hot-air corn poppers are particularly demanding in regard to how much coffee you roast, since they will not operate properly without the correct weight of beans to balance the upward thrust of the hot air. With oven and stove-top methods consistency in amount of coffee roasted per session is less important, particularly if you're the impulsive type who simply "roasts them until they're brown." But anyone carrying on systematic experiments should control this variable carefully.

Measuring green beans by weight on a kitchen food scale is more reliable than measuring them by volume, since beans differ in density. However, volume will work well enough in most home-roasting contexts.

Temperature Inside the Roasting Chamber. For professional roasters who attempt to subtly influence the flavor profile of the coffee during roasting this is the most important variable of all. Unfortunately, the simple technology available to home roasters makes sophisticated control of roasting-chamber temperature difficult if not impossible.

With most home-roasting equipment, store-bought or improvised, you have no choice about roast-chamber temperature. With fluid-bed roasters and hot-air corn poppers the temperature is built in. Stove-top roasting affords very rudimentary control. With convection ovens you can change temperature settings, but usually the only practical setting for coffee roasting is the highest available, so the question is moot. Only gas-oven roasting enables you to control roast-chamber temperature deliberately and measurably.

Consequently, the best approach for most home-roasting methods is to maintain the same temperature throughout your sessions and influence style or degree of roast simply by varying the length of time you keep the beans in the roasting chamber. If your method allows you a choice of roast temperature (essentially, if you are using either a gas oven or a stove-top roaster fitted with a candy thermometer), start with a temperature of about 500°F/260°C. If you have to wait longer than eight or ten minutes for the onset of pyrolysis, signaled by coffee-smelling smoke and crackling sounds, raise the temperature to 520°F/270°C and try again. On the other hand, if pyrolysis sets in sooner than four minutes into the roast, lower your beginning temperature to about 475°F/245°C for your next session. Never attempt to roast coffee at temperatures lower than about 460°F/238°C. With stove-top poppers never go higher than 520°F/270°C; with gas ovens, never higher than about 550°F/290°C. Once you settle on a workable temperature, which induces pyrolysis in less than eight or ten minutes but no sooner than three or four, stay with it until you learn a bit about the roasting process.

Identity of the Green Coffee. Green beans all roast slightly differently; some roast *very* differently. If you are carrying out systematic experiments to learn about roast flavors or styles, control this variable by using the same crop or blend of green beans for every session in your series of experiments.

The moister and denser the bean the slower it roasts and the higher the temperatures it will absorb on the way to the same roast style. Professional roasters often measure bean density and adjust roast-chamber temperatures accordingly. More intuitive professionals may compensate for differences among green coffees by regulating roast temperatures based on the history of their experience with a particular coffee.

Most home roasters can do neither, since the majority of home-roasting methods don't allow us to make adjustments to roast-chamber temperature for any reason. All we can do is be aware of differences in how quickly a given coffee may roast, and make very rough corresponding adjustments in our roast procedure. The following generalizations may be helpful, although in the context of home roasting only the last point concerning decaffeinated beans is of dramatic significance.

- Fresh beans less than a year old (new crop) from high growing areas (the best Guatemalan, Costa Rican, Kenyan, and Colombian coffees in particular) tend to be hard and moist, and may roast relatively slowly.
- Sumatran and Sulawesian coffees, which are often high in moisture content, may require longer roasting times or higher roast temperatures than those of other origins. Monsooned and aged coffees also tend to roast unpredictably or sluggishly.
- Older beans (a year or more since processing, called "past crop," plus some deliberately aged coffees) and beans from lower growing areas may roast faster, sometimes dramatically faster, than newer-crop, higher-grown coffees.
- Decaffeinated coffees can be very sensitive and may roast dramatically faster (15 to 25 percent) than fresh hard-bean coffees. With decaffeinated beans you should be prepared from the first sign of roasting smoke and crackling to check the appearance of the beans obsessively.

Time or Duration of the Roast. This is the most easily controlled and most important variable in home roasting. If you carefully control the other three variables and use the same roasting method from session to session, you should be able to correlate the time of the roast fairly accurately with the final color, style, and taste of the roasted beans. You can't achieve absolute consistency, since ambient temperature and atmospheric pressure both affect roasting time, but you can come close.

RECORD KEEPING

Take a look at the form on the following pages. Don't be intimidated by the number of columns or headings; several can be ignored by all but the most dedicated home roaster. Note that if you are consistent from session to session with roast-chamber temperature, quantity of coffee roasted, and quench method, you can obtain useful results by recording only five to six columns: the identity of the green coffee, the date of the roast, the final bean temperature (if your method permits), the elapsed time of the roast, the appearance of the roasted beans, and your tasting notes.

You may not know or care about the age of the beans. The temperature in the roasting chamber may not be measurable, or you may choose never to vary it once you start your experiments. Pyrolysis or first crack may come at about the same time if you are using a consistent method and roast-chamber temperature.

For advice on systematically tasting or cupping coffee see the list of tasting terms on pages 57–60 and the afterword on cupping on pages 208–214.

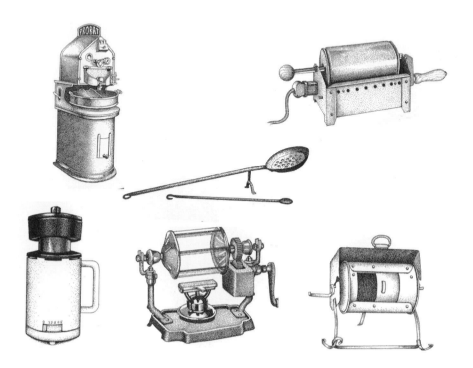

Sample Home-Roasting Log

Note that "roast 'em till they're brown" improvisors don't need to fool with charts like this one. Also note that not all columns are relevant to all roasting methods; fill in the columns that tell you what you need to know. Finally, be prepared to accept the fact that no matter how consistent you are, roasts still will differ from session to session. Home-roasting methods are still too offhand

Identity of Coffee	Approximate Age of Coffee	Roast Method	Date of Roast	Weight or of Volume Beans Roasted
Kenya AA	Current crop (less than a year old)	Fresh-Roast fluid-bed	6/3/03	3 ounces by weight
Brazilian Santos	New crop	Hot-air corn popper with thermometer installed	6/3/03	4 ounces by volume
Sumatra Mandheling	Old crop? (more than a year old)	Whirley Pop corn popper with thermometer installed	6/3/03	8 ounces by weight

to permit systematic compensation for subtleties like changes in atmospheric pressure and variations in green-bean density. Tasting and making observations about surface oils are activities ideally carried out the day following the roast. The examples are meant to suggest how the form might be used.

Roast Chamber Temperature (if measurable and variable)	Elapsed Time to "First Crack"	Final Bean Temperature (if measurable)	Elapsed Time of Roast	Quench Method (if variable)
NA	2 minutes	NA	3 minutes	Air (NA)
NA	4 minutes	450°F/230°C	9 minutes	Water
500°F/260°C	5 minutes	NA	8 minutes	Water

Home-Roasting Log

Identity of Coffee	Approximate Age of Coffee	Roast Method	Date of Roast	Weight or Volume of Beans Roasted

Roast Chamber Temperature (if measurable and variable)	Elapsed Time to "First Crack"	Final Bean Temperature (if measurable)	Elapsed Time of Roast	Quench Method (if variable)

Quick Guide to Home-Roasting Options and Procedures

Here are instructions for most of the ways it is possible to roast coffee at home, starting with manufactured-from-scratch devices and moving on to improvised methods. Near the end of this section (pages 191–193) you will find directions for two procedures related to improvised roasting methods: water quenching (accelerating the cooling of hot beans with a fine spray of water) and winnowing (separating chaff from roasted beans). A brief note about roasting decaffeinated and other specially handled coffees (page 194) concludes the section.

For background and overview on these machines and methods and their associated processes see Chapter 5. For ideas about things you can do to your beans after they're roasted see "Postroast Flavors and Frills."

Dedicated Home-Roasting Apparatuses

All currently available manufactured-from-scratch home coffee-roasting devices include a timer and controls that automatically trigger a cooling cycle, making all of these devices easier to use and less attention-demanding than improvised methods. They also efficiently remove chaff, the tiny, troublesome brown flakes liberated from coffee beans during roasting. These specialized home-roasting devices range in size and price from the little fluid- (or fluidized-) bed Fresh Roast, which currently sells for as little as $65 and roasts about three ounces of beans in a few minutes, to the gleaming and majestic Hottop Bean Roaster, which costs around $580 and roasts over a half-pound of coffee in fifteen minutes using classic drum-roaster technology.

Roasting with Dedicated Home Fluid-Bed Roasters

Fluid-bed roasting devices both agitate and roast beans with a powerful convection current of heated air.

ADVANTAGES

- Simpler and more automated than improvised roasting methods.
- Produce a consistent and uniform roast relatively quickly.
- Portable and easy to store, with small footprint.
- Cost considerably less than home drum roasters.
- Produce less smoke than home drum roasters.

DISADVANTAGES

- Roast considerably less coffee per session than home drum roasters and stove-top and oven methods.
- Currently available models are more expensive than ad hoc equipment used in improvised home-roasting methods, though cheaper by far than home drum roasters.

CURRENTLY AVAILABLE MODELS

- Original Fresh Roast: capacity per roast batch, 2.7 ounces (75 grams) by weight; costs around $65. Fresh Roast Plus: capacity per roast batch 3.5 ounces (100 grams) by weight, 5.5 ounces by volume; costs around $80.
- Hearthware Gourmet Coffee Roaster (also sold as Home Innovation Coffee Roaster): capacity per roast batch 3.5 ounces (100 grams) by weight, 5.5 ounces by volume; lists for $100 but often can be found for less.
- Brightway Caffé Rosto CR120: capacity 3.5 ounces (100 grams) by weight, 5.5 ounces by volume; lists for around $150 but often can be found for less.

The Hearthware Gourmet Coffee Roaster was one of the earliest of the current crop of home-roasting devices to come to market, and, at this writing, is still going strong on the basis of its simplicity and durability. The Hearthware Gourmet includes the standard set of features for such small fluid-bed machines. It roasts and agitates the beans by a current of hot air originating in the base of the machine, automatically initiates cooling based on the setting on the dial at the front of the unit, allows the user to observe the progress of the roast through a glass roasting chamber, and collects the chaff in a chamber that sits atop the machine.

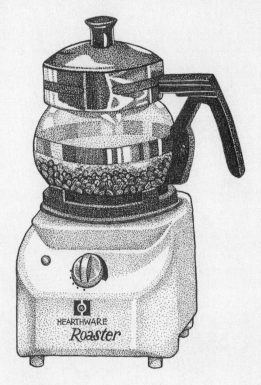

POINTS OF COMPARISON AMONG COMPETING MODELS

- Original Fresh Roast is fastest roasting, with smallest bean capacity.
- Hearthware Gourmet and Brightway Caffé Rosto are slower roasting, with larger bean capacity.
- All three models offer visual access to roasting beans. Brightway Caffé Rosto allows best views of roasting beans, but pouring beans out of roaster is awkward.
- Hearthware Gourmet Coffee Roaster is rather noisy, making it virtually impossible to hear the "second crack," an essential part of monitoring roast development by ear. Fresh Roast is quietest.
- Fresh Roast chaff collector is easiest to clean, Caffé Rosto chaff collector is hardest to clean.
- Fresh Roast roasting chamber sits rather precariously on roaster body and is easy to knock off and shatter.

- Hearthware Gourmet Coffee Roaster offers slightly more flexibility in terms of weight or volume of beans being roasted than does the Fresh Roast or Caffé Rosto. Bean movement in Fresh Roast or Caffé Rosto will stall if more beans than specified capacity are loaded. Fresh Roast is particularly sensitive in this regard.

TASTE NOTES

- In general, fluid-bed roasters emphasize bright, acidy notes in medium styles and pungency without charred notes in darker styles. Flavor profiles tend to be clean, sweet, and clearly articulated compared to the more complex and layered profiles of beans roasted in home drum roasters, gas ovens, and stove-top roasters and stove-top corn poppers.
- There may be subtle but substantial differences between coffees produced by fast-roasting fluid-bed machines like the original Fresh Roast (very bright, cleanly sweet) and those produced by slower-roasting units like Heartware Gourmet and the even slower Brightway Caffé Rosto (still cleanly articulated but somewhat lower-toned, rounder, fuller-bodied).
- Profiles can be altered slightly, brightening medium roasts and intensifying pungency in darker roasts by *slightly* (by 20 percent or so) decreasing volume or weight of beans being roasted.

WHAT YOU NEED

- Fluid-bed roasting device and accompanying instructions. See "Resources" for purchase information.
- Green coffee beans.

PROCEDURE

Fluid-bed devices may differ in details of operation. Follow the instructions that come with the device carefully. The following points may be helpful.

- Always start with the recommended weight or volume of green coffee beans. Too few beans may not roast properly, too many may not agitate sufficiently. Make sure beans begin to jostle and move at least slightly immediately after turning on device. If they do not begin moving until later in roasting cycle, reduce volume of beans for next round of roasting.

- Subtle adjustments in roast taste can be achieved by modestly reducing the volume of beans being roasted, particularly with Hearthware Gourmet and the Caffé Rosto. About 20 percent fewer beans will produce a faster roast and a brighter, more acidy/sweet profile in medium roasts and more pungency in darker roasts.
- If you seek precision in degree of roast, you may need to make adjustments on the fly, either advancing the dial to "cool" to stop the roast or by adding time to the roast cycle to extend it. See pages 143–145 for advice on controlling degree of roast using sound, smell, and bean color.
- *Empty the chaff collector after every roast batch.* To fail to do so will distort the performance of your roaster.
- Remove beans immediately after cooling cycle has been completed. Leaving beans in contact with a still-hot roasting chamber dulls flavor.

Roasting with Zach & Dani's Gourmet Coffee Roaster

Zach & Dani's Gourmet Coffee Roaster roasts coffee by means of a convection current of hot air but agitates the beans by means of a screw that rotates in the middle of the roasting chamber. Unique among home-roasting machines, it incorporates an electronic air cleaner that all but eliminates roasting smoke (though not roasting odor).

ADVANTAGES

- Roasts about 40 percent more coffee per batch at medium to moderately dark roasts than currently available devices using fluid-bed technology.
- Comes with a sophisticated air cleaner that substantially reduces the emission of roasting smoke.
- Controls are well designed, easy-to-use, and offer advantages both for those seeking walk-away automation and for those who want hands-on control.
- Costs considerably less than home drum roasters.

DISADVANTAGES

- Roasts considerably less coffee per session than home drum roasters and stove-top and oven methods.
- Requires much longer roast time than fluid-bed devices: 20 to 30 minutes.
- Has a somewhat larger footprint than fluid-bed roasters, though it is smaller and more portable by far than home drum roasters.
- Costs substantially more than ad hoc equipment used in improvised home-roasting methods and is somewhat more expensive than fluid-bed devices, though less expensive than home drum roasters.

CURRENTLY AVAILABLE MODEL

- Zach & Dani's Gourmet Coffee Roaster: capacity per roast batch 5 ounces (140 grams) by weight, 7 ounces by volume for medium to medium-dark roasts; 3.5 ounces (100 grams) by weight, 5.5 ounces by volume for dark roasts; costs around $200 for a kit that includes a grinder, a supply of green beans, and instructional materials.

TASTE NOTES

- Relatively slow roast produces a low-toned, round, complexly layered cup, less acidy and sweet than a fluid-bed cup but heavier bodied.

WHAT YOU NEED

- Zach & Dani's Gourmet Coffee Roaster and accompanying instructions. See "Resources" for purchase information.
- Green coffee beans.

PROCEDURE

Follow the instructions that come with the roaster carefully. The following points may be helpful.

- Although the Zach & Dani's machine is more forgiving with regard to weight of roast batch than fluid-bed devices, it roasts best at no more than the recommended weight or volume of green coffee beans.

- Reducing the volume or weight of the beans being roasted by about an ounce, or about 20 percent, will produce a faster roast with a brighter, sweeter taste in medium roasts and will help achieve a faster, richer-tasting dark roast.
- If you seek precision in degree of roast, you may need to make adjustments while roast is taking place, either by pressing the COOL button to stop the roast or by adding time to the roast cycle by pushing the triangular UP button, 1 minute per push. See the instructions that accompany the roaster.
- Roaster noise makes it difficult to time the roast by ear, but the slow pace of roast and excellent visual access to beans makes it easier to monitor roast by time or bean color. See pages 143–144 for advice on controlling degree of roast by bean color.
- *Empty the chaff collector after every roast batch.*
- I recommend removing beans immediately after the cooling cycle has been completed. Leaving beans in contact with a still-hot roasting chamber dulls flavor. Either use oven mitts, or handle components by touching plastic and rubber surfaces only, avoiding contact with hot metal and glass elements.

Roasting with Home Drum Machines

These are miniature, simplified versions of the classic professional drum roaster.

ADVANTAGES

- Roast considerably more coffee per session than competing dedicated home-roasting devices.
- Project more authority and coffee romance than competing fluid-bed machines or improvised equipment.
- Hottop Bean Roaster efficiently cools beans *outside the roasting chamber* and is at this writing the only dedicated home-roasting device to do so.
- Exterior surfaces of Swissmar Alpenrost are safe to touch throughout roasting cycle, a unique advantage among currently available home-roasting devices.

DISADVANTAGES

- Both machines roast slowly compared to fluid-bed devices or hot-air corn poppers. Hottop requires an additional 5-minute warm-up before roasting and an approximate 10-minute cool-down before roasting a second batch.
- Although both machines incorporate smoke-control features (Alpenrost, an adjustable ventilation port that helps direct smoke toward an exhaust fan or window; Hottop, a fiber filter), both produce considerably more roast smoke than competing dedicated roasting devices simply because they roast more coffee per batch than such smaller-capacity units. Do not buy either of these drum roasting devices unless your kitchen is equipped with an efficient ventilating range hood or you plan to roast out-of-doors or directly in front of an open window.
- Require considerable counter space.
- Cost more than smaller, less romantic roasting devices with smaller batch capacity and much, much more than improvised equipment.
- Hottop is appropriately named; the external surfaces of the machine become *very* hot during roasting and stay that way for a long time there-

Hottop home drum roasting machine. The Hottop felicitously combines traditional design (rotating drum, separate cooling outside the roasting chamber by means of fan and mechanical stirring) with features attractive to home users: excellent visual access to roasting beans through a glass panel at the front of the machine and a sophisticated computer chip that both automates the roasting procedure yet permits more experienced users some control over it.

after. The manufacturer hopes to offer an insulated version of machine shortly.

- Roasting beans cannot be seen or monitored visually in Alpenrost, although Hottop provides excellent visual access.

AVAILABLE MODELS

- Swissmar Alpenrost: capacity per roast batch 8 ounces (225 grams) by weight; costs around $290.
- Hottop Bean Roaster: capacity per roast batch 9 ounces (250 grams) by weight; costs around $580.

POINTS OF COMPARISON BETWEEN COMPETING MODELS

- Hottop is more expensive than Alpenrost.
- Hottop offers visual access to roasting beans; Alpenrost does not.
- External surfaces of Hottop become very hot during and immediately after roasting; exterior of Alpenrost remains safe to touch throughout roasting cycle.
- Hottop cools beans quickly outside roasting chamber, a technical advantage. Alpenrost's cooling is slow and rather inefficient, contributing to a low-toned cup profile with muted acidity and sweetness.
- Hottop is quieter, making it easier for those who roast by the sound of the crack to listen to the beans.
- Alpenrost's straightforward controls make it easier to use for first-time roasters, whereas Hottop's visual access to beans and more complex controls offer more information during the roast and more flexible control of degree of roast.
- Both are fine-looking appliances: Alpenrost is sleekly contemporary in appearance, Hottop romantically traditional.

TASTE NOTES

- Swissmar Alpenrost: low-toned, full-bodied, with muted acidity and sweetness.

- Hottop Bean Roaster: brighter, higher-toned, lighter-bodied, more pronounced acidity and sweetness, and a generally more classic cup than that produced by the Alpenrost but slightly rounder and fuller cup than produced by fluid-bed roasters.

WHAT YOU NEED

- Home drum roasting device and accompanying instructions. See "Resources" for purchase information.
- Green coffee beans.

PROCEDURE

Follow the instructions that come with the roaster carefully. The following points may be helpful.

- Don't overload either device with green beans, although Hottop is a bit more forgiving in this respect than Alpenrost. It is possible to alter the roast profile by modestly decreasing the charge of green beans: About 20 percent fewer beans will produce a faster roast with a sweeter, more acidy profile in medium roasts and a more pungent character in darker roasts.
- Alpenrost does not permit monitoring of roast by observing changing color of beans. If you wish to roast by sound and smell (see pages 143–144) with Alpenrost, start with a high or "dark" setting and stop roasting at desired juncture by pressing COOL button, because controls do not permit adding time during roast cycle. For more information on this procedure see Swissmar Alpenrost Experienced Roasters Guide at www.swissmar.com/exproast.shtmil.
- Hottop permits both stopping roast at will or lengthening roast by adding time in 10-second increments. Alarm sounds well before roast is about to conclude, allowing sufficient time to make such adjustments. Read the well-detailed instructions that accompany the roaster.
- *Always empty chaff collectors* and clean roasters regularly as indicated in the instructions.
- *Be careful not to touch the Hottop during or after operation;* all exterior surfaces become extremely hot.

Roasting with "Wave-Roast" Microwave Packets and Cones

Be advised that the microwave packets currently distributed by an organization called Smiles Coffee do *not* result in home-roasted coffee. The beans in the microwave pouches are already roasted when sold. All you do is heat them up. Perhaps there is some merit to the Smiles product, but I can't find it. Do not confuse Smiles Coffee with the genuine microwave-roasted coffee products described below.

At this writing an ingenious microwave coffee-roasting system tentatively called Wave Roast is on its way to market. The system is comprised of two products, one simpler and less expensive and the other more sophisticated and a bit more expensive.

The simpler product will consist of microwave packets, each filled with two ounces of green coffee, a cardboard stand to prop up the packets inside the oven, and a water reservoir. The water reduces energy in the microwave chamber to an appropriate level for coffee roasting and helps clean the air inside the microwave by absorbing roasting smoke. After the first popping sound indicates that roasting has begun, the user periodically stops the

Tentative design of Wave Roast microwave roasting cone and roller. The disposable cone is constructed of recyclable cardboard and is preloaded with green beans. A patented lining converts some microwave energy to radiant energy, which roasts the outsides of the beans while microwaves roast the insides. The cone sits atop a rechargeable battery-driven device that imparts a rolling motion to the cone, agitating the beans inside to assure even roasting.

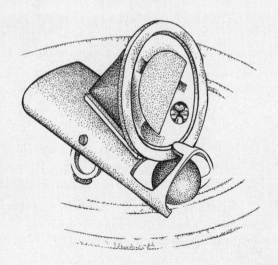

oven, reaches inside, and inverts the packet to help roast the beans evenly. The color of the roasting beans can be observed through a little transparent window. The entire procedure takes about four minutes.

The more sophisticated system seals the beans inside cardboard cones. The cones also will come preloaded with approximately two ounces of green coffee, which roasts in about four minutes. But, in the case of the cones, beans are agitated during roasting by a rolling motion imparted to the cone by an attractive, rechargeable battery-operated "roller" that sits atop and supplements the turning motion of the microwave turntable or by a small microwave oven specifically modified to roast coffee with the Wave-Roast cones. In both cases, an electronic sensor will monitor the roasting beans and signal when the desired roast level has been reached.

Neither packets nor cones are designed to be refilled. The manufacturer hopes to offer the packets at about $1 each. The cones probably will be sold in a starter kit, including seven cones charged with green beans, roller, and blade-type coffee grinder for around $40. Purchased singly, preloaded cones will sell for $1.75 to $3.50, depending on coffee origin.

ADVANTAGES

- Cones are very easy to use. (Packets are not.)
- Packets require no counter space, roller for cones requires very little.
- Little to no investment in specialized equipment is required.
- Virtually smokeless until a packet or cone is opened after roasting, at which point only a small puff of smoke is released.

DISADVANTAGES

- Roast relatively small volume of coffee per batch.
- Packets roast beans unevenly. (Cones roast relatively evenly.)
- On an ongoing basis, packets are expensive because of added cost of recyclable (but not reusable) cardboard packets and cones.
- Packets are awkward to use and require almost continuous observation during roasting. (Cones are easy to use.)
- Probably the least traditional and romantic of roasting methods.

TASTE NOTES

- *Packets:* uneven roast brings out complexity and depth of taste, since a range of roast styles may be present simultaneously in any given sample of beans. Acidity and sweetness are muted, body deepened. Produces the best results for those who like medium-dark (full-city) through moderately dark (espresso) styles. Should be avoided by those who prefer either very light or very dark roasts.
- *Cones:* At medium through medium-dark roast styles, produce a full-bodied cup with muted acidity and sweetness. They are at their best with darker roast styles, which remain roasty tasting but sweet and virtually completely free of charred and bitter tones.
- Taste notes are based on pre-product-release versions of the cones. Later alterations in cone design or microwave instructions may result in different cup profiles.

Stove-Top Roasting with the Aroma Pot Stove-Top Coffee Roaster

This contemporary variation on the traditional stove-top coffee roaster popular in nineteenth-century America and Europe can be purchased as part of a roasting kit on the Internet (see "Resources"). It looks like a small covered saucepan with a crank protruding from the top and must be used on a gas or electric burner or range top. The crank turns a pair of metal paddles that agitate the beans inside the pot during the roast.

ADVANTAGES

- More beans can be roasted per batch than with fluid-bed methods.
- Portable and easy to store.
- Coffee romantics may find the traditional design appealing.
- Has no motor or controls that can malfunction or wear out.

DISADVANTAGES

- Beans are roasted much less uniformly than with fluid-bed and drum devices.

- Beans cannot be observed easily during roasting.
- Roast temperature cannot be controlled with precision.
- Process requires continuous cranking during roast session plus occasional shakes, as well as a separate procedure for cooling beans.
- If vanes that agitate coffee jam or bend, there is no way of accessing interior of roaster to bend them back into place.
- Produces considerable roasting smoke and should only be used under an efficient kitchen exhaust fan or next to an open window.

CURRENTLY AVAILABLE MODEL

- Aroma Pot ½-Pound Coffee Roaster. Currently sold by The Coffee Project (see page 222) as part of a kit that includes the Aroma Pot itself, equipment for cooling coffee, storage canisters, and substantial quantities of green coffee, and costs around $140.

TASTE NOTES

- Performed carefully, roasting with the Aroma Pot produces a low-toned, full-bodied cup with muted acidity and sweetness and complexity in the lower range of the profile.

WHAT YOU NEED

- Aroma Pot ½-Pound Coffee Roaster (sold with colanders and spray bottle for cooling beans). See "Resources" for purchase information.
- Green coffee beans.
- Optional: Sample beans roasted to degree or darkness of roast you prefer.

PROCEDURE

Follow the instructions that come with roaster. The following points may be helpful.

- Start with a medium heat setting. If pyrolysis, signaled by a popping sound of the "first crack," occurs in less than 3 minutes, decrease heat and plan to do likewise with next roast batch. If more than 5 minutes elapses before the first crack, increase heat slightly and plan to do like-wise with next roast batch. After determining a heat setting that produces a first crack between 3 and 5 minutes, mark setting for future reference. Very hot ambient temperatures may accelerate roast times, in which case reduce heat slightly when such conditions occur.

- You don't need to turn the crank rapidly, and you can step away for a moment, but you must persist. Abandoning cranking for more than a minute will certainly cause bottom layer of beans to scorch. Important: Occasionally lift the roaster and shake it to further agitate the beans.
- Always dump beans from Aroma Pot into a colander for cooling immediately after removing the device from the heat. If you leave them inside the hot roaster you will seriously dull the flavor.

Stove-Top Roasting with a Crank-Type Corn Popper

ADVANTAGES

- Beans are accessible and can be studied easily as roast progresses.
- Beans roast somewhat more uniformly than with oven method or Aroma Pot.
- Portable and easy to store.
- More beans can be roasted per session than with fluid-bed devices.
- Costs considerably less than any manufactured-from-scratch roasting device.

DISADVANTAGES

- Beans are roasted less uniformly than with fluidized-bed or drum devices.
- Process requires continuous cranking and attention during roast session.
- Corn popper requires simple modification before it can be used for coffee roasting.
- Produces considerable roasting smoke and should only be used under an efficient kitchen exhaust fan or next to an open window.

TASTE NOTES

- Performed carefully, roasting with the Whirley Pop produces a low-toned, full-bodied cup with muted acidity and sweetness and complexity in the lower range of the profile.

WHAT YOU NEED

For roasting sessions:

- Whirley Pop stove-top corn popper (6-quart model) modified to accommodate candy thermometer as described below. At this writing popper is available for purchase already modified with a thermometer. See "Resources."
- Green coffee beans (approximately 9 ounces by weight or 12 fluid ounces per session for Whirley Pop 6-quart model).
- Colander for cooling that is large enough to accommodate about twice the volume of green beans you intend to roast.
- Kitchen exhaust fan or open window to dissipate roasting smoke.
- Oven mitt.
- Optional: Sample beans roasted to degree or darkness of roast you prefer.

For modifications to popper:

- Candy/deep-fry thermometer with dial and metal shaft that measures temperatures to 400°F/205°C or higher. Cooper, Springfield, UEI model T550, Comark, Pelouze, or Taylor brands all work well. See "Resources."
- Metal nuts or washers with holes large enough to slide onto shaft of thermometer and with sufficient total thickness to occupy about ½ to 1 inch of shaft length. (Not needed with UEI, Pelouze, or Comark 550F models or other thermometers with shaft of 5 or fewer inches long).
- ¼-inch high-speed drill bit and drill.

PROCEDURE

Modification to Whirley Pop corn popper (see illustrations on this page and on page 180).

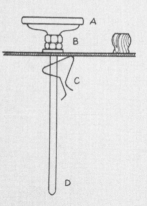

Correct installation of candy/deep-fry thermometer in the Whirley Pop stove-top corn popper. The thermometer enables the home roaster to monitor temperature inside the popper before and during the roast. See page 180 for an overview illustration of the popper with thermometer installed. (A) Thermometer dial. (B) Nuts and/or washers sufficient to raise the tip of the thermometer about ⅝ to ¾ inches above the inside bottom surface of popper. (C) Thermometer clip flush to the bottom surface of popper lid to secure the thermometer in place. (D) Tip of thermometer raised just high enough to clear stirring rods and roasting beans.

- Drill ¼ inch hole through popper lid. Lid has two hinged halves. Drill hole through center of half-lid that has clamp closure. Carefully remove and dispose of all aluminum shavings.
- Remove clip from thermometer. String sufficient metal nuts and/or washers on upper part of thermometer shaft to raise tip of thermometer about ⅝ to ¾ inch above bottom surface of popper. (See illustration on page 173).
- Insert thermometer in popper, with nuts and washers positioned between bottom of dial and upper surface of lid.
- Reach inside popper and slip clip back onto shaft of thermometer. Slide clip up to underside of lid to secure thermometer in place.
- (UEI/Pelouze/Comark 550F model has short shaft, so it requires no nuts or washers. It lacks clip and simply rests loosely in hole. It may rattle around but will be perfectly functional.)

ROASTING PROCEDURE

- Never use high heat under popper. On electric stoves start with a larger burner set to medium, on gas stoves start with a low flame.
- Never use popper without thermometer installed.
- Never abandon popper over heat.
- Make certain that cooling colander and oven mitt are at hand. If you wish to accelerate cooling of beans by water quenching (see pages 191–192), have a pump-spray bottle ready.
- Preheat popper by placing it over a medium heat setting (electric range) or low flame (gas range). Stand by and observe thermometer dial. The temperature will climb fairly rapidly. When indicator passes 400°F carefully modulate heat setting until temperature steadies at approximately 475°F to 500°F. (The candy thermometer may be calibrated only to 400°F. If so, the thermometer still can be used to accurately approximate higher readings. For example, 500°F is achieved when pointer circles past 400°F and returns to 100°F; 450°F is halfway between the two; and so on). Make note of burner setting. If you have a gas range, indicate approximate setting with a marking pen or bit of tape. Use this setting for future roasting sessions.
- Place green coffee beans in popper; close lid.

- Begin cranking handle of popper. You don't need to crank rapidly, and you can step away for a moment, but you must persist. Abandoning cranking for more than a minute will certainly cause bottom layer of beans to scorch. Occasionally beans may catch between stirring rod and bottom of popper causing crank to resist turning. If so, simply reverse direction of cranking. If crank still resists, see "Problems and Refinements" for this section.

- After beans are in popper, the temperature as indicated by the thermometer will gradually decrease. If temperature declines below 325°F turn up heat slightly.

- During remainder of session the thermometer will register slowly recovering temperatures, typically stabilizing at 350°F to 375°F. (Actual roasting temperatures on bottom of popper are higher.)

- About 1 minute after smoke and crackling begin (for lighter roasts) to 2 minutes (for darker roasts) check beans by lifting free half of popper cover. If you are deciding when to end the roast by bean color as well as by sound and smell (see pages 143–144), compare color of roasting beans with that of sample beans.

- Monitor roast at frequent intervals by sound or until beans reach same or slightly lighter color than your sample. When target is reached, immediately turn off heat and dump roasted beans into colander.

- Over sink or out-of-doors, stir or toss beans in colander until they are cool enough to touch and until most loose roasting chaff has floated free. To accelerate cooling, water-quench as described on pages 191–192. For more on chaff removal, see page 193.

PROBLEMS AND REFINEMENTS

If crank resists turning, heat may be causing bottom of popper to expand upward, interfering with movement of shaft that turns wire stirring vanes. Simply wait until popper is cool and place tip of kitchen spoon or similar long, blunt tool against bottom of popper next to shaft and press down firmly. Repeat on opposite side of shaft. Bottom of popper will depress slightly and (usually) permanently, freeing shaft to turn without interference. If your efforts produce slight indentations in bottom of popper don't be concerned; the operation still will be a success.

Roasting with Recommended Designs of Hot-Air Corn Popper

ADVANTAGES

- Somewhat simpler than other improvised methods, though it involves more effort and attention than that required by dedicated, manufactured-from-scratch home-roasting equipment.
- Produces more consistent and uniform roast than other improvised methods.
- Can accommodate installation of a thermometer for reliable monitoring of degree or color of roast.
- Portable and easy to store.
- Costs considerably less than manufactured-from-scratch roasting devices.

DISADVANTAGES

- Requires considerably more attention during and after roasting than that required by manufactured-from-scratch roasting devices.
- Only those units with the recommended popping chamber design (see

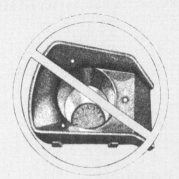 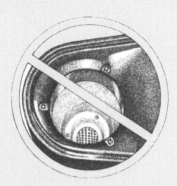 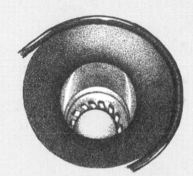

Interiors of popping chambers in three typical hot-air corn poppers. *Use only designs like the one on the right for coffee roasting,* in which hot air issues into the chamber from diagonal slots in the chamber wall. *Do not use designs like those pictured in center and on left,* in which hot air issues into the popping chamber from the bottom of the chamber.

illustration page 176) should be used to roast coffee. Other designs are potentially dangerous when employed for that purpose.

- Roasts considerably less coffee per session than home drum roasters and stove-top and oven methods.
- Regular use to achieve very dark roasts (dark brown and shiny with oil, common names Italian or dark French) will shorten life of popper. However, hot-air poppers can be used to produce moderately dark roasts of the kind usually called Viennese or espresso. See the "Quick Reference Guide to Roast Styles," pages 68–69.

TASTE NOTES

- Hot-air poppers emphasize sweet, acidy notes in medium styles and pungency without charred notes in darker styles. Flavor profiles tend to be clean, sweet, and clearly articulated compared to the more complex and layered profiles of beans roasted in home drum roasters, gas ovens, and stove-top roasters and corn poppers.

WHAT YOU NEED

- Hot-air popper of recommended design only (see illustration page 176). Other designs may be dangerous when used to roast coffee.
- Large bowl to collect chaff.
- Green coffee beans (same volume per batch as that of popping corn recommended by manufacturer of popper, usually about 4 fluid ounces or 1/2 cup).
- Colander for cooling that is large enough to accommodate about twice the volume of green beans you intend to roast.
- Two oven mitts or pot holders.
- Optional: Sample beans roasted to degree or darkness of roast you prefer.

A hot-air corn popper with bowl positioned to catch roasting chaff as it drifts out of the popper.

PROCEDURE

- Position popper under kitchen exhaust fan or near open window to dissipate roasting smoke. Can be positioned out-of-doors, but only in clement weather;

low ambient temperatures (under 50°F/10°C) may prevent coffee from roasting properly.

- Place in popping chamber same volume of green beans as volume of popping corn recommended in instructions accompanying popper. Do not exceed this volume.
- Make certain plastic chute (hoodlike component above popping chamber) is in place. Do not operate without chute; it assists in maintaining the proper temperature in popping/roasting chamber.
- Place large bowl under chute opening to catch chaff (see illustration on page 177).
- Place sample roasted beans where they can be easily seen for color comparison with beans inside popper. Make certain cooling colander and oven mitts are at hand. If you wish to accelerate cooling of beans by water quenching (see pages 191–192), have a pump-spray bottle ready.
- Plug in or turn on popper.
- In approximately 3 to 4 minutes coffee-smelling smoke will appear and beans will begin to crackle. Turn on a kitchen exhaust fan if indoors.
- About 1 minute after smoke and crackling begin (for light to medium roasts) to 2 minutes (for moderately dark roasts) begin checking color of beans by lifting out butter cup with oven mitt and peeking into popping chamber. If popper design does not incorporate a butter cup, either check color by lifting off entire hood, or monitor roast by listening to the crack, a reliable method of control described on pages 143–144.
- Roast develops relatively quickly with hot-air poppers, typically 5 to 6 minutes to medium roast, 7 to 8 minutes to medium-dark, 9 to dark.
- Monitor roast continuously by sound or until beans reach same or slightly lighter color than your sample. When desired degree of roast is achieved, unplug or turn off popper and, using oven mitts, immediately lift popper and pour beans out of popping chamber through chute opening into cooling colander.
- Place colander under kitchen exhaust fan and stir or toss beans until warm to touch. To accelerate cooling, water quench as described on pages 191–192.

Hot-air popper with candy/deep-fry thermometer installed. The thermometer measures the approximate internal heat of the roasting beans, permitting monitoring of the progress of the roast by temperature.

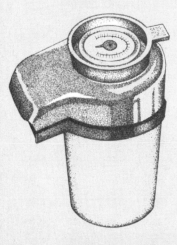

PROBLEMS AND REFINEMENTS

Hot-air poppers can be easily fitted with metal candy thermometers to monitor the approximate inner temperature of the roasting beans. Since the internal temperature of the beans correlates to the degree or style of roast, this modification permits the emulation of the procedure of technically inclined professionals who use the approximate internal temperature of beans to determine when to conclude the roasting session.

This modification differs in purpose from the somewhat similar procedure suggested for the Whirley Pop stove-top popper discussed earlier in this section. Here the goal is to monitor the temperature of the roasting beans, not the air temperature.

What you need for modification (see illustrations page 180)

- Candy/deep-fry thermometer with dial and metal shaft that measures temperatures to 400°F or 500°F or 550°F. Shaft must be long enough to project from bottom of plastic butter cup or hood to a point about 2 to 3 inches above bottom of popping/roasting chamber. The Cooper brand thermometer fits most poppers perfectly. The Taylor brand has a shaft about ½ inch longer than the Cooper's; Insta-Read is longer still. The shaft of the UEI/Pelouze/Comark 550F thermometer is 5 inches long, too short for some popper models. (Measure before you buy!) See "Resources" for thermometer availability.
- ¼-inch high-speed drill bit and drill.
- If necessary: metal nuts or washers with holes large enough to slide onto shaft of thermometer. These may be required as spacers between underside of thermometer dial and top surface of butter cup or hood to raise tip of thermometer shaft to recommended minimum 2 inches from bottom of popping/roasting chamber.

Modification procedure (see illustrations page 180).

- Drill ¼-inch hole through center of plastic butter cup or top of popper hood. Carefully remove and dispose of all plastic shavings.
- Remove clip from thermometer. If necessary, string sufficient metal nuts and/or washers on upper part of thermometer shaft to raise tip of ther-

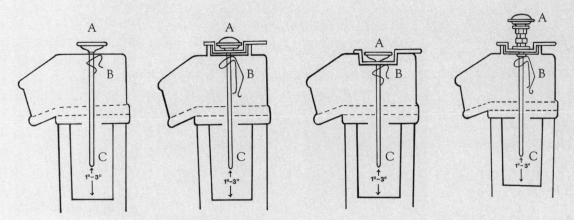

Installation of a candy/deep-fry thermometer in the recommended designs of hot-air popper. Use recommended design poppers only (see page 176). The thermometer permits monitoring the approximate internal temperature of the beans as they roast. (A) Thermometer dial. (B) Thermometer clip flush to the bottom surface of the butter cup to secure the thermometer in place. (C) Thermometer tip protruding to within 1 to 3 inches of the bottom surface of popping/roasting chamber. The green beans may not touch the thermometer tip at the start of roasting but will expand and surround it as roasting proceeds. (If the thermometer tip extends to closer than 1 inch from the bottom of the popping chamber, insert sufficient nuts or washers between the underside of the thermometer dial and the surface of the butter cup to raise the tip to a minimum 1 inch above the bottom.)

mometer a minimum of approximately 2 inches above bottom of popping/roasting chamber.

- Insert thermometer in popper with nuts and washers (if necessary) positioned between underside of dial and upper surface of butter cup or hood.
- Slip clip back onto shaft of thermometer. Slide clip up to underside of butter cup or hood to secure thermometer in place.

Monitoring the progress of the roast with the installed thermometer:

- Consult the "Quick Reference Guide to Roast Styles" on pages 68–69 for equivalents of bean temperature and roast style.
- When temperature on thermometer approximately matches temperature for your preferred roast style, unplug or turn off popper and, using oven mitts, immediately remove plastic chute and thermometer from top of popper, lift popper, and pour roasted beans into cooling colander.
- Your candy thermometer may be calibrated only to 400°F. If so, the thermometer still can be used to accurately approximate higher temperature

readings. For example, 450°F is achieved when pointer has circled the dial and centers between 400°F and 100°F.

- With hot-air poppers do not attempt to achieve roasts with final internal temperatures higher than about 460°F/240°C (moderately dark to dark brown color; common names Viennese or espresso).

Roasting in a Gas Oven

ADVANTAGES

- Temperature in roasting chamber (i.e., oven) is easily controlled and roughly repeatable.
- With most gas ovens, roasting smoke is effectively vented.
- More coffee can be roasted in a given session than with most other methods.
- Control over temperature enables those who roast systematically to compensate roughly for differences in density of green beans and broadly influence the taste of the roast.

DISADVANTAGES

- Hot spots inside some ovens and lack of strong convection currents may cause beans to roast unevenly: some beans lighter, some darker, some between. Solutions to this problem may require patience and experiment.
- Timing roast can be difficult because color of beans may not be uniform, and beans may be difficult to see and the sounds they produce difficult to hear inside oven.
- Precision in roast style may be difficult to attain owing to uneven roasting.

TASTE NOTES

- A somewhat uneven roast brings out complexity and depth of taste, since a range of roast styles may be present simultaneously in any given sample of beans. Acidity and sweetness may be muted, body deepened. Gas-oven roasting probably produces the best results for those who like medium-dark (full-city) through moderately dark (espresso) styles. It probably should be avoided by those who prefer either very light or very dark roasts.

WHAT YOU NEED

- Ordinary kitchen gas oven. (Do not attempt to use an electric range or a toaster or microwave oven for coffee roasting. Conventional electric kitchen ovens can be used following these instructions but typically produce roasts too uneven for most tastes. For electric convection ovens consult the section on pages 139–140).
- One or more flat, perforated pans with raised edges. Perforated baking pans designed to crisp bottom crusts of breads or pizzas work well. Perforated vegetable steamers with folding, petallike edges also work, though they are much less handy than perforated baking pans. Perforations should be relatively close together (no more than ⅛ inch apart) and small enough to prevent coffee beans from falling through (maximum about 3/16-inch diameter). Pan should have raised lip around edges. See examples of such pans below and on page 183 and suggestions for obtaining them in "Resources." In larger ovens more than one baking pan can be used per roasting session.
- Enough green beans to densely and uniformly cover surface of baking pan(s) one bean deep.

A typical perforated pan for gas-oven and convection-oven roasting.

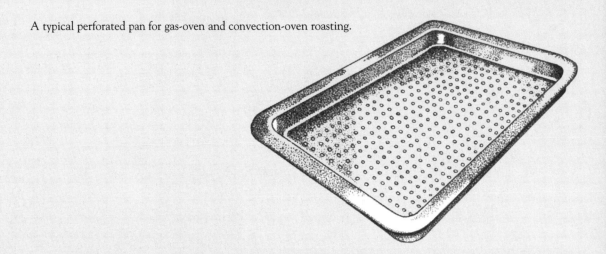

- Colander for cooling that is large enough to accommodate about twice the volume of green beans you intend to roast.
- Two oven mitts or pot holders.
- Flashlight (necessary only if interior of oven is not illuminated and remains dark when you peer through window or crack open door).
- Optional: Sample beans roasted to degree or darkness of roast you prefer.

PROCEDURE

- Note: Virtually all gas ovens will produce a reasonably consistent and very flavorful roast, but success may require patience and experimentation. If your first roast emerges uneven in color, don't give up. Consult "Problems and Refinements" for this section.
- Preheat oven to 500°F/260°C to 540°F/280°C, depending on condition of green coffee and desired taste characteristics. For fresh, new-crop coffees, set to 540°F/280°C; for past-crop, aged, or monsooned beans, set to 520°F/270°C; for decaffeinated beans, set to 500°F/260°C. For a brighter, more acidy taste in medium roasts and more pungency in dark roasts try upper range of temperature, for more body and less acidity/pungency use lower end of range. If beans take longer than 15 minutes to reach a medium roast or 20 minutes to reach a moderately dark to dark (espresso) roast, or if they taste bland or flat, start with a higher temperature on subsequent sessions.

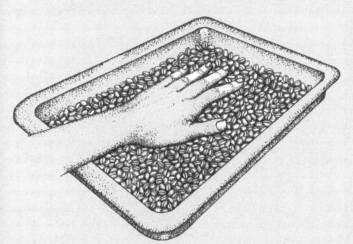

Patting the surface of the green beans with an open hand is a good way to make certain the beans are distributed evenly, one deep, across the entire surface of the perforated pan used for oven roasting.

- Spread green beans closely together, one bean deep (no deeper) across entire perforated surface of baking pan. Pat beans down with a flattened hand until they are densely but evenly distributed, touching or almost touching, but not piled atop one another. Make certain entire surface of pan is covered with a single layer of beans. See illustration on page 183.
- Place baking pan charged with beans on middle shelf of preheated oven.
- If you intend to control degree of roast by color of beans, place sample roasted beans where they can be easily seen for color comparison with beans inside oven. Make certain cooling colander and oven mitts are at hand. If you wish to accelerate cooling of beans by water quenching (see pages 191–192) have a pump-spray bottle ready.
- In about 7 to 10 minutes you should hear crackling from inside oven and smell coffeelike scent of roasting smoke.
- About 2 minutes after crackling begins (for lighter roasts) to 3 minutes after crackling begins (for darker roasts) peek inside oven, with a flashlight if necessary. If oven has no window, crack open oven door only for as long as it takes to compare color of beans inside oven with that of the sample of roasted beans.
- Continue peeking at about 1-minute intervals, comparing roasting beans to sample beans. When average color of roasting beans is satisfactory or approximately same as that of sample, pull baking pans out of oven using oven mitts and dump beans into colander.

Details of two perforated baking pans or sheets appropriate for roasting coffee in a gas or convection oven. The important features for any oven coffee-roasting pan are holes sufficiently close together to permit circulation of hot air and small enough to prevent the beans from falling through or catching, and a raised lip around the edge of the pan.

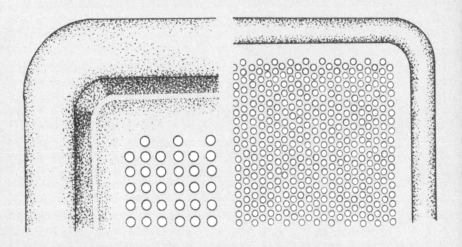

- Over sink or out-of-doors, stir or toss beans in colander until they are cool enough to touch and until most of loose roasting chaff has floated free. To accelerate cooling, water quench as described on pages 191–192. For more on chaff removal, see page 193.

PROBLEMS AND REFINEMENTS

Actual temperatures in ovens may differ from control settings. Consider comparing the actual temperature as indicated by an oven thermometer to the temperature setting on oven before your first roasting session. Compensate for any difference when setting temperatures thereafter.

Beans always will roast somewhat unevenly. Nevertheless, they may taste as good as or better than uniformly roasted beans. Try them. If you don't like the flavor complexity, or if the range between dark and light beans is too great (if darkest beans are almost black and lightest beans medium-brown, for example), one or more of the following adjustments may be needed.

- Make certain beans are tightly and uniformly spread one bean deep but no more over entire surface of pan.
- Use middle oven shelf. If results on middle shelf are unsatisfactory, experiment with higher or lower placement.
- Place one or more cookie sheets on lower shelf of oven to break up flow of hot air through oven and thus dissipate "hot spots." Arrange pans charged with coffee beans on upper shelf above cookie sheets. Position cookie sheets in relation to bean-charged pans so as to break up pattern of hot spots revealed by previous roast sessions. In other words, if beans in middle of roasting pan emerge darker than beans at sides, position a cookie sheet directly below roasting pan. If darker beans are at back of pan, position a cookie sheet somewhat farther back in oven than roasting pan, etc.
- If cookie-sheet strategy is successful (it usually is), beans may take longer to reach pyrolysis. If beans take longer than 15 minutes to reach a medium roast or 20 minutes to reach a moderately dark (espresso) roast, or if they taste bland or flat, start with a higher temperature on subsequent sessions.

- If you are using more than one shelf in oven and beans roast unevenly from shelf to shelf, arrange pans on one shelf only (middle shelf is usually best).
- If cookie-sheet strategy fails and beans still roast unevenly across surface of pan, rotate pan about a half turn approximately every 3 minutes during roasting. This is a last resort and seldom required.

Oven roasting offers the potential for control over temperature and timing. Keep records of oven settings and elapsed time of roasts while roasting the same amount of similar green beans. When you achieve a roast you enjoy use the same oven setting and set a kitchen timer for 2 minutes or so before the termination of the roast, thus minimizing time spent peeking into oven to check roast color. You still must make a final decision when to stop the roast based on visual observation of the bean color, since differences in atmospheric pressure and ambient temperature alter the length of a roast from session to session. See pages 149–153 for more advanced experiments with record keeping.

Roasting in a Convection Oven

Note: Only convection ovens with maximum settings of 450°F/230°C or higher can be used to roast coffee. Test the oven for actual heat output. Preheat the oven to a maximum temperature setting (usually 450°F/230°C to 500°F/260°C) with an oven thermometer positioned inside. If the actual temperature inside the oven as registered by the thermometer peaks at 475°F/245°C to 500°F/260°C the oven will produce an acceptable to excellent roast. If the actual temperature is 450°F/230°C to 460°F/240°C try a roast, but most likely the beans will not expand and the coffee will taste flat. If the temperature registers below 450°F/230°C do not attempt to use the oven for coffee roasting.

ADVANTAGES

- Temperature in roasting chamber (i.e., oven) is easily controlled and repeatable.
- More coffee can be roasted in a given session than with most other methods.

- Produces a relatively consistent and uniform roast.
- Most convection ovens permit easy visual inspection of roasting beans, making monitoring roast color easier than with many other methods.

DISADVANTAGES

- Maximum temperature in most convection ovens (see note at head of this section) is barely high enough to induce a proper roast.
- Monitoring of roast must be done mainly on the basis of bean color, since the cycle of the crackling beans typically cannot be heard above the sound of the oven fan.

TASTE NOTES

Important: Most convection ovens, owing to low heat output relative to roasting requirements, produce a mild, sweet roast with muted acidity and relatively weak aroma.

WHAT YOU NEED

- Convection oven with maximum temperature of at least 450°F/230°C, preferably 500°F/260°C. (See note at head of this section. Do not purchase a convection oven for coffee roasting unless it incorporates a maximum temperature setting of at least 500°F/260°C and permits easy visual inspection of roasting beans through clear, nontinted glass.)
- Perforated baking or pizza pan of kind recommended for gas-oven roasting (see page 184).
- Sample beans roasted to your preferred style.
- Enough green beans to densely cover entire surface of baking pan(s) in a single layer.
- Colander for cooling that is large enough to accommodate about twice the volume of green beans you intend to roast.
- Two oven mitts or pot holders.
- Optional: Sample beans roasted to the degree or darkness of roast you prefer.

PROCEDURE

- Make certain a raised rack or shelf is in place in oven. Do not place perforated baking pan directly on a carousel or floor of oven; use raised rack or shelf. Do not use microwave or mixed microwave/convection function in ovens that offer both convection and microwave options.

- Preheat oven to highest available temperature setting but no higher than 530°F/270°C. If oven offers more than one air velocity setting, experiment. Use highest velocity that does not blow chaff out of beans, usually low. Until you have established a roasting routine through experimentation with your particular oven, set timing function for 25 minutes. Coffee will roast in approximately 12 to 25 minutes, depending on heat-transfer rate of oven and desired degree of roast.

- Spread green beans closely together, one bean deep (no deeper) across entire perforated surface of baking pan. Pour beans onto pan, then pat them down with a flattened hand until they are densely but evenly distributed.

- Place baking pan charged with beans in preheated oven.

- Place sample roasted beans where they can be easily seen for color comparison with beans inside oven. Make certain cooling colander and oven mitts are at hand. If you wish to accelerate cooling of beans by water quenching (see pages 191–192), have a pump-spray bottle ready.

- In about 10 to 15 minutes you should begin to smell coffeelike scent of roasting smoke. If oven is built-in and vents efficiently you may not smell smoke and will need to make frequent visual checks of color of roasting beans through oven window until you have established your own timing routine for roasting.

- After appearance of roasting smoke observe beans through oven window at 1- to 2-minute intervals, comparing them to sample beans if you wish. When average color of roasting beans is satisfactory, or approximately same as that of sample, stop oven, pull baking pan out of oven using oven mitts, and dump beans into colander.

- Over sink or out-of-doors, stir or toss beans in colander until they are cool enough to touch and until most loose roasting chaff has floated free. To accelerate cooling, water quench as described on pages 191–192. For more on chaff removal, see page 193.

PROBLEMS AND REFINEMENTS

If you roast the same amount of green beans per session and record the elapsed time of each session you can begin to predict the approximate time your oven requires to achieve a given roast style. Then set a kitchen timer for approximately 2 minutes before you anticipate concluding the roast. You still must make a final decision when to stop the roast based on visual obser-vation of bean color, since differences in atmospheric pressure and ambient temperature alter the length of a roast from session to session.

A few convection ovens may roast unevenly (beans at front or back of pan may roast more darkly than beans at opposite end, for example). Roasts that are only mildly inconsistent may taste as good or better than more con-sistent roasts. But if lack of uniformity is extreme or bothers taste, try repo-sitioning the roasting pan in a different part of the oven, usually toward front or back. If that doesn't work, open the oven every 3 to 4 minutes and, using oven mitt, rotate the pan a quarter or half turn. This strategy is a last resort and is usually not necessary.

Ovens Combining Conventional and Convection Functions

Some contemporary electric ovens permit cooks to chose options ranging from conventional thermal operation through pure convection to combinations of the two. With such ovens try the combined convection-thermal setting.

Preheat the oven to 425°F to 450°F/220°C to 230°C. For brighter, more acidy taste in medium roasts and more pungency in dark roasts try upper range of temperature, for more body and less acidity/pungency use lower end of range. Follow the instructions given earlier in "Roasting in a Gas Oven."

Getting the Roast Color You Want

Look at the chart on pages 68–69 to help determine your preferences in terms of "color" or degree of roast. Because the longer beans roast, the darker their color, beginning roasters often focus too rigidly on elapsed time as a way of controlling the roast. Remember that the time it takes to achieve a given degree of roast is relative and determined by many variables including the density and moisture of green beans, the ambient temperature of the room in which you are roasting, and, if relevant, fluctuations in the electrical current. You may need to make adjustments during roasting, either stopping the roast by intervening to initiate the cooling cycle or adding time to the roast cycle, in order to achieve a precise degree of roast.

To understand how to read the roast by eye, ear, and nose, read pages 143–144. Learning to listen to the roast is particularly helpful. To summarize: For sweet, briskly acidy medium roasts, stop the roast after the first loud popping ends but before the quieter, crinkling-paper sound of the second crack begins. For round, sweet roasts stop the roast just as the crinkling sound of the second crack starts. For darker espresso-style roasts wait until the crinkling sound of the second crack is just beginning to rise toward a continuous crescendo and the beans begin producing dark, intense-smelling roasting smoke. Wait only briefly beyond this moment for extremely dark "French" roasts. Things happen very quickly once the second crack begins. Don't wait too long into the crescendo of the second crack or you will outright burn the beans.

Cooling Beans After Roasting

Precise, rapid cooling of freshly roasted beans is essential to good flavor. Ideally, beans should be warm to the touch within 2 to 3 minutes after the conclusion of the roast.

Dedicated, made-from-scratch home-roasting devices all incorporate a built-in cooling cycle. Typically, the heating element kicks off while a fan continues to circulate room-temperature air through the hot beans, which remain in the same chamber in which they were roasted. Cooling beans inside the roasting chamber produces a good cup in home devices because the volume of beans being roasted is small. Larger-batch professional roasting machines must cool the coffee outside the hot roasting chamber to avoid completely destroying the flavor by slow, sluggish cooling.

Among currently available dedicated home-roasting devices only the Hottop drum roaster (pages 164–167) dumps the beans into a separate cooling tray outside the roasting chamber, where they are cooled by a current of room-temperature air supplemented by mechanical stirring.

Kicking off the cooling process for just-roasted beans with a few one-second bursts of purified water, applied with a very fine spray. Done correctly, such *water quenching* will improve the quality of the roast by decisively initiating cooling. Done incorrectly, it can harm the roast by promoting staling.

With improvised home-roasting methods the beans must be cooled manually by immediately removing them from the roasting chamber and stirring or tossing them in a colander. The cooling process can be accelerated by subjecting the beans to a light, brief spray of purified water (water quenching) immediately after removing them from the roast chamber or by placing the beans in a freezer compartment until they reach room temperature.

Never allow hot beans to sit untouched in a receptacle and cool of their own accord. They will lose considerable aroma and liveliness.

Cooling beans by stirring or tossing them in a colander should be performed over a sink or out-of-doors, since roasting chaff will be released in the process.

I strongly recommend careful, restrained water quenching for cooling all coffee roasted by improvised methods, although for small batches (4 to 6 ounces by weight or volume) simply stirring or tossing the hot beans in a colander can be sufficient. If you roast ½ pound or more beans in one session you should consider water quenching. Commercial roasting companies that drench the coffee after roasting to increase its weight have given water quenching a bad name, but all experiments I have conducted indicate that water quenching, performed properly, increases the cup quality of the coffee.

The water-quenching procedure has an added virtue: it reduces the volume of smoke released by the just-roasted beans. However, it is important that the water quenching be performed immediately after roasting, sparingly, and with care. No more water must be used than will evaporate almost instantly from the hot beans. Coffee that has been allowed to sit in droplets of moisture during cooling will stale rapidly in the days that follow.

WHAT YOU NEED

- Trigger-spray bottle with adjustable nozzle.
- Two colanders that are large enough to accommodate about twice the volume of green beans you intend to roast.

PROCEDURE

- Fill trigger-spray bottle with distilled or filtered water.
- Adjust nozzle to as fine a spray as possible.
- Prepare bottle before beginning roasting and have it and colanders close at hand.
- Apply water immediately after dumping beans from roasting chamber into one of two colanders.
- Holding bottle 6 to 10 inches from hot beans, apply a single short (1-second) burst of water to beans while stirring or tossing them in colander. See illustration on page 191.
- Wait a second or two to allow water to evaporate from surface of hot beans, then apply a second short burst and wait a second or two again. Repeat intermittent bursts while stirring or tossing beans. Repeat only as long as water continues to vaporize upon contact with beans. Normally this will be about one short burst of spray per 1 to 2 ounces of beans.
- Do not attempt to completely cool beans with water. Your goal is to initiate cooling with a quick application of water, then finish cooling by stirring or tossing. If in doubt stop spraying sooner rather than later.
- Transfer beans, which still will be hot, to second dry colander. Stir or toss them until they are merely warm. Some moisture may remain beaded on surface of beans immediately after quenching, but if you have performed procedure with restraint this moisture will evaporate well before beans are cool.

Chaff Removal after Roasting

Most green coffee beans are delivered with fragments of the inner, silver skin of the fruit still adhering to them. During roasting these fragments dry and loosen, turning into roasting chaff. Decaffeinated beans retain no chaff. Other beans may retain more or less chaff depending on whether they have been subjected to a final cleaning procedure during processing, called *polishing*.

All manufactured-from-scratch devices remove chaff during roasting and deposit it in a chaff collector, which must be emptied between roast batches. Hot-air corn poppers pressed into service as coffee roasters also blow the chaff off the roasting beans and deposit it into a bowl situated next to the popper.

With other improvised methods the recommended cooling procedure—tossing the beans in a colander—will remove most of the loose chaff. Colanders with larger, slotlike openings will evacuate chaff more effectively than colanders with smaller, circular openings. Occasionally swirling the beans around the inside of the colander with a circular motion will help free the more stubborn chaff fragments.

If you water quench, first quench, then focus on removing the chaff as you toss the beans in the second dry colander.

Occasionally a coffee will be delivered virtually covered with chaff. In this case pour the beans to and fro between two colanders, tossing and swirling them between pours. Occasionally blow on the beans as you pour them.

Do not become obsessive with this procedure. Winnow out as much loose chaff as you can without making yourself dizzy, then enjoy the coffee. Very large amounts of chaff can dampen flavor slightly, but smaller amounts have no impact whatsoever on the cup.

If the last bits of chaff bother you for cosmetic reasons, you can always pour the offending beans back and forth in front of a fan, out-of-doors.

Resting Coffee after Roasting

Coffee flavor is at its peak twelve to twenty-four hours after roasting, but don't hesitate to enjoy freshly roasted coffee immediately.

Accommodations for Differences Among Green Coffees

All coffees roast somewhat differently. If you have been roasting one coffee regularly and you begin roasting another, do not expect it to behave exactly like the first. Older coffee (past crop, mature, vintage) tends to roast somewhat faster than a fresh (new-crop) coffee.

More important for the home roaster are the delicacy of decaffeinated coffees and the confusing color of aged and monsooned beans. Decaffeinated beans often roast dramatically (15 to 25 percent) faster than nontreated beans and must be observed with great care after pyrolysis sets in to avoid overroasting.

A second problem with decaffeinated, aged, and monsooned beans is reading their color during roasting. They all begin the roasting process anywhere from light yellow (monsooned beans) to brown (aged and decaffeinated beans). This difference in color means that you must be particularly observant if you monitor the roast by color rather than by sound and smell and that you compensate for the original color of the bean when determining when to end the roast.

Roasting Blends of Beans from Different Origins

Separate batches of beans from different origins that together make up a blend can be combined before or after roasting. It is undoubtedly best to roast the individual components of blends separately, then combine them, because every lot of green beans differs in density, moisture content, and bean size, and consequently develops at a different pace in the roaster.

If you do blend before roasting for the sake of convenience, compose the blend some days before you plan to roast it. Allowing the blended green beans to rest together helps even out moisture among them and promotes a more consistent and better-tasting roast.

The only situation in which two components of a blend absolutely must be roasted separately is in the case of blends of decaffeinated and regular beans, because decaffeinated beans often roast much more quickly than untreated beans.

Chapter 6

AFTERWORDS

Postroast Flavors and Frills

 At this writing producing elaborately flavored coffees with names reminiscent of soda fountains and cocktail lounges—French vanilla, blueberry cheesecake, piña colada, and so on—is the one roasting act you can't pull off at home. These coffees are created with powerful flavoring substances that use a special medium—propylene glycol—to carry the flavor from roasted bean through the brewing process and into the cup. Ordinary kitchen flavorings use water, alcohol, or glycerin as media, all of which fade during brewing. Even the few flavorings available to the home roaster that do make use of propylene glycol are too feeble to persist into the cup. As this book goes to press no supplier of the concentrated professional flavorings is willing to provide them to the home market, presumably for fear that children may find a bottle and overdose on essence of blueberry cheesecake.

If you like extravagant flavors with your home-roasted coffees, add them directly to the cup after brewing, not to the beans before. You can choose from all-purpose extracts and flavorings sold in the spice section of most supermarkets, from the Flavor-Mate brand of unsweetened flavorings packaged in purse- or pocket-sized bottles, from the Italian-style soft-drink syrups used to sweeten and enhance drinks in the espresso cuisine, or from the various powders used to garnish the frothy heads of those drinks. The general books on coffee or espresso listed in "Resources" (including mine) offer recipes and suggestions for using these flavorings.

What you *can* combine successfully with your freshly roasted coffee beans before brewing are various natural, traditional flavorings. You may want to dress up one of your freshly roasted coffees as a special gift to a friend, for example, or simply experiment with the exotic. If so, here are just a few suggestions for combining traditional ingredients with freshly roasted coffee beans.

Some Prerecipe Caveats

Note that suggested proportions of flavorings to coffee are simply recommended starting points for your own experiments. Spices vary greatly in strength depending on their age and packaging. Furthermore, I generally have gone lightly with flavoring in an attempt to supplement rather than to overwhelm the taste of the coffee. If you prefer dramatic culinary gestures like pesto that can be smelled from the front porch or hot sauces that turn dinner parties into sauna sessions, plan to increase the flavoring proportions from the outset.

My suggestions for pairing specific flavorings and roast styles are even more tentative. The recommended flavorings will enhance any roast style, but the combinations I've noted seem particularly agreeable.

I have avoided specifying powdered spices because one of the advantages of traditionally flavored coffees is the opportunity to grind spice and coffee together. The flavor oils of both are liberated at the same moment, just before brewing.

Choosing Green Coffees for Flavoring

After absorbing the loving descriptions of the world's fine coffees in Chapter 4, readers may wonder about the effect of flavoring on the many subtle taste distinctions I cited and celebrated.

In fact, unless carried out with the greatest discretion, flavorings largely obscure the distinctions among fine coffees. The best coffee for flavoring purposes probably is a good, clean, low-keyed Latin American coffee: a Peru, Mexico, or Brazilian Santos, for example. Indonesian coffees also flavor well. The intense acidity of many East African and high-grown Latin American coffees may compete with some flavors while complementing others.

A Warning on Mills and Grinders

Use only blade-style mills or grinders (the kind that work like blenders and whack the coffee apart) to grind coffees combined with other ingredients. Substances other than coffee can clog or even ruin feed-through, burr-style grinders.

Preparing Dried Citrus Zest

Many of the following recipes depend on the delightful fragrance of the dried outer peel of the orange (the orange *zest*, as cooks rightly call it). Dried lemon zest also can be attractive in combination with other ingredients.

Suppliers often coat citrus fruits with resins, waxes, or other harmless (yet hardly tasty) substances to preserve their freshness. You might want to

A few of the spices and dried fruits that can enhance freshly roasted coffee: star anise; vanilla bean; cinnamon; orange peel; dried, unsugared pineapple.

make a detour to a natural foods store for organically grown, untreated fruits when using the skins to make zest.

To prepare your own zest:

Remove strips of the outer peel of oranges with a paring knife or potato peeler. With oranges feel free to dig into the white inner skin; with lemons use a potato peeler only and try to take as little as possible of the white skin, or *pith*, which will taste bitter.

Place the strips of fresh zest on a cookie sheet in an oven preheated to 200°F/95°C. Remove after 1½ hours or when the zest is dry and leathery.

Typically one orange will produce six to eight strips of zest; one lemon, five to six strips.

Orange-Based Coffees

Orange combines particularly well with darker roasts, even the darkest.

Orange-Peel Coffee

For every fluid ounce of roasted coffee beans:
½ strip dried orange zest

Break or cut strips into smallish pieces and combine them with freshly roasted coffee beans. Prepare for brewing with blade grinder only.

VARIATIONS: Partly substitute lemon zest for orange. Or try the zest of bitter Seville oranges.

Vanilla-Orange Coffee

The vanilla both intensifies and softens the orange flavor notes.

For every fluid ounce of roasted coffee beans:
½ strip dried orange zest
¼ inch fresh vanilla bean

Break or cut orange strips and vanilla bean into approximately ¼-inch pieces and combine them with freshly roasted coffee beans. Prepare for brewing with blade grinder only.

For every fluid *ounce of* roasted *coffee beans:*
$1/2$ *strip dried orange zest*
$1/4$ *teaspoon coriander seeds*

Orange-Coriander Coffee

Break or cut orange strips into approximately $1/4$-inch pieces and thoroughly combine them with coriander seeds and freshly roasted coffee beans. Prepare for brewing with blade grinder only.

For every fluid *ounce of* roasted *coffee beans:*
$1/2$ *strip dried orange zest*
$1/8$ *to* $1/4$ *teaspoon chopped dried gingerroot*

Ginger-Orange Coffee

Break or cut orange strips into approximately $1/4$-inch pieces and thoroughly combine them with chopped dried ginger and freshly roasted coffee beans. Prepare for brewing with blade grinder only.

This combination produces a superb flavored coffee. If you try any of these recipes make it this one.

Cinnamon-Orange Coffee

For every fluid *ounce of* roasted *coffee beans:*
$1/2$ *strip dried orange zest*
$1/2$ *inch stick cinnamon*
$1/4$ *inch fresh vanilla bean*

Break or cut orange strips, cinnamon, and vanilla bean into approximately $1/4$-inch pieces and thoroughly combine them with freshly roasted coffee beans. Prepare for brewing with blade grinder only.

Cinnamon and Other Spices

Cinnamon alone and nutmeg and cinnamon together are traditional and splendid enhancements to coffee, particularly to light through moderately dark-roast styles. Also see earlier recipes combining orange zest and spices.

Anise and various mints similarly resonate well with coffee.

Cinnamon-Stick Coffee

For every fluid ounce of roasted coffee beans:
1 inch cinnamon stick

Break cinnamon stick into smallish pieces and thoroughly combine them with freshly roasted coffee beans. Prepare for brewing with blade grinder only.

Cinnamon-Vanilla Coffee

The previous recipe allows more coffee taste to emerge; the vanilla in this recipe emphasizes the cinnamon notes.

For every fluid ounce of roasted coffee beans:
1 inch cinnamon stick
1/4 inch vanilla bean

Break or cut cinnamon stick and vanilla bean into approximately 1/4-inch pieces and thoroughly combine them with freshly roasted coffee beans. Prepare for brewing with blade grinder only.

Cinnamon-Nutmeg Coffee

This coffee is delicious, but take care with the very powerful nutmeg or it will overwhelm everything else.

For every fluid ounce of roasted coffee beans:
3/4 inch cinnamon stick
1/12 nut (approximately) nutmeg
1/4 inch vanilla bean

Lightly crush nutmeg into small crumbs. Break up or cut cinnamon stick and vanilla bean into approximately 1/4-inch pieces. Thoroughly combine all ingredients with freshly toasted coffee beans. Prepare for brewing with blade grinder only.

Anise Coffee

The perfume of star anise is a particularly effective enhancement for those moderately dark through dark roasts used for espresso cuisine.

For every fluid ounce of roasted coffee beans:
1/2 (approximately) star-anise cluster

Break up anise clusters into small pieces and thoroughly combine them with freshly roasted coffee beans. If anise clusters are already fragmented when purchased, use 2 to 3 pods or star points to every fluid ounce of roasted beans. Prepare for brewing with blade grinder only.

Mint Coffee

I like the gentle taste of spearmint with coffee, but any mint can be used. Some will prefer the brighter, sharper tones of peppermint. Both are particularly pleasant with medium-dark through moderately dark (full-city through espresso) roasts.

For every fluid ounce of roasted coffee beans:
¾ teaspoon dried spearmint

If spearmint is in leaf form, crumble it. Thoroughly combine spearmint with freshly roasted coffee beans. Prepare for brewing with blade grinder only.

VARIATION: Substitute ½ teaspoon dried peppermint for spearmint, or ½ teaspoon of the two combined.

Lemon-Mint Coffee

For every fluid ounce of roasted coffee beans:
½ teaspoon dried spearmint

½ teaspoon lemongrass
¼ strip dried lemon zest

See pages 197–198 for instructions for preparing lemon zest. Cut or tear zest into approximately ¼-inch fragments. Combine zest, mint, and lemongrass with freshly roasted coffee beans. Prepare for brewing with blade grinder only.

Vanilla Bean

Vanilla is a magic ingredient when flavoring coffee; in addition to adding its own fragrance it rounds out and intensifies many other flavors, which is why it appears so often in these recipes. Fresh vanilla is another flavor that seems to resonate best with medium-dark through dark (full-city through espresso) roasts.

Vanilla-Scented Coffee

Simply placing vanilla beans and freshly roasted coffee beans together in a sealed container will scent the coffee. Those who take their coffee black may enjoy the sweet, subtle fragrance that results. If you lace your coffee with sugar and milk, however, try the more direct approach embodied in the next recipe.

For every fluid ounce of just-roasted coffee beans:
$1/2$ inch fresh vanilla bean

Break vanilla bean into $1/2$-inch pieces. Combine them with just-roasted coffee beans in a sealed zip-tight plastic bag. Allow to rest for at least 2 days. Before grinding, separate the vanilla fragments from the coffee beans to be ground and return the vanilla fragments to the container with the remaining beans.

Vanilla-Bean Coffee

For every fluid ounce of roasted coffee beans:
$1/4$ inch vanilla bean

Cut vanilla bean into $1/4$-inch pieces and combine them with freshly roasted coffee beans. Prepare for brewing with blade grinder only.

Chocolate

America's second-most-favorite flavoring after vanilla is best added to the cup following brewing in the form of syrup, extract, or hot chocolate. When added to coffee before brewing, most chocolate is wasted; it fades under the impact of grinding, hot water, and filtering.

However, the following recipe produces a delicately flavored cup that black-coffee drinkers in particular may enjoy. The recipe contains no sugar, but the combination of buttery baking chocolate and fresh vanilla contributes a smooth, sweet sensation to the cup. The beans also look attractive in their chocolate coating. A medium-dark through moderately dark (full-city through espresso) roast will best accentuate the chocolate tones.

Chocolate-Covered Coffee

For every fluid ounce of green coffee beans:
$1/4$ square ($1/4$ ounce) unsweetened baking chocolate
1 inch vanilla bean

Grate chocolate. In warm, moist weather, chocolate may require chilling before grating. Place half of grated chocolate into glass, metal, or ceramic bowl. Arrange the following near roasting apparatus: bowl containing chocolate; second, empty bowl; remaining chocolate; and mixing spoon.

Roast coffee. When it reaches your desired style, dump it directly from the roasting chamber into the bowl with the grated chocolate. Immediately begin stirring the hot beans while gradually adding the remaining chocolate. Continue stirring until the beans are warm and thoroughly coated with chocolate. Dump the beans into the second, empty bowl and continue to stir until cool. Refrigerate for a few minutes, then remove and break apart any clusters of beans that remain stuck together.

Cut the vanilla bean into ¼-inch pieces and lightly mix with the chocolate-covered beans. Store in a cool, dry place. Prepare for brewing with blade grinder only.

Orange-Chocolate Coffee

For every fluid ounce of green coffee beans:
¼ square (¼ ounce) unsweetened baking chocolate
1 strip dried orange zest (see pages 197–198)
1 inch vanilla bean

Follow the preceding recipe for Chocolate-Covered Coffee. Break orange-zest strip into approximately ¼-inch fragments. Combine zest and vanilla-bean pieces with cooled and separated chocolate-covered beans. Prepare for brewing with blade grinder only.

Dried Fruit

Any fruit sufficiently dry to fragment in a grinder can be combined with roasted coffee beans and successfully brewed. Most fruit simply makes the cup heavier and sweeter, however, without adding recognizable flavor notes.

Note that *fruit must be thoroughly dry but not completely brittle*. Think of the consistency of old shoe leather. Most dried fruit sold in markets is too soft; rather than pulverizing, it converts to a sticky mess inside the grinder. Natural-food stores often sell dried fruits that have no sugar added, however, and are stiff to the touch. You may want to experiment by combining some of these fruits with freshly roasted beans. Here is one possibility.

Pineapple-Sweetened Coffee

Look for thinly sliced, unsugared pineapple rounds dried to a leathery consistency. In addition to sweetness and considerable body, they add a muted but recognizable pineapple taste to the cup.

For every fluid ounce of roasted coffee:
¹/₂ thoroughly dried, unsugared pineapple round

Cut or tear pineapple round into smallish fragments and combine them with freshly roasted coffee beans. When brewing use half again as much of the pineapple-coffee mix as you would unenhanced coffee. Prepare for brewing with blade grinder only.

Storing and Handling Roasted Coffee

Since the primary reason for roasting at home is experiencing the perfume of truly fresh coffee, you obviously should store and handle your roasted coffee with care. Coffee in its green state keeps very well, but the moment it is roasted it begins a rapid, relentless journey from flavorful to flavorless. The taste components of roasted coffee—the elements that make the difference between sour brown water and aromatic pleasure—compose a tiny part of the roasted bean. The enemies of these perfumes are moisture and heat, which destroy them, and oxygen, which stales them. Roasted coffee can be protected from moisture and heat easily enough by storing it in a cool, dry place, out of the sun. But what about oxygen?

The flavor oils are temporarily protected by two elements of the bean: its physical structure and the carbon dioxide gas produced as a by-product of roasting. If you wait to grind your coffee until just before brewing, the physical structure of the bean will do its part. The carbon dioxide is another matter. It steadily filters out of the bean at first, then gradually diminishes in flow as the chemical changes associated with roasting conclude and the roasted bean restabilizes. Meanwhile the ubiquitous oxygen lurks, pressing in with vulturelike persistence, awaiting its moment to seep into the bean and begin its destruction of the delicate oils.

Coffee tastes best a few hours to a day out of the roaster. By two days after roasting, a good part of the aroma has fallen prey to the opportunistic oxygen; a week later taste is also compromised; in two weeks aroma has virtually vanished, and taste has lost its complexity and authority.

Here are some steps to take to preserve and maximize the fragrance of your home-roasted coffee.

Roast small quantities of coffee often. Obviously the best way to drink absolutely fresh coffee is to roast every three to four days.

Store coffee in a cool, dry place, away from direct sunlight. After allowing the coffee to rest for a day uncovered, place it in a sealed jar or canister. A canister with a rubber seal and metal clamp is probably best. Caution: *Do not fill a tight-sealing canister or jar more than halfway with just-roasted coffee that has not been rested for a day or so;* the gas escaping from absolutely fresh coffee can exert considerable pressure on the walls and lid of a filled and tightly sealed container.

Grind your coffee immediately before brewing. The purpose of grinding coffee is to break open the bean and make the flavor oils available to hot water and thus to our palates. Unfortunately, breaking open the bean also makes the flavor oils available to oxygen and staling. Grinding is a devastating procedure that should be undertaken only a few moments before you brew.

Resist the refrigerator reflex. Don't store coffee in refrigerators; they're damp inside, and dampness compromises aroma and flavor. Refrigerators also harbor a variety of odors that can taint freshly roasted beans. Refrigeration seems to mute the flavor even of coffee stored in tightly sealed containers.

Freeze coffee that you can't consume within a few days after roasting. Whether or not it's a good idea to freeze whole-bean coffee is one of those peculiar controversies that run unresolved through the rhetoric of the coffee world. Two of the country's leading technical experts on coffee roasting are diametrically opposed on this issue, one touting the freezer as the perfect place to preserve roasted whole-bean coffee and the other excoriating freezers as the best way to destroy the structural integrity of the bean and its capacity to protect flavor.

I would argue that freezing whole coffee beans while they're fresh is silly, but if you absolutely have to keep your roasted beans around for more than three or four days before brewing, I find the freezer helps considerably more than it hurts. Put the beans in a sound zip-tight freezer bag and squeeze as much air as possible out of the bag before sealing it. Remove only as many beans as you intend to consume for the day and immediately reseal the bag and return it to the freezer. Allow the beans to thaw before grinding and brewing.

Drink your coffee immediately after brewing. It does little good to roast, then grind, and brew superbly fresh coffee if you let it sit on a hot plate for ten minutes while the aromatics evaporate. If you must keep brewed coffee around before you drink it, hold it in a preheated insulated carafe, which will preserve the flavor if not the aroma.

All of these rules and instructions can be taken either as symptoms of a pointless obsessiveness or, if you love coffee, as a way of being, of stopping to savor a small but exquisite space in the onrush of life.

For more information on coffee brewing, see my books *Coffee: A Guide to Buying, Brewing & Enjoying* and *Espresso: Ultimate Coffee.*

Cupping Coffee at Home

Obviously the most reliable long-term way to evaluate coffee is to drink it the way you usually drink it, but mindfully. If you're after a knowledge of coffee in its larger complexity and variety, however, you may want to approach tasting more systematically.

The professional cupping ritual has a relatively long history. It appears to have been well established in its present form by the mid-nineteenth century. Variations of it are used today by coffee growers, agricultural boards and graders, exporters and importers, and roasters and blenders as a way of evaluating coffee and what we do to it.

Traditional cupping is redolent of a sort of mahogany-toned, nineteenth-century romance. The gestures are arcane yet functional, and the trappings—sample roasters, water kettles, silver spoons, and spittoons—as solid yet mythic as the fittings of an old ship or country store.

Although turning a part of your house into a permanent cupping facility is not a practical alternative even for fanatics, a simple, portable adaptation of the professional cupping ritual is. Home cupping provides an effective way to compare similar coffees roasted to different styles, different coffees roasted to the same style, and your own blending experiments.

Setting Up for Cupping

Before cupping you might review the tasting terms defined on pages 57–60 and the reference guide to roast styles on pages 68–69.

    You will need identical or almost identical cups or heatproof glasses, one or more for each coffee, roast, or blend you plan to taste, and a round metal soupspoon. Cups or glasses that flare out a bit at the top are best.

    Ideally you also need a burr grinder, one that has settings from fine to coarse, so you can be certain that you are grinding each sample exactly like

The professional coffee-cupping ritual, taken from a 1920s photograph. Nothing much has changed today except the hats and the gender of some of the cuppers. Coffee growers, exporters, buyers, and roasters regularly cup coffees for purposes of evaluation. Samples of green beans are prepared in small roasters like those pictured on page 27 and in the same background here, uniformly ground, and brewed in identical cups. The tasters sample the aroma of each coffee, then repeatedly taste the coffee by sucking it explosively from round spoons, spraying it across their palates. The tasted mouthfuls are finally deposited in the large spittoon in the foreground.

the others. However, since burr grinders are relatively expensive ($50 and up) you may end up using a blade grinder, one that whacks the coffee apart like a blender. If you do use a blade grinder make sure to time yourself, so that you produce an approximately similar grind for each sample coffee.

You also should have two glasses of water, one to sip from to clear your palate and one in which to rinse the spoon between samples. Finally, you will need a bowl or large mug in which to dispose of mouthfuls of coffee and floating grounds scooped off the surface of the brewed coffee.

Have paper and pencil at hand to take notes. You may find the sample tasting charts reproduced at the end of this section useful.

If you are comparing several green coffees at one sitting, do your best to bring each sample to the same color or degree of roast, and cool each in an identical manner. Roast all of the samples for a given cupping session on the same day.

Cupping Procedure

Grind small samples of each of the coffees you plan to cup. The grind or degree of granulation should be as uniform as possible from one sample to the next. About a medium grind is best. Without becoming obsessive about it, try not to mix coffees from your various samples while grinding. Sometimes coffee will cake up in various spots in a grinder receptacle. In this case, try to knock out the caked portions of one sample before grinding the next.

Place the same volume of ground coffee in each cup or glass. Use about 2 level tablespoons or one standard coffee measure per 6-ounce cup. Meticulous professional cuppers weigh out ¼ ounce (7 grams) of coffee per 5 ounces (150 milliliters) of hot water. Such precision is not important in general cupping, but consistency is.

When all of your samples are prepared, sample the fragrance, which is the odor of the freshly ground, not-yet-brewed coffee. Stick your nose in the cup or glass, shake it to agitate the ground coffee, and sniff. The fragrance gives you a useful preview of the aromatics and even the taste of the hot coffee.

Next, fill each cup with an identical volume of water heated to brewing temperature (a little short of boiling). As you pour the water over the coffee make certain you wet all of the grounds. Fill the cups to about a $1/2$ inch below the lip. Allow the coffee to brew for about 3 minutes before beginning the cupping.

The cupping itself is in three parts.

Breaking the Crust and Sampling the Aroma. A layer of saturated grounds will cover the surface of the coffee. Bend over the cup, with your nose almost touching the coffee, and gently break this crust with your spoon. As you do so, *sniff.* Sniff deeply and repeatedly, while lightly agitating the surface of the coffee with your spoon. Make mental and perhaps written note of the characteristics and intensity of the aroma of each sample. Be active; move back and forth between samples, gently agitating the surface of each coffee again to refresh the aroma.

Tasting the Coffees Hot. Breaking the crust and agitating the surface usually provide sufficient activity to sink most of the grounds floating on the surface of the coffee to the bottom of the cup. However, you may need to remove the froth plus some of the more stubbornly buoyant fragments of ground coffee with your spoon before tasting, particularly if you used a blade grinder.

The professional cupper lifts a spoonful of the coffee and, in a quick, explosive slurp, sprays the coffee across the entire range of membrane in the oral cavity. This is not an easy act to master, particularly given the training most of us receive in how to behave at table. Nevertheless, give it a try. The idea is to get a quick, comprehensive jolt of simultaneous taste and aroma. Note acidity, nuances of acidity, and taste; if the roast is a dark one note the balance of pungent, sweet, and acidy notes. *Don't swallow the coffee.* Instead, roll it around in your mouth, chew it, wiggle your tongue in it. Get a sense of its weight or body and the depth and complexity of its flavor. Observe how the various sensations develop as the coffee remains in your mouth; some coffees may grow in power and resonance while others may peak and fade.

Now once again you need to defy table manners and spit out the coffee. Professional cuppers use three-foot-high spittoons for this purpose. Obviously you don't need a spittoon; a bowl or mug will do.

Taste repeatedly. Rinse the spoon between samples, and occasionally take a sip of water to clear your palate. Record your observations before moving on to the final part of the cupping.

Tasting the Coffees Lukewarm. Certain characteristics emerge most clearly at lukewarm or even room temperatures. Let the coffees sit for a few minutes, then return to repeat the cupping, refining and confirming your earlier observations.

Cupping Experiments

You can amuse yourself plus establish some general sensory reference points for cupping by conducting a few simple exercises.

Cupping Roast Styles. I give rather elaborate instructions for experimenting with roast styles on pages 208–214. Essentially, you roast the same green coffee to four or five progressively darker styles, then line them up and taste them. This gives you some genuine experience to attach to the generalizations about the changing taste profiles of roast styles given in the reference guide on pages 68–69.

Cupping Unblended or Varietal Coffees. Here the emphasis is on the taste characteristics the green coffee brings to the roast, rather than vice versa. Consequently, bring a variety of green coffees to the same, light-to-medium roast (often called a "cupping roast"). As a palate-training exercise, I suggest you start with very different green coffees, one from each of the general categories proposed in the blending lists on pages 98–100. For example, a Sumatran Mandheling, a Kenyan, a Brazilian Santos, and one of the cited Costa Rican coffees. Taste for the full body, low-toned rich acidity, and often quirky musty and fruity tones of the Sumatra; the intense acidity and dry fruit and wine notes of the Kenya; the smooth sweetness and nutty and (perhaps) dry fruit tones of the Brazil; and the bright acidity and clean balance of the Costa Rica.

Then perhaps explore within each flavor family. Cup an Ethiopian Harrar, an Ethiopian Yirgacheffe, and a Kenya, for example. Observe the rather wild, often overripe fruitiness and fullish body of the Harrar (and, if you are lucky, the blueberry notes); the dry, crisp fruitiness and medium body of the Kenya; the distinct lemon and floral high notes of the medium- to light-bodied Yirgacheffe.

Professional cuppers who evaluate green coffees for purchase typically brew at least five cups of each coffee sample to determine whether the sample is uniform in its characteristics. If you want to learn about this approach, you might taste five cups of a Costa Rica, a famously consistent coffee, and five of a Sumatran Mandheling, well-known for its surprises and inconsistency. Some home roasters enjoy the adventure of inconsistency, others value predictability in a coffee.

Cupping Your Own Blends. Obviously the idea here is to evaluate your blending experiments. Either maintain the same blend constituents and cup a variety of proportions among them, or keep the proportions the same and cup a series of blends that vary one of the constituent coffees.

Sample Cupping Forms

Use the first chart for cuppings in which your goal is to distinguish among green coffees or blends of green coffees. Use the second to compare roast styles, the way in which a given coffee or blend responds to different degrees or styles of roast, and so on. Also use the second chart to compare coffees and blends brought to dark-roast styles. The first three terms—*aroma, acidity,* and *body*—represent key traditional coffee-tasting categories. The categories that follow are less fixed by tradition and usage. Everyone who cups coffee has favorite terms and categories; these last are mine. See pages 58–62 for definitions.

CUPPING FORM FOR COMPARING GREEN COFFEES
AND LIGHT- TO MEDIUM-ROAST BLENDS

Name of coffee, mark or estate, grade, crop or age; description of blend:

Date of Cupping:

Tasting Category	Rating*	Notes
Fragrance		
Aroma		
Body/Mouthfeel		
Acidity		
Complexity		
Depth		
Regional distinction		
Sweetness		
Balance		

*5 = Extraordinary; 4 = Outstanding; 3 = Satisfactory; 2 = Weak; 1 = Negligible

CUPPING FORM FOR COMPARING DIFFERING ROAST STYLES OR COFFEES BROUGHT TO DARK ROASTS

Name of coffee, mark or estate, grade, crop or age; description of blend:

Approximate roast style and other roast notes:

Date of Cupping:

Tasting Category	Rating*	Notes
Fragrance		
Aroma		
Body/Mouthfeel		
Acidity		
Complexity		
Depth		
Regional distinction		
Sweetness		
Pungency (for darker roasts)		
Balance		

*5 = Extraordinary; 4 = Outstanding; 3 = Satisfactory; 2 = Weak; 1 = Negligible

RESOURCES

The Internet and the home-roasting community developed virtually simultaneously. It is difficult to imagine today's lively hobbyist roasting scene developing without the World Wide Web's capacity to connect far-flung roasting enthusiasts with one another and with equally far-flung resources. Which is a nice way of breaking the news that readers without access to a computer and an Internet connection may find themselves at a disadvantage in obtaining green coffee and home-roasting equipment.

The Internet allows anyone with a computer, a desk, and a garage to set up business. And when you have an entire country, if not the entire world, available as customers on the Internet, it hardly makes sense to set up a corner home-roasting establishment to cater to the dozen or so enthusiasts who might live close enough to burn some gasoline driving to your store.

Mostly Text and Fed-Ex

So the home-roasting community largely has become a digitally based community, mostly text and FedEx rather than faces and places. And it almost goes without saying that a digital community has its advantages and its drawbacks.

The advantage is that you can shop for green coffee and equipment and browse for information from almost anywhere at any time. The disadvantages are: (1) Businesses are as easy to stop as to start on the Internet, and you may find yourself attempting to log on to a site I mention here, only to turn up a white screen with some discouraging news from your browser. (2) Information on the Internet goes through no systematic editing procedure: Anyone can declare anything as fact or any procedure as sound and useful, simply by typing in some words on a screen. Particularly in the early days of home roasting I read some wildly misleading hot tips about home roasting that either were dangerous or produced truly appalling-tasting coffee.

However, things have settled down considerably since then, and most of the sites I cite here have been up and running for at least three or four years, and most members of the home-roasting community have accumulated enough experience to recognize the difference between roasting coffee and baking or burning it.

Finally, there are some opportunities for face-to-face buying and information exchange available to home roasters living in larger cities, which I note in the following pages.

Buying Green Coffee in Person

Buying green coffee from small roasting companies that roast their coffee on the premises or nearby is one of those opportunities. Such companies usually will sell you green coffee, particularly if you are willing to buy five or ten pounds at a time. You should pay about 15 to 25 percent less than the roasted price, although some stores will insist on charging the same price for both green and roasted.

Selling unroasted coffee is a fussy inconvenience for most conventional coffee stores because it is an exception to their normal routine. You may not be offered much choice in the way of exotic or out-of-the-way coffees unless you establish a special relationship with the proprietor or manager. Also, be prepared to tolerate arrogant or uncomprehending store clerks ("What? You roast coffee?")

The other face-to-face (or at least voice-to-voice) buying opportunity is arranging to buy 100- to 150-pound bags of green coffee directly from a roaster or large green-coffee dealer. Depending on where you live, you may be able to pick the coffee up yourself from a warehouse, making such money-saving purchases even more economical. Consult pages 219–220.

Buying Green Coffee via the Internet or Phone

The easiest way to access a large range of green-coffee origins is via the Internet (see pages 218–219). The problem can be freshness. Over the course of the crop year, many green coffees gradually fade in flavor. If they have been stored in damp conditions they also may turn mildly mildewed tasting or baggy.

If a coffee you order arrives light-brownish or straw-colored but if it is not aged, monsooned, or decaffeinated, and if it tastes disappointingly dull or vaguely ropelike and mildewed, you have been supplied with a faded or baggy coffee. Ask your supplier whether the coffee he sent you was "new or current crop." If the answer is no or a vague equivocation, change your supplier. The sites I list on pages 218–219 have a proven reputation at this writing, but, again, situations change quickly on the Internet.

Besides current-crop coffee, you should also expect a fairly wide selection of coffees that have been cupped or evaluated by your supplier, not simply by the dealer who sold the coffees to your supplier. You should also expect a price break for larger purchases, purchases of over ten or twenty pounds of the same coffee, for example.

Buying Equipment via the Internet or Phone

Dedicated home-roasting equipment, as well as an assortment of equipment for use in improvised methods, can be purchased through the sites listed on page 218 under "One-Stop Internet Shopping." Dedicated equipment also can be purchased via the Web sites of the companies that manufacture or distribute this equipment. See the listings in this section under the headings for each roasting method (i.e., "Home Fluid-Bed Roasters," "Home Drum Roasters," etc.)

One-Stop Internet Shopping for Green Coffee and Equipment

The following Internet-based companies reliably offer a mix of green coffee, roasting equipment, and information.

Sweet Maria's
www.sweetmarias.com
Voice 888-876-5917, 510-601-6674
Fax 888-876-5917, 510-601-6674
At this writing, arguably the leading home-roasting site on the Internet. Good selection of green coffee, cupped and rated; extensive selection of equipment (including the Whirley Pop stove-top corn popper with thermometer installed and thermometers for use in other improvised equipment); information; newsletter.

Coffee Bean Corral
www.coffeebeancorral.com
Voice 800-245-2569 (Hawaii only)
Voice 877-987-1233 (elsewhere in the U.S.)
Fax 808-246-9065
Excellent green-coffee selection. Equipment selection includes both original Fresh Roast and Fresh Roast Plus models, voltage regulator for small coffee roasters, reasonably priced 1-kilo tabletop roaster. Extensive information. At this writing a rather slow but well-organized Web site.

The Coffee Project
www.coffeeproject.com
Voice 800-779-7578
Good selection of green coffee, outstanding selection of roasting equipment, coffee plants, newsletter. Carries the difficult-to-find Aroma Pot stove-top roaster.

Home Coffee Roasters
www.homeroasters.com
Voice 800-803-7774
Fax. 678-494-3433
Large selection of green coffee, including organic, fair-traded, and decaffeinated selections; some equipment; information.

Roast Your Own
www.roastyourown.com
Voice 888-30-ROAST
Selection of quality green coffee focused on social and environmental causes and issues. Well-organized site; information, books, equipment.

Coffee Wholesalers
www.coffeewholesalers.com
Voice 541-431-1103
Fax 541-431-1103
Good selection of green coffee, cupped for quality by proprietors. Some equipment.

Macaw Import Export (Canadian site)
www.macawcoffee.com
Voice 888-810-0024
Fax 613-567-8035

Buying Green Coffee in Bulk

By "in bulk," I mean seriously in bulk: a full-sized, 100- to 150-pound bag. Such a purchase can net impressive savings per pound but requires special arrangements with either a large roaster or a green-coffee dealer, usually by telephone. If you can find a local source and pick up the coffee yourself you will save yourself the considerable hassle and expense of arranging shipping for your bag of coffee. Remember that the firms you are calling are not mail-order emporiums. They are wholesale dealers who expect their customers to make their own shipping arrangements.

One approach is to call larger roasting firms (places that roast for more than one store) in your area to see if someone will sell you a single bag from their warehouse stock at a good price. By a "good price," I mean at least one-half the typical per-pound roasted retail price for a given coffee. Remember that you are calling roasters, not green-coffee dealers; don't importune or feel badly if they brush you off. You are asking them to make a possibly inconvenient exception to their ordinary procedure.

An approach that has the potential of netting even more savings is buying a full bag directly from a wholesale green-coffee dealer. At one time these firms were concentrated in large port cities, but since the advent of faxes and e-mail, their offices, and often their warehouses, have been dispersing all over the country. If you live in a large metropolitan area you might check the heading. Coffee-Brokers in the yellow pages (in the business-to-business listings if your phone company divides things up that way). "Brokers" as a blanket term for all green-coffee wholesalers is actually a misnomer. True coffee brokers are usually middle people who arrange for green-coffee sales but never take possession of the coffee. Green-coffee dealers actually purchase the coffee and store it under their name in warehouses. Obviously you are looking for a green-coffee dealer rather than a broker, despite the partiality of telephone companies for the latter term.

At any rate, call the numbers you find under the broker heading and ask the respondents if they sell single bags. A few will do so happily, many won't even think about it. Some—those who are true coffee brokers rather than dealers—may deal only in enormous containers of coffee. If you do find a source, you should pay about one-quarter to one-third (certainly no more than one-half) of the typical roasted price for that coffee.

Again, you will need to call or e-mail these suppliers. At most, their Web sites may provide a list of coffees available on a "spot" basis, meaning coffees that are available for sale out of a warehouse in the indicated metropolitan area. For example, "Spot SF" indicates a coffee currently available in a warehouse near San Francisco. However, wholesale green-coffee dealers' sites almost never invite ordering via the Internet. Wholesale green-coffee trading remains a clubby sort of business built on personal contacts.

Burlap Bags for Coffee Storage

Those who wish to seriously support their roasting hobby by establishing a cellar of green coffees will need something suitable in which to store medium-size quantities of those coffees. The burlap "sand" bags used to control flooding are technically sound, hold about 20 to 25 pounds of green coffee when filled, look suitably professional, come with a simple string closure, and currently cost less than a dollar per bag.

At least two suppliers listed on pages 218–219 (Sweet Maria's and Coffee Bean Corral) sell smaller, 5-pound cloth storage bags. But, at this writing, for the larger 20- to 25-pound bags you need to look in your local yellow pages under a heading that has "Bags" in the title. In my area the heading is reassuringly specific "Bags—Burlap & Cotton." Names of several concerns in obscure industrial parts of town should follow. Make sure you buy the burlap and not the plastic bags. Some bag suppliers may have additional sizes and styles of smaller burlap and cotton bags available as well.

Home Fluid-Bed Roasters

Fresh Roast. Original Fresh Roast, capacity per roast batch 2.7 ounces (75 grams) by weight; around $65. Fresh Roast Plus, capacity per roast batch 3.5 ounces (100 grams) by weight; lists for around $80. Most Internet suppliers listed on pages 218–219 offer one or both of these reasonably priced little machines.

Hearthware Gourmet Coffee Roaster (also sold as Home Innovation Coffee Roaster). Capacity per roast batch 3.5 ounces (100 grams) by weight; lists for $100 but often can be found for less. www.hearthware.com; 800-566-3009, x109, plus other suppliers listed on pages 218–219. Hearthware also promises a new roaster with high-end features and sophisticated controls by 2004.

Brightway Caffé Rosto CR120. Capacity 4 ounces (120 grams) by weight; lists for around $150 but often can be found for somewhat less. www.bright way.com; 800-949-0072, plus other suppliers listed on pages 218–219.

Zach & Dani's Gourmet Coffee Roaster

Capacity per roast batch 5 ounces (140 grams) by weight for a medium- to moderately dark roast, 3.5 ounces for a dark roast; around $200 in a kit that includes grinder, supply of green beans, and instructional materials www.coffeeroasting.com; 877-470-0330.

Home Drum Roasters

Swissmar Alpenrost. Capacity per roast batch 8 ounces (225 grams) by weight; lists for around $280. www.swissmar.com; 905-764-1121. Other suppliers are listed on pages 218–219.

Hottop Bean Roaster. Capacity per roast batch 9 ounces (250 grams) by weight; lists for around $580. At this writing available at www.vineus usa.com; 877-955-1229.

"Wave-Roast" Microwave Packets and Cones

Packets. Microwave packets, each prefilled with 2 ounces (60 grams) by weight of various green-coffee origins, $1 to $3 each depending on origin. Packets are recyclable but not refillable.

Cones. Starter kit of seven cones, each prefilled with 2 ounces (60 grams) by weight of green coffee, plus rechargeable battery-operated roller device for agitating cones/beans inside microwave and blade-type coffee grinder, probably will list for around $40. Cones are recyclable but not refillable. Single cones precharged with coffee will sell for $1.50 to $3.50 depending on coffee origin.

The preceding information is based on prerelease plans, and prices and configurations may change. Consult www.mojocoffee.com.

Aroma Pot ½-Pound Coffee Roaster

Sold as part of a kit that includes the Aroma Pot itself, equipment for cooling coffee, storage canisters, substantial quantities of green coffee, and extensive informational materials; lists for around $140. www.coffeeproject.com; 800-779-7578.

Whirley Pop Stove-Top Corn Popper

Six-quart model modified for coffee roasting, including thermometer, sells for around $26 at Sweet Maria's: www.sweetmarias.com; 888-876-5917. Six-quart model with no thermometer (but including popcorn!); around $25 at www.whirleypop.125west.com; 888-921-9378.

Hot-Air Corn Poppers

Use only the recommended design popper (see page 176) for coffee roasting. Currently two widely distributed brands incorporate the proper coffee-friendly design. Most discount department stores carry one or the other at $15 to $25. If you find more than one brand incorporating the recommended design, buy the model with the higher wattage indicated on the bottom.

Voltage Regulators

One of the baffling variables for those who try to maintain the same roast level from batch to batch using small-scale home equipment (particularly with fluid-bed roasters and hot-air corn poppers) is the variability of household electrical current. Actual voltage can change from hour to hour or minute to minute, turning a six-minute Viennese roast into a six-minute espresso roast without warning.

A solution is a transformer that will maintain voltage at a level you set. Coffee Bean Corral (www.coffeebeancorral.com; 877-987-1233) currently sells two such devices. The better one, the Variac 2090, sells for around $120 at this writing. Those fastidious and focused hobbyists who seek advanced control and consistency might consider this piece of equipment.

Candy/Deep-Fry Thermometers

Inexpensive metal-stemmed thermometers designed for candy making or deep frying are widely sold in kitchenware departments and stores as well as on the Internet. Be sure to buy one that has a metal rather than glass stem. Those manufactured by Cooper and Taylor and by Springfield are both all about the right length to monitor either air temperature (with the Theater II popper) or internal bean temperature (with recommended designs of hot-air poppers).

Most Cooper and Taylor candy/deep-fry thermometers for sale in consumer outlets are calibrated only to 400°F, too low (it would seem) for coffee-roasting applications. However, you should have no trouble approximating readings to 500°F or higher with either brand. See pages 173–174.

A smallish pocket-sized thermometer calibrated to 550°F/290°C is widely available. It has been sold over the years under a variety of names, including Pelouze, Comark, and UEI. Its 5-inch shaft is a bit too short for use in monitoring internal bean temperatures in most designs of hot-air poppers, but it can be used successfully to register air temperature in the Theater II stove-top popper.

Simply searching under "Candy Thermometers" using your Internet browser should turn up a variety of vendors for these $12 to $15 devices. Home-roasting supplier Sweet Maria's (www.sweetmarias.com; 888-876-5917) carries two thermometers at this writing. Or log on to the general kitchenware site Cook's Corner (www.cookscorner.com; 800-236-2433) and select "Timers & Thermometers."

Oven-Roasting Pans and Supplies

Perforated pizza and oven pans with the right size and pattern of perforations for oven coffee roasting are distributed by Wearever, AirBake and Mirro. These sometimes can be found in well-stocked kitchenware stores and departments, but are almost always available on the Internet or by telephone at Cook's Corner (www.cookscorner.com; 800-236-2433). To order by Internet, access the Cook's Corner home page, then select "Bakeware," then "AirBake," then "Perforated Pizza Pan Large." It lists for around $12. The model number for this particular pan is 08353.

Convection Ovens

These devices produce a coffee that may taste pleasantly mild to some, bland and without aroma to others. See pages 139–140. If possible roast coffee in someone else's convection oven and taste it before buying a convection device purely for that purpose.

Convection ovens are sold in most large appliance and department stores. They can cost as little as $70 to as much as $250.

Professional Roasting Equipment

Sample roasters. Small professional sample roasters of the traditional drum design roast from 4 ounces to 1 pound of coffee, and are both wonderfully picturesque and essentially indestructible. Prices start at around $4,000 and range up to $8,000 or more, making these units unlikely choices for the coffee hobbyist. Still, who am I to make assumptions about how much discretionary income others are willing to expend on a culinary obsession?

One persuasive choice for the passionate and affluent hobbiest is Probat's elegant PRE-1 one-barrel sample roaster, which works much like full-size classic drum roasters, allowing control of both heat and airflow; operates on standard household current; and is an impressive object in gun-metal blue and brass on a wooden base. It roasts up to 4 ounces (100 grams) by weight per batch and lists for around $5,400. Order from Equip for Coffee (www.equipforcoffee.com; 650-259-7801).

A Colombian company produces a Probat-style sample roaster called the Quantik, with digital temperature readout and automatic, temperature-triggered shutoff that runs on household current and roasts up to 5 ounces (150 grams) by weight per batch. It can be ordered through Roastery Development Group (www.coffeetec.com, 650-556-1333). Although it is not as handsome as the Probat PRE-1, it is cheaper at around $4,200, and the digital electronic thermometer is an improvement over the simpler thermometer on the PRE-1.

The San Franciscan SF1-LB sample roaster is essentially a tiny replica drum roaster with most of the features and all of the charm of the larger shop machines. It roasts from 4 ounces to 1 pound per batch (100 to 450 grams) by weight and is available from Coffee/PER (www.coffeeper.com; 775-423-8857) for around $4,200. Note, however, that it requires either natural gas or 220-volt current. Upgrades, including a very useful electronic thermometer that measures bean temperature, add around $850 to the basic price.

Tabletop roasters. This is the current terminology for small professional machines that roast from about 1 to 6 pounds per batch. Prices start at around $2,000 and range up to $10,000 or more. All variously require 220-volt current, a natural gas hookup, or propane.

The two leading fluid-bed options currently are the Sonofresco (www.coffeekinetics.com; 360-757-2800), a 1-pound-per-batch machine with total automation (uses propane), which lists for around $4,000, and the machines manufactured by technical pioneer Michael Sivitz (www.sivitzcoffee.com), which list for $2,000 and up and require 220-volt current. Sivitz, who pioneered fluid-bed roasting in the United States, manufactures roasting machines that, from a technical and quality point of view, are impeccable and offer the operator much more precise control than the Sonofresco. Unfortunately, Sivitz's smallest-volume tabletop machine, a 1.25-pound-per-batch bargain at $2,000, lacks niceties like chaff control, meaning you may need to vacuum the garage after every roasting session.

A wide range of tabletop-scale drum roasting machines is available, although virtually all require either propane, natural gas, or 220-volt current. The best are configured along traditional drum roaster lines (see illustration on page 53). They apply heat using a combination of convection, radiation, and conduction principles, and enable the operator to control both airflow and heat input. The best also incorporate an electronic thermometer that reads bean temperature (see pages 173 and 180). I would advise buyers to opt for this feature. Some of these machines may cut costs by cooling the beans inside the drum rather than dumping them into a cooling tray outside the drum. I have not experimented sufficiently with these shortcut machines to take a position, but it is wise to be wary of any roasting device that attempts to cool more than a pound of coffee inside the heating chamber rather than outside. If you are considering buying a machine that cools inside the drum rather than outside, make certain that the beans are warm to the touch within three (certainly no more than four) minutes after the heating element turns off.

Most smaller manufacturers of drum roasting devices produce starter tabletop machines. Check the Web site for Roastery Development Group (www.coffeetec.com; 650-556-1333) or call or log on to the Web sites for Diedrich Coffee Roasters (www.diedrichroasters.com; 877-263-1276), CoffeePER (www.coffeeper.com; 775-423-8857), Primo Roasting Equipment (www.primoroasting.com; 800-675-0160) or Ambex Coffee Roasters (www.ambexroasters.com; 727-442-2727). Drum roasters with less conventional configurations include the RoastMaster 9002 (1 to 2.2 pounds per batch; around $3,000) and the Caffé Rosto Pro 1500 (1 to 3.3 pounds per batch; around $6,000).

Tabletop roasting devices are often used to effect a transition from home roasting to small-scale roasting as a start-up business. The tradeoffs among technologies and machines become much more complex at this point, too complex to fully explore here. A point to consider in terms of choice of technology: it is much easier to obtain consistent, predictable, clean-tasting roasts with fluid-bed technology than with drum roaster technology, although some manufacturers of drum roasters have made impressive advances in control and automation. The greater complexity of input in drum roasting, with its combination of convection and conduction/radiation, gives the operator more creative control during the roast, but with control comes responsibility and the risk of ruining flavor through inexperience. Those who buy conventionally configured drum roasters for potential use in a small-scale coffee business should be prepared to spend considerable time studying roasting theory and practice in order to understand fully what is going on inside the roaster. In particular, it is all too easy to produce burned, rubbery-tasting dark roasts with drum roasting equipment.

Professional Cupping Equipment

A comprehensive source for classic cupping-room supplies, apparatuses, and furnishings (cups, spoons, spittoons, scales, etc.) is the Roastery Development Group (www.coffeetec.com; 650-556-1333). The Specialty Coffee Association of America Resource Center (www.scaa.org; 562-432-7222) carries a selection of smaller equipment.

Flavorings

Professional-strength unsweetened flavorings, the kind used by professional roasters to create flavored whole-bean coffees with names like hazelnut-vanilla, Irish crème, banana split, etc., are not available for sale to home roasters at this writing. Apparently no one in the flavor-vending network wants to risk selling these potent products to nonprofessionals. The situation may change. If it does, I am sure that you will find these flavorings for sale at the Internet sites listed on pages 218–219.

For whole spices, unsweetened dried fruit, and similar traditional flavorings, try large natural foods stores or upscale supermarkets.

More Home-Roasting Information

You are holding in your hand the only currently available book-length print source for information on home-roasting (and the only practical guide to roasting on any scale). Those who are computer-enabled can browse through the many home-roasting sites on the Internet and subscribe to the e-newsletters available through many of these sites.

As well as the one-stop home-roasting sales and information sites listed on pages 218–219, the site www.homeroast.com offers an outstanding set of links to a wide range of other home-roasting–related sites, some substantial and informative, some quite limited but engaging. *The Flamekeeper* is the on-line publication of the Roasters Guild, an association of professional coffee roasters and green coffee dealers (www.roastersguild.org).

General Coffee Information

Although I have provided a solid, practical summary of general coffee information in the preceding pages, aficionados doubtless will want to learn more about their passion. Here are a good many books, a few magazines, and some selected Web sites.

GENERAL WEB SITES ON COFFEE

There are hundreds running into the thousands, ranging from sites managed by coffee-roasting companies, coffee farms, and coffee magazines to one-guy or gal sites that share personal perspectives and, on occasion, obsessions. Here are just a few.

My own Coffee Review www.coffeereview.com is both periodical publication and reference Web site. The search and archiving functions permit accessing over six years and counting of monthly coffee reviews and articles as well as a succinct but comprehensive set of coffee reference materials.

The Specialty Coffee Association of America's site www.scaa.org provides a growing matrix of information, rotating articles and links. www.coffeeresearch.org offers authoritative and regularly updated coffee information. www.coffeegeek.com is a lively all-around shopping-and-information site, and www.ineedcoffee.com and www.coffeeuniverse.com are spirited on-line publications. For espresso, try www.coffeegeek.com, The Espresso Index at www.espresso.com, and David Schomer's www.espressovivace.com.

GENERAL BOOKS ON COFFEE

When I published my first book about coffee in 1975, there was only one other book in print on the subject. Today there are at least a couple hundred. Here are just a few. Buy them through the Specialty Coffee Association of America's Resource Center (www.scaa.org; 562-432-7222) or Bellissimo Coffee Info Group (www.espresso101.com; 800-655-3955).

General Practical Guides to Coffee. My own *Coffee: A Guide to Buying, Brewing & Enjoying*, now in its fifth edition and completely updated, remains the most detailed general introduction to specialty coffee in print. Other general introductions cover roughly the same ground in perhaps a bit less detail but provide a variety of differing and valuable perspectives and insights. They include books by the very knowledgeable long-time coffee insiders Kevin Knox (*Coffee Basics*) and Timothy Castle (*The Great Coffee Book*, with Joan Nielson) and food writer Corby Kummer (*The Joy of Coffee*).

A step up in price and quality of illustration but a step down in practical kitchen and coffee-buying detail are coffee-table introductions like Riccardo and Francesco Illy's *The Book of Coffee: A Gourmet's Guide* and Felipe Ferre's splendidly illustrated *Adventure of Coffee*.

Finally, William Ukers's *All About Coffee* (2nd edition), is an obviously dated (1935!) but superb compendium with almost biblical stature in the coffee industry. Reprints are available through the Specialty Coffee Association of America's Resource Center (www.scaa.org; 562-432-7222).

Technical References. These are rather expensive books focused purely on information and aimed at a specialized professional and technical audience. None are page-turners, but they can provide invaluable information for serious aficionados and beginning professionals willing to pay rather stiff business-to-business prices. Buy them through the Specialty Coffee Association of America's Resource Center (www.scaa.org; 562-432-7222).

The standard reference work on sourcing green coffee is Philippe Jobin's *The Coffees Produced Throughout the World*. With its wealth of detail presented in list format, this is an invaluable volume but one best consulted after reading a more general, expository introduction to coffee origins like the kind offered by my books.

A good overview of coffee-roasting theory and technology is contained (along with much valuable, well-researched coffee history) in Ian Bersten's *Coffee Floats, Tea Sinks*. Michael Sivitz and Norman Desrosier's *Coffee Technology* is arguably the best technical overview of coffee technology generally, including roasting, but the writers assume their readers share a basic knowledge of chemistry and engineering. Those readers interested in roasting technology also should be aware that the researches of Bersten and Sivitz have led them both to conclude that variations on fluid-bed technology provide the best conditions for coffee roasting, a sound position but one that many members of the coffee technical community would dispute.

Caffeine, a technical anthology edited by Gene A. Spiller, contains an excellent chapter on the chemical components of coffee. Those interested in the details of how green coffee is traded will find a clear, succinct untangling of complex commercial and grading procedures in the International Trade Center's *Coffee: An Exporter's Guide*, which can be purchased at www.interacen.org/publications.

Finally, *Coffee Futures: A Source Book of Some Critical Issues Confronting the Coffee Industry*, edited by P. S. Baker, is a concise, authoritative but nontechnical summary of the current state of the world coffee industry and the immediate issues it faces. Purchase through CABI Commodities (www.cabicommodity.org).

Coffee History. Interest in the colorful and complex history of coffee has produced several valuable new books over the last few years, though most are rather expensive hardcovers ($35 to $100). William Ukers's classic 1935 *All About Coffee* projects an accurate but romantic vision of the history of coffee. Ian Bersten's *Coffee Floats, Tea Sinks* is particularly strong on the history of coffee technology. Mark Pendergrast's *Uncommon Grounds: The History of Coffee and How It Transformed Our World* is a thorough, well-researched, engagingly written history of coffee that is especially effective at untangling some of the political and economic complexities behind coffee's recent history. It presents a more detailed and critically balanced view of coffee history than either Ukers's outdated view of coffee as the wine of democracy or the antiromantic vision of Gregory Dicum and Nina Luttinger's *The Coffee Book: Anatomy of an Industry from Crop to the Last Drop*, a sketchy and rather dyspeptic history of coffee that focuses on its destructive role as a globally traded commodity. The chapters in *The Coffee Book* outlining how the international coffee market works are clear and concise, however, and probably in themselves worth the modest price of this paperback.

Edward and Joan Bramah's *Coffee Makers: 300 Years of Art and Design* is another excellent, expensive, and profusely illustrated technical history of coffeemaking, emphasizing the British experience. Ulla Heise's *Coffee and Coffee Houses* is a large-format book focusing on the social and cultural history of coffee. The early story of coffee in the context of Islamic culture is elegantly and authoritatively covered in Ralph Hattox's crossover academic work *Coffee and Coffeehouse: The Origins of a Social Beverage in the Medieval Near East*, available in an inexpensive paperback edition.

Ian Bersten's *Coffee, Sex & Health: A History of Anti-Coffee Crusaders and Sexual Hysteria* is a witty, amusing, and convincing history of the medical arguments for and (mostly) against caffeine and coffee. Bersten's research persuasively suggests that the anticoffee bias that for so many years dominated the medical professions and continues today in some circles had its roots in a hysterical fear that coffee and caffeine provoked an unruly sexual excitement.

Coffee Travel. Daniel and Linda Rice Lorenzetti's *The Birth of Coffee* is a skillfully and knowledgeably annotated collection of black-and-white (sepia-and-white as printed) photography recording some of the most celebrated coffee-growing regions of the world, including one of my favorites, the little-visited highlands of Yemen. Although the text is authoritative, this is not a general introduction to coffee history and coffee production, but rather a splendidly photographed coffee travel book probably best enjoyed by those who already have some familiarity with coffee. Stewart Lee Allen's *The Devil's Cup*, in contrast to the sober tone of the Lorenzetti book, is charmingly irreverent and profoundly caffeinated, a sort of backpacking adventurer's travels through the romantic geography of coffee history.

Cupping. The main source for professional cupping terminology and procedure is Ted Lingle's *The Coffee Cupper's Handbook* (or the shorter version, *The Basics of Cupping Coffee*). Both versions are reasonably priced and available from the Specialty Coffee Association of America (www.scaa.org; 562-432-7222).

Espresso. My own paperback *Espresso: Ultimate Coffee* is the most thorough of currently available overviews for the aficionado. For ultimate fanatics and those considering espresso as a business I recommend David Schomer's *Espresso Coffee: Professional Techniques*. The most thorough available technical work on espresso is Andrea Illy, R Viani, and Rinantonio Viani's *Espresso Coffee: The Chemistry of Quality*.

VIDEOTAPES

At this writing, no authoritative videotapes on coffee roasting, either home- or professional-scale, are available.

As for more general coffee videos, *The Passionate Harvest*, which I wrote and coproduced with my colleague Bruce Milletto (distributed by Bellissimo Coffee Info Group, www.espresso101.com, 800-655-3955), is an authoritative and engaging visual introduction to coffee-growing production, focusing in particular on Ethiopia, Guatemala, Brazil, and Kona, Hawaii. Bellissimo also distributes an excellent visual introduction to coffee brewing, *The Art of Coffee*, as well as respected industry-training tapes on espresso production and other retailer concerns and issues. *The Passionate*

Harvest and all of the Bellissimo videos except *The Art of Coffee* are sold at a rather daunting business-to-business price, however. *Gourmet Coffee: Your Practical Guide to Selecting, Preparing and Enjoying the World's Most Delicious Coffees* is an introductory video sold at a consumer price point. It is an entertaining and accurate, though not particularly detailed, overview of specialty coffee generally, and is available from the SCAA Resource Center (www.scaa.org; 562-432-7222).

PRINT MAGAZINES AND NEWSLETTERS

No print coffee magazines or newsletters aimed at consumer coffee aficionados are published at this writing, although several appear on-line, including, again, my own "Coffee Review" (www.coffeereview.com), an on-line journal that has reviewed coffees on a monthly basis since 1997; Coffee Universe (www.coffeeuniverse.com); and the vivacious www.coffeegeek.com and www.ineedcoffee.com.

In the print realm, several informative trade publications flourish. *Tea and Coffee Trade Journal* (with a nicely designed on-line version at www.teaandcoffee.net) is the granddaddy of coffee trade magazines. It attempts to appeal both to larger traditional coffee concerns as well as to the specialty segment of the coffee industry. *Fresh Cup* (www.freshcup.com; 503-236-2587) is a well-established and lively Portland-based publication that focuses mainly on the roasting through retail side of specialty coffee, as does *Specialty Coffee Retailer* (www.retailmerchandising.net/coffee/). *Cocoa & Coffee International* (www.siemex.biz/coffee/), an authoritative though pricey London-based publication, focuses on the green-coffee end of the industry from an international and often commodity-based perspective. *Coffee and Beverage Magazine* (www.coffeeandbeverage.com; 416-596-1480, x229) serves both the coffee and general beverage market in Canada. The Specialty Coffee Association of America's informative publication "Specialty Coffee Chronicle" comes with membership in the Association.

KITS AND POSTERS

The Agtron/SCAA Roast Classification Color Disk System is available from the Specialty Coffee Association of America (SCAA members, $195, non-members, $295; www.scaa.org; 562-432-7222). Intended for small-scale professional roasters, this kit will be of interest only to the most committed and technically obsessive of home roasters. See page 56.

The SCAA also sells a coffee-cupping kit, a poster, and kits that help beginning green-bean buyers understand coffee grading systems, plus two taste-training kits, including the amazing if recondite Nez du Café (Nose of Coffee), a collection of vials of isolated aromas that help cuppers learn to identify key aromatic components of coffee.

SEMINARS AND CLASSES

At this writing the only roasting and coffee seminars aimed specifically at home roasters and coffee hobbyists are offered by the non-for-profit Specialty Coffee Association of America SCAA). These seminars are designed especially for the association's e-members (emember@scaa.org). Far more roasting and coffee seminars are aimed at those in or entering the specialty-coffee industry as professionals. These events include those offered by the SCAA and its associated organization, Coffee Roasters Guild (www.roastersguild.org; membership open to roasting professionals only). The for-profit, somewhat more consumer-oriented Coffee Fest (www.coffeefest.com; 800-232-0083) also offers instructional activities at its events, as does the North American Specialty Coffee and Beverage Retailers' Expo (NASCORE; www.nascore.net; 503-236-2587) and, in Canada, the Canadian Coffee & Tea Expo (www.coffeeandbeverage.com; 416-1480, x229). Professional seminars on roasting and related matters are offered by Agtron, a well-known and innovating manufacturer of coffee laboratory apparatus, and by Diedrich Coffee Roasters (www.diedrichroasters.com; 877-263-1276), as well as other producers of roasting equipment.

ASSOCIATIONS

The Specialty Coffee Association of America (SCAA) is a dynamic, well-established catalyst for coffee professionals (www.scaa.org; 800-562-432-7222). For $18 to $45 per year, consumer aficionados and home roasters can join the SCAA's e-member program, which makes the monthly SCAA e-newsletter and a selection of other electronic information available to members together with substantial discounts on SCAA Resource Center products and other benefits. For more information contact the SCAA at emember@scaa.org. A visit to the SCAA's annual conference and exhibition can be an informative and eye-opening experience. Current membership guidelines for The Roasters Guild, an association of roasting professionals who are already members or employed by members of the SCAA, would seem to exclude hobbiest roasters ("Roasting must be an integral part of your profession"), but home roasters and aficionados will find a visit to The Roasters Guild Web site enlightening (www.roastersguild.org).

INDEX

Page numbers in italics denote illustrations.

ABOUT THE AUTHOR

Kenneth Davids is widely recognized as one of America's foremost authorities on coffee. He has published three books on the subject, including *Coffee: A Guide to Buying, Brewing & Enjoying* (over 270,000 copies sold in five editions) and *Espresso: Ultimate Coffee* (now in its second edition and nominated for a James Beard award).

He coproduced, hosted, and wrote the script for "The Passionate Harvest," an hour-long documentary film on coffee production that has won numerous awards, including a prestigious Platinum Award at the Houston International Film Festival.

He has assisted growers in finding wholesale markets for their coffees, trained cuppers, and designed blends for a variety of clients. His workshops and seminars on coffee sourcing and evaluation have been featured at professional coffee meetings in the United States, Canada, South America, Europe, and Japan.

His influential coffee reviews appear regularly in a variety of publications, including the prize-winning World Wide Web publication *coffeereview.com* and the print magazine *Tea & Coffee Trade Journal* and *Fresh Cup*. Reviews and other notices of his work have appeared in the *Los Angeles Times*, the *Wall Street Journal*, the *Manchester Guardian*, the *New York Times*, on CBS news and CNN Headline News, and in many smaller publications. In 1996 he was awarded a Special Achievement Award for Outstanding Contributions to Coffee Literature by the Specialty Coffee Association of America.